Lancastrians to Tudors

England, 1450–1509

Andrew Pickering

CAMBRIDGE
UNIVERSITY PRESS

CAMBRIDGE UNIVERSITY PRESS
Cambridge, New York, Melbourne, Madrid, Cape Town, Singapore, São Paulo

Cambridge University Press
The Edinburgh Building, Cambridge CB2 8RU, UK

www.cambridge.org
Information on this title: www.cambridge.org/9780521557467

First published 2000
Reprinted 2003, 2005

A catalogue record for this publication is available from the British Library

ISBN 978-0-521-55746-7 paperback

Transferred to digital printing 2008

Text design by Newton Harris Design Partnership

The cover illustration is a portrait of Richard III, by an unknown artist. It is
reproduced by courtesy of the National Portrait Gallery, London.

ACKNOWLEDGEMENTS
(Lat 1158, f.27v), The Neville family at prayer, by the Master of the
Golden Legend in Munich, Neville Book of Hours (1430–35),
Bibliothèque Nationale, Paris, France/Bridgeman Art Library: p.14;
*(Ms Lat. 9471, f.194), The Last Judgement, c.*1418–25 (vellum), by
Master of the Hours of Rohan (fl.1418–25), Grandes heures de
Rohan, *(c.*1418), Bibliothèque Nationale, Paris, France/BAL: p.145;
*(Ms 265, f.IV), Edward IV, with Elizabeth Woodville, Edward V and
Richard, duke of Gloucester, later Richard III,* English, Dictes of
Philosophers, *(c.*1477), Lambeth Palace Library, London/BAL: p.49;
The Princes Edward and Richard in the Tower, 1878 (oil on canvas)
by Sir John Everett Millais (1829–96), Royal Holloway and Bedford
New College, Surrey/BAL: p.71; *Portrait of Arthur, prince of Wales*
(1486–1502), *c.*1499 (oil with gold leaf on panel) by English School
(15th century), private collection, courtesy of Philip Mould/BAL:
p.85; *Henry VII, bust,* perhaps by Pietro Torrigiano (1472–1528),
Italian, 16th century (painted gesso on wood), Victoria and Albert
Museum/BAL: p.122; by permission of The British Library: p.35
(ms Add. 40742, f.10), p.92 *(ms Egerton 616, f.6),* p.125 *(Flemish*

*illustrated ms. known as the Golf Book, c.*1500); in the collection of
the duke of Buccleuch & Queensberry, KT: p.62; College of Arms,
from the *Rous Roll:* p.69; © Crown copyright NMR: p.130;
reproduced by permission of the Dean and Canons of Windsor:
p.54; Mary Evans Picture Library: pp.5, 17, 51, 83, 142; Ghent,
University Library: p.33 *(ms 236, f.7v),* p.42 *(ms 236, f.5r);* Hugo
Van der Goes, *James III and his Son,* © H.M. The Queen, on loan to
the National Gallery of Scotland: p.55; Hulton Getty Picture
Collection: pp.12, 53, 172; 'By courtesy of the National Portrait
Gallery, London': pp.26, 31, 82, 121; by permission of
Northampton Museums and Art Gallery: p.36; Public Record
Office: p.114 *(Coram Rege Roll, Trinity 15, Henry VII KB, 27/956 m
1),* p.154 (PRO C81/1546 (103)); *Edward IV,* unknown artist, 'The
Royal Collection © 2000, Her Majesty Queen Elizabeth II': p.164;
Copyright The Society of Antiquaries of London: p.70.

Picture Research by Sandie Huskinson-Rolfe of PHOTOSEEKERS

Contents

Fifteenth-century kingship and the reign of Henry VI

Focus questions

- How was England governed in the mid-fifteenth century?
- How strong was the monarchy before the reign of Henry VI?
- What factors undermined Henry VI's rule before 1455?
- Why was Henry VI usurped by Edward, earl of March, in 1461?

Significant dates

1421	Henry VI is born.
1422	Henry V dies, Henry VI becomes king.
1437	Henry VI's minority ends.
1444	The Truce of Tours is made with France. Henry VI is betrothed to Margaret of Anjou.
1445	Henry VI marries Margaret of Anjou.
1450	Normandy is lost to the French. Suffolk is murdered and Cade's rebellion breaks out.
1452	*February to March* the duke of York's first insurrection begins.
1453	Henry VI becomes insane. Henry VI's son and heir, Edward, prince of Wales, is born.
1454	*November* York's first protectorate begins.
1455	Henry VI recovers and York's protectorate ends. *May* The First Battle of St Albans takes place. *November* York's second protectorate begins.
1459	*September* The Battle of Blore Heath takes place. York flees to Ireland.
1460	*July* The Battle of Northampton takes place. *December* York is killed at the Battle of Wakefield.
1461	*February* The Battle of Mortimer's Cross takes place. Queen Margaret defeats the Yorkists at the Second Battle of St Albans. Edward IV usurps the throne. *March* Edward IV defeats the Lancastrians at the Battle of Towton.

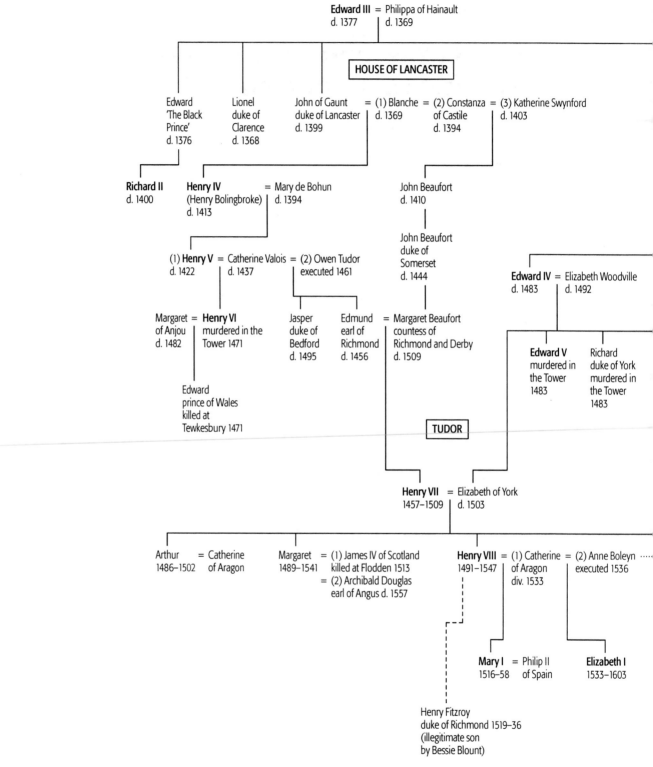

Edward III = Philippa of Hainault
d. 1377   d. 1369

HOUSE OF LANCASTER

Edward   Lionel   John of Gaunt = (1) Blanche = (2) Constanza = (3) Katherine Swynford
'The Black   duke of   duke of Lancaster   d. 1369   of Castile   d. 1403
Prince'   Clarence   d. 1399   d. 1394
d. 1376   d. 1368

Richard II   **Henry IV**   = Mary de Bohun   John Beaufort
d. 1400   (Henry Bolingbroke)   d. 1394   d. 1410
        d. 1413

                                           John Beaufort
                                           duke of
(1) **Henry V** = Catherine Valois = (2) Owen Tudor   Somerset
d. 1422   d. 1437   executed 1461   d. 1444   **Edward IV** = Elizabeth Woodville
                                                 d. 1483   d. 1492

Margaret = **Henry VI**   Jasper   Edmund = Margaret Beaufort
of Anjou   murdered in the   duke of   earl of   countess of
d. 1482   Tower 1471   Bedford   Richmond   Richmond and Derby   **Edward V**   Richard
                       d. 1495   d. 1456   d. 1509   murdered in   duke of York
                                                         the Tower   murdered in
Edward   1483   the Tower
prince of Wales   1483
killed at
Tewkesbury 1471   **TUDOR**

                                           Henry VII = Elizabeth of York
                                           1457–1509   d. 1503

Arthur   = Catherine   Margaret = (1) James IV of Scotland   **Henry VIII** = (1) Catherine = (2) Anne Boleyn
1486–1502   of Aragon   1489–1541   killed at Flodden 1513   1491–1547   of Aragon   executed 1536
                               = (2) Archibald Douglas   div. 1533
                                   earl of Angus d. 1557

                                                            Mary I   = Philip II   **Elizabeth I**
                                                            1516–58   of Spain   1533–1603

Henry Fitzroy
duke of Richmond 1519–36
(illegitimate son
by Bessie Blount)

The houses of York, Lancaster and Tudor.

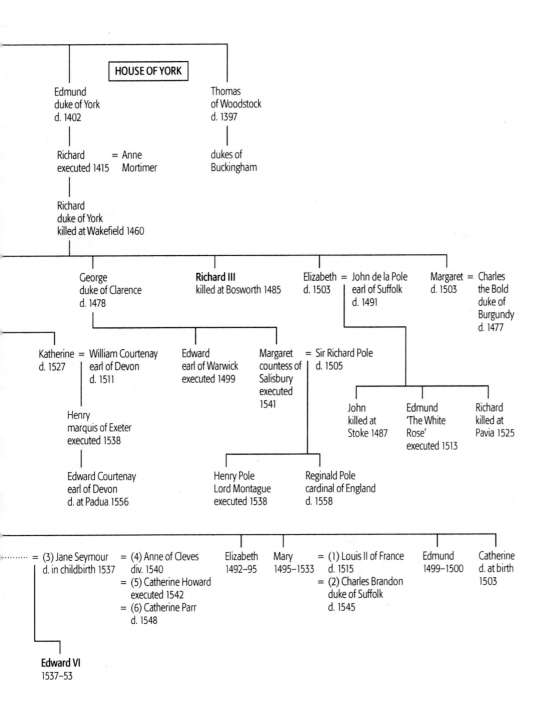

HOUSE OF YORK

Edmund
duke of York
d. 1402

Thomas
of Woodstock
d. 1397

Richard = Anne
executed 1415 Mortimer

dukes of
Buckingham

Richard
duke of York
killed at Wakefield 1460

George
duke of Clarence
d. 1478

Richard III
killed at Bosworth 1485

Elizabeth = John de la Pole
d. 1503   earl of Suffolk
             d. 1491

Margaret = Charles
d. 1503   the Bold
           duke of
           Burgundy
           d. 1477

Katherine = William Courtenay
d. 1527   earl of Devon
           d. 1511

Edward
earl of Warwick
executed 1499

Margaret = Sir Richard Pole
countess of   d. 1505
Salisbury
executed
1541

Henry
marquis of Exeter
executed 1538

John
killed at
Stoke 1487

Edmund
'The White
Rose'
executed 1513

Richard
killed at
Pavia 1525

Edward Courtenay
earl of Devon
d. at Padua 1556

Henry Pole
Lord Montague
executed 1538

Reginald Pole
cardinal of England
d. 1558

.... = (3) Jane Seymour
           d. in childbirth 1537

= (4) Anne of Cleves
  div. 1540
= (5) Catherine Howard
  executed 1542
= (6) Catherine Parr
  d. 1548

Elizabeth
1492–95

Mary
1495–1533

= (1) Louis II of France
      d. 1515
= (2) Charles Brandon
      duke of Suffolk
      d. 1545

Edmund
1499–1500

Catherine
d. at birth
1503

Edward VI
1537–53

Overview

> The reign of Henry VI has strong claims to be considered the most calamitous in the whole of English history.
>
> B. P. Wolffe, 'The personal rule of Henry VI', in S. B. Chrimes, C. D. Ross and R. A. Griffiths (eds.), *Fifteenth-century England 1399–1509*, Stroud, 1972

Henry VI (1421–71) was the third and last of the Lancastrian monarchs, king of England and, for a time, France. The first, Henry IV, had been the duke of Lancaster – hence the adjective 'Lancastrian' which is used to describe his dynasty and its supporters.

The first misfortune of Henry VI's reign was that it began in 1422 in his early infancy, although his formal coronation was delayed until 1429, shortly before his eighth birthday. A strong council of 17 nevertheless governed effectively during Henry's minority in spite of '**protector**' duke of Gloucester's attempts to extend his own authority. On coming of age in 1437, however, Henry proved inept. He was too forgiving towards high-profile offenders, showed too much favouritism to the ruling elite and he imposed high levels of taxation. All these faults were listed among the king's shortcomings by his contemporaries.

The contrast between the stability of Henry's minority and the disasters of the reign after he came of age is striking. From 1437 to 1450 he played the central role in creating a situation in which once-loyal subjects were driven to contemplating that most terrible of crimes – the deposition of their anointed king.

Worst of all, perhaps, Henry VI was blamed for undoing Henry V's greatest achievement by losing almost all of the huge French empire his father had gained after his victory at Agincourt in 1415.

Henry VI became king of France on the death of his maternal grandfather, Charles VI of France, whose daughter, Catherine, had married Henry V in accordance with the terms of the Treaty of Troyes of 1420. He only made one single boyhood visit to this troubled second kingdom in which, from about 1429, the spirit of French nationalism threatened to cast out the English presence. In May 1430, both Henry and the recently captured Joan of Arc were in English-held Rouen. Henry made his way to Paris and Notre Dame Cathedral to be crowned king of France while Joan of Arc, convicted as a witch, stayed in Rouen to face execution by burning at the stake. Henry's formal coronation was an attempt to counter the crowning of a French claimant to the throne, Charles VII, in the previous year. For 15 years, Charles VII was accepted only in the south and centre while the English king retained Paris, Aquitaine and much of the north.

Two humiliating defeats, Formigny in 1450 and Castillon in 1453, helped push the English out of Aquitaine and Normandy. By 1461 a single outpost,

protector Whereas regents were granted virtually full authority to act as king, protectors were more accountable for their actions. Henry VI's youth made it necessary to create this office and his first protectors were his uncles, John of Lancaster and Humphrey of Gloucester, between 1422 and 1429. During his breakdown from 1454 to 1455, Richard of York claimed the position. When Edward IV died in 1483 Richard of Gloucester stepped in as protector for his brother's son, Edward V, prior to usurping the throne.

On the death of his grandfather, Charles VI of France, in October 1422, Henry VI was proclaimed King Henry II of France. This painting shows his coronation eight years later.

Calais and its **Pale**, remained. It was finally relinquished in 1558 during the reign of Mary I, although English monarchs continued to claim a title to the French throne until 1802.

Careless in his use of the royal **patronage**, Henry showed particular favour to the dukes of Somerset and Suffolk, giving them titles, land and favours, while denying the same to other great and powerful families. Among these was Richard, duke of York, a descendant of Edward III, who, before the birth of Henry's son in 1453, was regarded by many as the legitimate heir to the throne.

The fact that Richard of York was ignored in this way, together with the king's general misfortunes and personal weaknesses, resulted in rebellion. Thus began the first of the **Wars of the Roses** – 30 years of intermittent warfare which, in 1461, ended the reign of Henry VI and, finally, in 1485, destroyed the Lancastrian dynasty.

Pale The Pale was the land around the town of Calais that was under English control. Similarly, the land around Dublin under English control was called the Dublin Pale.

patronage A patron is one who holds the power of appointing others to offices or titles, many of which have privileges of various kinds attached to them. The king, as patron, could use his powers of patronage by giving offices and titles to his friends or supporters.

Wars of the Roses The term 'Wars of the Roses' was coined in the nineteenth century by Sir Walter Scott. War between 1455 and 1485 was not continuous and historians now see these events as a series of separate wars rather than a single lasting conflict.

How was England governed in the mid-fifteenth century?

Kings and kingdoms

scrofula Scrofula was an unpleasant skin disease which it was commonly believed could be cured by the touch of the monarch.

Kingship by the fifteenth century had acquired a mystical quality; kings were not like other men: their touch alone could cure **scrofula** and it had become customary to approach them on bended knee and address them as 'Majesty'. It was assumed that kings ruled by 'divine right', that is that they were appointed by God – a belief emphasised by the fact that they were anointed with holy oil at their coronation. There was a general acceptance of the concept of the 'royal prerogative', the monarch's right to rule, in such areas as foreign policy, by issuing proclamations which had the force of law. However, it was generally accepted that the king should consult a parliament before making new statute laws or imposing new taxes.

The king's strength in the fifteenth century lay in the combination of traditional respect for his authority with the fact that the nobility depended on royal patronage. The traditional feudal bonds between king and subject were largely broken down by the later Middle Ages. Loyalty was only likely when it was in each party's mutual interest. As the king was the richest man in the kingdom and had power to bestow positions and other gifts on those he chose to patronise, he was well equipped to gain the service and support of the nobility.

The mystique of monarchy was reinforced by the stories associated with its lineage. English kings claimed an ancestry that included King Arthur, the Emperor Constantine and the great-grandson of Aeneas of Troy. These enduring legends were written down as 'history' in about 1130 by Geoffrey of Monmouth in his *History of the kings of Britain*.

Marcher lords The Marches were the border regions between England and Wales, and England and Scotland. Since Norman times, these troublesome areas had been placed under the jurisdiction of Marcher lordships. The Marcher lords had a long tradition of independence and, during the fifteenth century, they posed a considerable threat to England's kings. The Act of Welsh Union with England (1536, 1543) finally curbed the powers of the mighty Welsh Marcher lords.

The kingdom which the later-fifteenth-century monarchs ruled, in effect, was made up of England, Wales and a part of Ireland – Dublin and the area around it known as the Pale. Assumptions were made regarding the ancient allegiance owed to the English crown by the Welsh, Irish and Scottish, but these were not really enough to unite all the peoples of the British Isles. Much of Ireland and all of Scotland were fiercely independent and frequently in conflict with England. Despite its 'conquest' in the twelfth century, most of Ireland was not subdued and certainly not anglicised despite the influence of certain Anglo-Irish families. Here the English king's title was that merely of 'lord of Ireland'. The Welsh **Marcher lords** and the northern earls enjoyed a good deal of autonomy too, having secured privileges, 'liberties', in return for their loyalty and willingness to defend the king's most vulnerable borders.

Henry V had won a second kingdom for English kings after defeating the French at Agincourt in 1415. This kingdom comprised half of France, but all except Calais and its Pale was lost by 1453. The war in which it was lost, the Hundred Years' War, probably encouraged a sense of national identity and encouraged a cultural cohesion within the realm. French, a language long cultivated by the English nobility, went into decline in England as English fortress towns in France were recaptured by French armies. Until Calais was lost in 1558, English kings were active in asserting their French dynastic claims. Calais was an immensely important outpost during the period since it provided the main port through which English cloth entered continental Europe.

What were the foundations of the king's power in the fifteenth century?

The council

The king's council was the body on which the monarch was most reliant for advice. Traditionally it comprised some of the greatest **magnates**, but stronger medieval kings also surrounded themselves with advisers who were capable, yet could claim no 'natural' right to enjoy the privilege of joining the king's inner sanctum. A strong council was necessary during the minorities of both Richard II and Henry VI until they came of age. The turbulent years of the second half of the fifteenth century, moreover, encouraged a less informal relationship between king and council, as monarchs with a fragile power base tried to strengthen their position. Thus the king's council became more of a permanent institution during the fifteenth century.

magnates Magnates were the most powerful nobles of all.

Parliament

In medieval England, parliament was already divided into two chambers: the Lords (the upper house) and the Commons (the lower house). Those sitting in the latter were representatives of the shires and boroughs, elected from 1429 by freeholders worth 40 shillings a year in land. Two knights were selected for each shire and two burgesses for each borough, in all totalling around three hundred. The members of the upper house were the heads of the great landowning families. By the fifteenth century, the two houses had evolved into vitally important elements in the process of England's government. Parliament acted as an advisory body to the monarch, administered and could act as a court of law. The Commons was valuable to the crown for its ability to approve and give its consent to taxation proposals. The Commons, in return, presented petitions to the crown regarding issues considered to be of common interest. Monarchs had the right to accept or reject petitions but they could not alter them.

By the middle of the fifteenth century, the struggle between king and parliament for the authority to govern was an old one. In the 1380s, parliament for a time triumphed over King Richard II, by calling for the arrest, trial and punishment of those royal favourites thought to be responsible for a despotic approach to government which neglected the traditional involvement of the council and Commons. Led by the 'Lords Appellant' – so called because they 'appealed' (accused) five of the king's closest advisers of treason, the 'Merciless Parliament' of 1388 initiated a full-scale purge of the royal household.

The law and local administration

Time-honoured customs were the substance of common law – a law based on precedent in the form of written or reported statements of judges. Some laws (statutes) were always written down and usually came from parliament. Common law and statute law were enforced by the king's courts, King's Bench and Common Pleas, both of which usually sat at Westminster. Their work in the counties was carried out by itinerant judges through such institutions as courts of assize. In some areas lords of manors still held their own private 'manorial' courts for the handling of their tenants' minor misdemeanours, and many towns had the equivalent by which the town corporation could try cases involving such matters as weights and measures in the market place, the pollution of waterways, the maintenance of fences and ditches, and the creation of dunghills. All over the country there were 'liberties' – places where the king had handed over full judicial authority to a local magnate. Cases involving issues like divorce and the reading of wills were still the province of the church and its courts. Cases that could not be resolved by common law or statute law were heard in Chancery. The system was, therefore, complex to say the least and corruption was rife.

The single most important legal and administrative post in the provinces during the fifteenth century was that of justice of the peace (JP). These JPs were nominated and unpaid. From 1363 they were required to hold sessions four times a year. At these quarter sessions, minor cases were resolved and more serious ones were brought to trial, perhaps at the county court presided over by the sheriff. Details of the sessions were recorded by the JP's 'clerk of the peace'. JPs also had the right to arrest people accused of a breach of the peace.

What was the difference between common law and statute law?

How strong was the monarchy before the reign of Henry VI?

The study of history has much to do with cause and effect. Modern historians seek explanations for events and reflect upon how one chain of events led to another. In their studies historians identify short-term and long-term factors. These might then be arranged into a hierarchy of importance. The history of the second half of the fifteenth century can only be fully understood when it is set in the context of a broad chronology. This section outlines the histories of the reigns of the four kings who ruled England before Henry VI. The dramatic developments that occurred in his reign are rooted in the reigns of his predecessors.

The reign of Edward III, 1327–77

The origins of the Wars of the Roses, the struggles between the houses of York and Lancaster and between York and Tudor during the second half of the fifteenth century, have been traced by some historians to the reign of Edward III. In 1328 Edward laid claim to the French throne when Charles IV died. Edward's mother was the sister of Charles but, according to French custom, which did not recognise inheritance through the female line, the throne had been granted to Edward's cousin, Philip of Valois. In the continuing wars against France, which Edward had begun in 1337, England was victorious at Sluys (1340), Crécy (1346) and Poitiers (1356). Although much of the territory won was subsequently lost, England held five French towns and the Calais Pale on Edward's death. As well as providing his kingdom with a claim to the French throne Edward also produced 13 children, some of whose descendants, ultimately, would wage war with one another in pursuit of the crown. Five of his sons were married to rich heiresses and became some of the most powerful magnates in the kingdom.

The reign of Richard II, 1377–99

Edward's eldest son, Edward, the Black Prince, died before his father and the throne was inherited by his nine-year-old son, Richard II. Unlike his prolific grandfather, Richard died in 1400 without children. Richard II's choice of unpopular and incompetent advisers, the fact that he sometimes ignored parliamentary decrees and his unspectacular foreign policy turned powerful members of the nobility against his regime. In 1387 the Lords Appellant rose against the king's favourite, Robert de Vere, earl of Oxford, and defeated him at the Battle of Radcot Bridge in Oxfordshire. The earl escaped and fled abroad, to die a few years later after being gored by a boar while out hunting. His estates were confiscated and he was condemned to death by the so-called 'Merciless Parliament' of 1388.

Cowed by the actions of the Lords Appellant in 1387, Richard ruled for a time with restraint and he was fairer in his patronage of the aristocracy. By the late 1390s, however, he had reverted to his former practice and worse. He determined to rule without parliament, considered himself the font of law, promoted a new and unpopular favourite, his cousin Edward, earl of Rutland, and began plotting his revenge upon the Lords Appellant. Murders, arrests and executions followed. His cousin, Henry Bolingbroke, the son of John of Gaunt – the mightiest of England's magnates – was banished for ten years in

How did Richard II manage to turn most of the nobles against him?

Owen Glendower
Owen Glendower led the last major revolt against English rule in Wales. In the first decade of the fifteenth century, the castles of Harlech and Aberystwyth were held by the rebels, and Welsh parliaments met in 1404 and 1405. Henry IV regained control after 1408, although Glendower remained at large, fermenting further rebellion, until his death around the year 1416.

Lollard Lollard was a term of abuse for a follower of the preacher, John Wycliffe. He attacked the doctrine of transubstantiation, whereby the bread and wine taken at mass are thought to turn into Christ's flesh and blood when consecrated by the priest. Lollards opposed clerical riches, believing the most truly Christian priest was a poor one, and they wanted the common people to have access to the Bible. In the 1390s, Wycliffe produced an English translation of the Scriptures. During the fifteenth century, Lollard beliefs were regarded as heretical by the authorities and Lollards risked the punishment of death by burning.

1398. When his father died the next year, Bolingbroke's vast estate was confiscated and distributed to the king's favourites.

On 4 July 1399, Bolingbroke, the new duke of Lancaster, returned to England with a few hundred supporters, determined to win back his inheritance. Richard II was abroad in Ireland and Bolingbroke met no resistance as he began to gather an army around him. When Richard returned, arriving in south Wales in late July, he found himself deserted by his uncle, Gaunt's brother, the duke of York. Even Rutland now abandoned him and pledged his support to Lancaster. In despair Richard fled to Conway Castle. Persuaded to surrender he was then taken to London and placed in the Tower. Here he was forced to abdicate and, on 29 September 1399, he gave up his throne. This was now to be occupied by Henry Bolingbroke. Thus began the reign of Henry IV, the first king of the House of Lancaster.

The reign of Henry IV, 1399–1413

A plot to rescue Richard II from the Tower prompted Henry to have him murdered in February 1400. His dubious claim to the throne, financial difficulties and **Owen Glendower**'s nationalist revolt in Wales made for a perilous start to Henry's reign. In 1403 he was almost dethroned by the mighty Percy family, rebelling in alliance with Glendower. Although they had helped Henry snatch the crown from Richard II in 1399, they now claimed they had supported him in his recovery of his Lancastrian inheritance but never intended to promote his seizure of the throne or the killing of the king. In fact it is more likely that they sought revenge on Henry, who had failed to provide them with the rich rewards they expected in return for their support. Lack of organisation among the rebels' leaders saved Henry, who defeated them at the Battles of Shrewsbury (1403) and Bramham Moor (1408).

The last years of Henry's reign saw peace which, by reducing his financial demands, improved his relationship with parliament, but during this time he suffered from chronic ill-health. He died in 1413 at the age of 46, to be succeeded by his eldest son, Henry.

The reign of Henry V, 1413–22

Within a few months of his accession, Henry V faced a rising led by Sir John Oldcastle. Although a personal friend of the new king, Oldcastle had run into trouble, having been revealed as a closet **Lollard**. His desperate endeavour to save himself by engineering a coup against the king was unsuccessful and he went into hiding, a wanted man for the combined crimes of blasphemy and treason. After three years he was captured, hanged and burned in 1417.

In 1415 a second attempted coup, designed to replace Henry with Edmund Mortimer, earl of March, was thwarted when Edmund himself betrayed the conspirators to the king. The plot was uncovered just as Henry was about to embark for France in order to re-assert the ancient claim of English kings to the throne of France. In October he and the English archers achieved heroic status by pulling off a staggering victory at Agincourt against a larger and more heavily armed French force. With the full support of a delighted parliament and people, he was able to continue his campaign and bring large areas of northern and a greater part of south-west France under English control. The Treaty of Troyes in 1420 was the crowning glory for, by its terms, the French king, Charles VI, betrothed his daughter, Catherine of Valois, to Henry and made him his heir. He would not live to inherit, however, for he died a short time later of dysentery while still campaigning in France, leaving behind a baby son – the new king, Henry VI.

What factors undermined Henry VI's rule before 1455?

Losses in France

> … the conduct of the war in France and the problems of government at home were quite inseparable to contemporaries and cannot be considered separately by historians.
>
> B. P. Wolffe, 'The personal rule of Henry VI', in S. B. Chrimes, C. D. Ross and R. A. Griffiths (eds.), *Fifteenth-century England 1399–1509*, Stroud, 1972

Chief among Henry's concerns at the beginning of his personal rule was the war with France. England was desperately engaged in a struggle to hold on to the territories captured by Henry V and the regency government of Henry VI's minority, and was beginning to lose the contest. The situation deteriorated further, as relations with England's most important ally, **Burgundy**, worsened, and its duke, Philip, gravitated towards a truce with France. When Philip finally broke his alliance with England in 1434 there were riots in London, and Flemish settlers, whose homeland was subject to Burgundy, were lynched in the streets. In September 1435 the Treaty of Arras bound together the interests of France and Burgundy.

In April 1436 the French recaptured Paris and, by 1442, Pontoise was surrendered too, despite five attempts to relieve the besieged English garrison. By 1444, after years of expensive and largely futile campaigning, some of the most powerful men in England wished to relieve England of the full burden of Henry V's French ambitions. These included **Edmund Beaufort, duke of Somerset**, and **William de la Pole, duke of Suffolk**, who was rapidly emerging as the leader of the dominant faction in Henry's court. The king shared their

Burgundy During the fifteenth century, most of the Low Countries (now The Netherlands and Belgium) were acquired by the mighty dukes of Burgundy – Philip the Good (1419–67) and Charles the Bold (1467–77). Because of England's long-established trade with the Low Countries, Burgundy, therefore, became England's natural ally. In 1468 Edward IV's sister, Margaret, was married to Charles the Bold.

Edmund Beaufort, duke of Somerset (c. 1406–55) Somerset's feud with Richard, duke of York, sparked off the Wars of the Roses. He was the prime mover in the surrender of Normandy and was then appointed captain of Calais in 1451. He used his position and influence over the king to make himself rich, much to the disgust of his opponents.

William de la Pole, duke of Suffolk (1396–1450) William de la Pole was leader of the dominant faction at Henry VI's court during the later 1440s. He played a central role in the disastrous plan to take Fougères in 1449.

Margaret of Anjou (1430–82) Margaret of Anjou was the daughter of René of Anjou and niece of Charles VII of France. Her need to win supporters at court contributed to the split between the Suffolk–Somerset and the York–Warwick factions.

disenchantment with the French war. Suffolk negotiated a two-year truce with France at Tours in 1444 which included arrangements for Henry's marriage to **Margaret of Anjou**, the 15-year-old niece of Charles VII. In order to secure this valuable marriage alliance Henry promised to surrender Maine to Charles, to expect no dowry from his bride (much to the disgust of the duke of Gloucester – see p. 14) and to foot the bill for the cost of the wedding. Knowing how unpopular the abandonment of such hard-won territory would be, care was taken to keep this part of the proposal a carefully guarded secret until such time as the truce could be converted into a lasting peace.

In April 1445, 23-year-old Henry married his beautiful bride, Margaret of Anjou. Represented as a triumph of diplomacy by the Beauforts and their supporters, who wanted peace with France, the marriage would soon be associated with national humiliation by those of Gloucester's inclination. Not

The wedding of Henry VI and Margaret of Anjou. In this portrait the artist has shown the bride as pregnant, even though she was not, in order to emphasise the queen's vital role as the begetter of an heir.

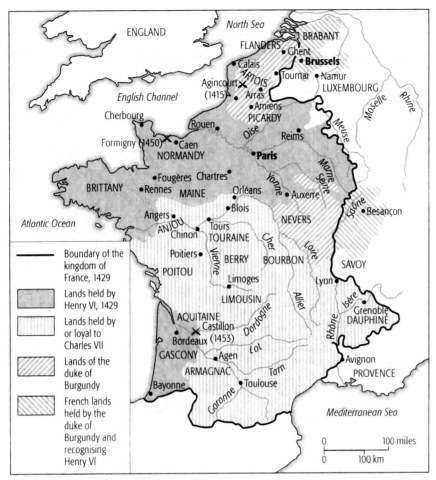

France in 1429, showing the lands held by Henry VI. By 1461, only Calais remained in the hands of the English king.

surprisingly, Margaret sought allies in the Beaufort faction and her preferential treatment of the Beauforts further alienated their opponents.

Henry had yet to fulfil his part of the bargain – the surrender of Maine – and as the end of the two-year truce approached so too did the day of reckoning. Henry vacillated while Charles sent envoys to pressure England's king into an early settlement. Meanwhile Queen Margaret nagged him incessantly on behalf of her uncle. As news leaked out regarding Henry's intent, Gloucester and other magnates, particularly those with personal interests in France, raged.

Maine was finally surrendered in March 1448 but only after the French had threatened the English garrisons with a massive army. Between 1445 and 1449 an uneasy peace was maintained until Charles VII brought this phase of the Hundred Years' War to a conclusion when he launched the assault on Normandy that smashed the English forces at Rouen and Formigny in 1450.

How had Henry VI managed to lose most of his French possessions by 1453?

English aggression provoked the French attack – an ill-conceived and foolhardy decision in 1449 to capture Fougères on Brittany's border. By 1453 Henry had lost virtually all of the remaining French territories.

Gloucester, York and Suffolk

Events in France in the 1440s contributed a great deal to the deepening rivalries between the most powerful of the English families which eventually led to civil war. **Humphrey, duke of Gloucester**, Henry V's surviving brother and Henry VI's uncle, was the most influential advocate of the policy of conquest during the period. This brought him into conflict with the then dominant Suffolk faction which, by and large, endorsed the king's policy of appeasement. In 1447, as tensions between England and France increased over the fate of Maine, Suffolk had Gloucester arrested, together with almost 30 of his associates, on treason charges. He was accused of planning to usurp the throne and smearing the queen's reputation by spreading rumours of an alleged affair with Suffolk. Five days later, the 57-year-old prisoner was dead. He probably died of a stroke after years of debauchery but rapidly the 'Good duke' became a martyr for those despairing of the present government and many believed Suffolk had engineered his murder.

Humphrey, duke of Gloucester (1390–1447) Humphrey, duke of Gloucester, was the youngest son of Henry IV and acted as occasional protector and regent during the minority of Henry VI. He was a strong supporter of the aggressive foreign policy of his brother, Henry V, and clashed with Suffolk over French affairs in the 1440s.

Richard Neville and his 12 children. Large families such as this were able to extend their influence in politics and the church through marriage and by exploiting royal patronage.

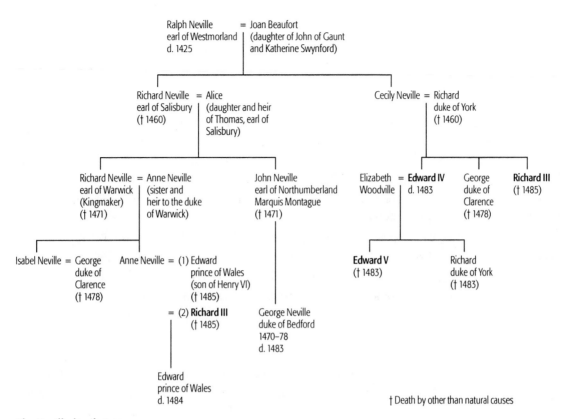

The Neville family tree.

Ralph Neville
earl of Westmorland
d. 1425
= Joan Beaufort
(daughter of John of Gaunt
and Katherine Swynford)

Richard Neville
earl of Salisbury
(† 1460)
= Alice
(daughter and heir
of Thomas, earl of
Salisbury)

Cecily Neville = Richard
duke of York
(† 1460)

Richard Neville
earl of Warwick
(Kingmaker)
(† 1471)
= Anne Neville
(sister and
heir to the duke
of Warwick)

John Neville
earl of Northumberland
Marquis Montague
(† 1471)

Elizabeth
Woodville
= **Edward IV**
d. 1483

George
duke of
Clarence
(† 1478)

Richard III
(† 1485)

Isabel Neville = George
duke of
Clarence
(† 1478)

Anne Neville = (1) Edward
prince of Wales
(son of Henry VI)
(† 1485)

= (2) **Richard III**
(† 1485)

George Neville
duke of Bedford
1470–78
d. 1483

Edward V
(† 1483)

Richard
duke of York
(† 1483)

Edward
prince of Wales
d. 1484

† Death by other than natural causes

Gloucester's death left **Richard, duke of York**, heir to the throne. York owned vast estates in England, Wales and Ireland and held several castles, including his stronghold at Ludlow in the heart of his Welsh Borders domain. Not only was Richard the wealthiest of Henry's subjects but some maintained his claim to the throne was even greater than that of the king's. Hard-featured and arrogant, York extended his influence through marriage to Cecily Neville, the 22nd child of Ralph Neville, earl of Westmorland. In all, York sired 12 children. Thus he, like his sons after him (Edward IV and Richard III), was at the centre of a great web of aristocratic relations and a powerful force to be reckoned with by those who crossed him.

York served as Henry's lieutenant in France in 1436–37 and then as governor of France and Normandy from 1440 to 1445. He had worked hard to save Henry V's crumbling French kingdom (and his own Norman estates) and shared Gloucester's dislike of appeasement. After two years of prevarication, his command in France was not renewed but, in 1447, granted to Suffolk's ally, Edmund Beaufort, the duke of Somerset. In the same year, York was made lieutenant of Ireland – a post he was reluctant to fill. He doubtless regarded his appointment as banishment, designed to keep him away from

Richard, duke of York (1411–60) Richard, duke of York, was descended on both sides of the family from Edward III. York was the obvious heir to the throne in the event of Henry VI dying childless, yet he had become alienated from the king and the dominant faction at his court by the later 1440s. No doubt York's opponents supposed he might have inherited the disaffection of his father, the earl of Cambridge, who was executed for his part in the Southampton plot of 1415, an attempt to displace his cousin, Henry V, and replace him with Edmund Mortimer, earl of March.

white roses The white rose was one of the badges used by the house of York. It had become the most popular of these badges by 1485, when Henry Tudor defeated Richard III at Bosworth. The red rose, one of the house of Lancaster's badges, became the principal badge of Henry VII after his accession.

the king and a court dominated by Suffolk. He was further annoyed by the crown's failure to pay him monies owed for his services in France. He reluctantly pawned his most precious possession – a heavy jewel-studded golden collar, decorated with the **white roses** of York: next to the crown jewels, the most valuable treasure in the kingdom. By the time he finally left England for Ireland in 1449, his financial difficulties had forced him to sell some of his manors. Meanwhile Somerset faced no such problems and his requests for outstanding payments, much to York's chagrin, were usually met with alacrity. To add insult to injury, in 1449, York lost further assets as Normandy fell to Charles VII, for which the duke, and the country at large, blamed Somerset and Suffolk.

Somerset shared York's descent from Edward III but, unlike York, he was also descended, like the king himself, from John of Gaunt, the duke of Lancaster. When, early in 1450, Suffolk made arrangements for his son to marry Somerset's niece, Margaret Beaufort, it must have seemed likely to York that, in the event of Henry dying without issue, his claim to the throne would be challenged by Suffolk and his 'Lancastrian' allies.

Suffolk's days, however, were numbered for, identified as a prime mover in the plans to seize Fougères in 1449, he was blamed for the loss of Normandy. Made the scapegoat for a humiliating foreign policy, the crown's bankruptcy and an embargo placed on English cloth exports by the duke of Burgundy, parliament sent him to the Tower in 1450 on a treason charge. Among other things, he was accused of planning to place his son on the throne, having arranged his betrothal to Margaret Beaufort, the direct descendant of John of Gaunt. Henry declared him innocent of the treason charge but, nevertheless, banished him for five years to save him from further condemnation. Having escaped a lynching in London, he set sail from England with a small entourage but his ship was intercepted off Dover by his enemies. They forced him aboard one of their own boats and after a few days on board, having been found guilty by an impromptu kangaroo court, he was sentenced to death and beheaded with half-a-dozen strokes of a rusty sword.

Why did Suffolk make so many enemies?

Cade's rebellion

The fear of reprisals against the people of Kent for the murder of Suffolk, together with general disaffection with the regime, high taxes, and the shock of the military disasters in France, precipitated Jack Cade's revolt in Kent in 1450. The rebels' demands, as described in their 'Complaint of the Commons of Kent', were for greater political equity among the aristocratic elite, the bringing to justice of Gloucester's 'murderers', an inquiry into the losses in France, and for financial efficiency – the king should **live of his own**. By 1450 the government was in debt to the tune of £372,000 and the sum was

live of his own The perpetual complaint of parliaments, forced by kings to impose extraordinary taxes in order to fund their extravagant royal activities, was that kings should try to 'live of their own'. This meant that they should cover their

Jack Cade's revolt was genuinely popular and highlighted the weaknesses of fifteenth-century kings and their governments. This lesson was not lost on Richard of York.

increasing at the rate of around £20,000 per annum. However, the rebels declared that they had no desire to depose their sovereign.

Cade's army was substantial (one contemporary source estimated it at 46,000) and it included many gentry. Among them were two members of parliament and three sheriffs. Henry VI, convinced the rebellion was a dynastic coup masterminded by York in Dublin, donned armour and marched a substantial army from Leicester towards London to meet the rebels. Half of the king's army confronted the rebels at Sevenoaks in Kent and was routed after a short but bloody fight. As mutiny spread through his army and Cade's popularity grew, Henry decided to withdraw to Kenilworth Castle in Warwickshire, leaving the archbishop and most of the council sheltering in the Tower. For a few days in July London fell into rebel hands. A number of courtiers, including Lord Say, the treasurer of England, were captured and executed but Cade's inability to keep control of his undisciplined army, together with the resentment of Londoners, soon forced him, after a bloody fight against the retinue in the Tower of London, to disperse his troops and abandon the cause. Though promised a free pardon, Cade was then pursued into Sussex and killed by the sheriff of Kent at Heathfield on 12 July. His body was brought back to London where it was beheaded and quartered. His head was boiled

expenses with revenue from the royal estates and from fines and other regular methods of raising money. Henry VI clearly failed to 'live of his own' for, by 1450, the royal debt stood at £372,000. This was at a time when the king's regular income amounted to probably less than £33,000. Henry VI's reputation was also tarnished by the corrupt practices of his courtiers and his own ill-considered and excessive patronage of favourites. The cost of running the royal household almost doubled within ten years of his minority ending.

and its fleshless skull replaced those of his own victims, impaled on spikes on London Bridge. Alison Weir, in *Lancaster and York* (1995), has illuminated the significance of these events:

> The rebellion had achieved nothing ... However, what had been made strikingly manifest by Cade's uprising was the inability of king and council to cope with such a crisis. A king was supposed to lead his armies, protect his people and enforce justice, but this king had fled, and in his absence the government of the realm had all but broken down. What had also been made alarmingly clear was how easy it had been for the insurgents to occupy the capital.

The troubles were not confined to London and the south-east. Simultaneous risings and riots occurred in the Midlands, the south and west. In June the congregation of Edington Church in Wiltshire hacked to death the bishop of Salisbury, Suffolk's friend and the king's chaplain, after he had said mass.

The return of Richard of York

The revolt had not been an attempt to depose Henry, although Cade had claimed connections with the house of York and declared his opposition to the dominant Beaufort faction. Absent in Ireland during these events, Richard of York was not directly implicated but he soon returned to England, probably with a view to declaring his loyalty as well as hoping to win political favour from a king scared by Yorkist supporters. His return was greeted with enormous public support and he soon rallied around him an 'army' several thousands strong. He marched on London and demanded to see the king, to whom he pledged his loyalty but also harangued for the misgovernment of the country. Shortly afterwards, he presented the king with a list of personal demands regarding payment of monies owed and recognition of his position as heir presumptive, together with a list of more general grievances echoing those contained in Cade's manifesto. A frightened king now admitted him onto the council but refused to abandon York's deadly enemy, Somerset. Returning to London, now that he had been admitted to the 'inner sanctum', York brought with him 3,000 armed retainers. However, while York's supporters dominated parliament, Somerset maintained his supremacy within the council. He was confident of the king's approval, which was confirmed in early 1451 by his appointment as captain of Calais. Despite attempts to impeach Somerset through parliament and the submission of a petition concerning York's position as heir apparent, it soon became clear that Henry would not be budged by protest and public demand alone. York began to prepare for an armed confrontation, certain that if he could not shift Somerset he stood to lose all.

In 1452 York raised an army and met with the king at Dartford, but submitted in the face of a stronger royal force. This was, however, only after an assurance from the king that he would arrest Somerset. In a remarkable scene that followed, York, having dispersed his army, rode into the king's camp with just 40 of his retainers, and stumbled upon a row in the royal tent between the king and queen concerning the fate of the newly arrested Somerset, who was also present. The tables rapidly turned on York, who now found himself a virtual prisoner, while Somerset regained his liberty. York's popularity saved him and, after making a solemn vow in St Paul's Cathedral never to rebel against the king, he retired to his castle at Ludlow under what amounted to a suspended sentence of **attainder** should he offend the king again. Without a blow being struck, the first engagement in the 'Wars of the Roses' was over.

The madness of King Henry VI

The crisis was made worse in August 1453 when, a few days after receiving news of an English defeat at Castillon and Charles VII's capture of Bordeaux, which marked England's final defeat in the Hundred Years' War and the loss of all territories except Calais, Henry, according to his contemporaries, 'went mad'. For a year-and-a-half he would be completely incapacitated and his eventual recovery was only a partial one, leaving him, it seems, a schizophrenic and, in the historian Charles Ross's memorable phrase, a 'useful political vegetable'. Then, in October 1453, Henry's queen, Margaret of Anjou, bore a son. Immediately rumours spread regarding the child's supposed illegitimacy, some of which maintained he was Somerset's bastard. The fact that Henry, in his madness, did not (because he could not) acknowledge the baby as his son merely heightened speculation.

Whether Henry survived his illness or not, the kingdom needed a regent and to this Richard of York, the king's nearest adult blood relation, promptly laid claim. His eventual success was the result of a swing in the political allegiances of the biggest and most powerful of the great families in fifteenth-century England, the Nevilles.

Richard Neville, the earl of Warwick, and a close relative to York by marriage, disputed the right to the lordship of Glamorgan granted to the duke of Somerset by Henry in 1453, even though Warwick had held it and administered it well for three years. Sharing York's sense of having been wronged by Somerset and the king himself, Warwick began to support York and abandoned the family's old loyalty to the house of Lancaster. The new alliance vastly improved York's position for, some said, Warwick was as rich as, maybe richer than, York himself. Moreover, his power was apparent in his massive fortresses and great armies of retainers, all of whom wore his livery of red

Why were York and Somerset such bitter opponents?

Why did the queen take Somerset's side?

attainder An Act of Attainder was the means by which parliament imposed punishment without trial on those accused of treason. It might result in execution and could mean the confiscation of all property and title.

jackets embellished with the insignia of a white bear and ragged staff. A considerable number of peers in the House of Lords were closely connected to him by blood or marriage. He was popular in both the north and at London. At his residence in the capital, six oxen were boiled and roasted for breakfast each day and members of his 600-strong retinue were endowed with the right to share with their friends as much meat as they could carry away on the blade of a dagger.

As the regency was being debated in parliament and at court, York and Warwick sought support and demonstrated their strength and determination by bringing with them to London a couple of thousand armed retainers.

In March 1454 York was made protector of the realm at the request of the king's council. In the likely event of Henry failing to recover his sanity, York seemed set to rule the kingdom for the next 14 years. Somerset had been vanquished. He was sent to the Tower and the queen banished to Windsor to tend her ailing husband. She had failed in the struggle for the regency and it was clear York intended to deny her further participation in courtly intrigues. It is likely that at this point Margaret saw a future, perhaps imminent, Yorkist bid for the throne and the disinheritance of her baby son.

What were the political consequences of the king's madness?

Why was Henry VI usurped by Edward, earl of March, in 1461?
The beginning of the Wars of the Roses

When Henry recovered at the end of 1454, the tables once again were turned on York. The king, remembering nothing of the past 16 months, recognised his son and had Somerset released. He was reinstated as captain of Calais, a position of considerable military strength recently usurped by York. York and Warwick retired to the north. Formally deposed as protector in February, York once more raised an army in order to march on London and persuade the king to abandon Somerset – a pre-emptive strike designed to defeat his rival before he found some means of destroying York himself. The king and Somerset learned too late of York's preparations and only managed to put around 2,000 men in the field to confront York's estimated 3,000. They met at St Albans on 22 May 1455. The battle was preceded by prolonged negotiations, which failed due to the king's absolute refusal to hand over Somerset and York's refusal to back down. After three hours of fighting, the royalist army began to flee; the king fell into York's hands and was placed in the abbey for safety and Somerset took refuge with the duke of Buckingham in an inn. A contemporary account, found in the archives in Dijon, France, described what happened next:

> ... after the doors were broken down the duke of Somerset, seeing that
> he had no other remedy, took counsel with his men about coming out
> and did so, as a result of which he and all his people were surrounded
> by the duke of York's men. And after some were stricken down and the
> duke of Somerset had killed four of them with his own hand, so it is
> said, he was felled to the ground with an axe and being so wounded in
> several places there he ended his life.

Buckingham fell with him. The king, meanwhile, wounded in the neck by an
arrow, was met by Richard of York in the abbey. Here the duke pledged his loyalty and begged forgiveness for endangering the king's life. The king, needless
to say, forgave all and accepted York as his unrivalled first minister. Warwick
replaced Somerset as captain of Calais – a role in which he was to distinguish
himself and become a hero of the southern ports for his success in clearing the
Channel of privateers and destroying a Spanish fleet.

St Albans was the first battle of the Wars of the Roses, so called because of
the badges worn by the two sides, the Lancastrian red rose and the Yorkist
white rose, at the Battle of Bosworth 30 years later.

The 'Loveday' – detente and war, 1455–59

For four years an uneasy peace was maintained. Henry, prone to insanity and
seemingly anxious to end the feuding, was easily contained by the new regime.
Margaret of Anjou, the Yorkists' bitterest enemy now that Somerset was dead,
was more of a threat. She established a rival court in the Midlands, made up of
members of families hostile to York and vengeful for the defeat at St Albans. As
the niece of Charles VII of France, she was blamed by some, undeservedly, for
the losses in France. Some believed it was the Frenchwoman's loyalty to her
kin that had shaped the disastrous half-hearted and pacifist foreign policy of
her weak, easily influenced husband. What was certainly true, however, was
the fact that she had needed to cultivate friendships among the leading noble
families. The patronage and favouritism by which this need was fulfilled contributed to the formation of factions and the feuds between them.

In February 1456 Henry felt sufficiently confident and well enough (it is
likely he suffered a relapse in 1455) to remove York from office, although he
retained his dominant position within the council. As a pay-off York was
granted over £1,800 arrears from his first protectorate and the promise of
more to come for expenses incurred during the second. Of even greater value
to the Yorkist cause was Henry's appointment of Warwick to the captaincy of
Calais, the military base from which he would later launch his invasion of
England. Peace continued for the next three years, propped up in 1458 by a
public show of reconciliation engineered by the king, the 'Loveday' of

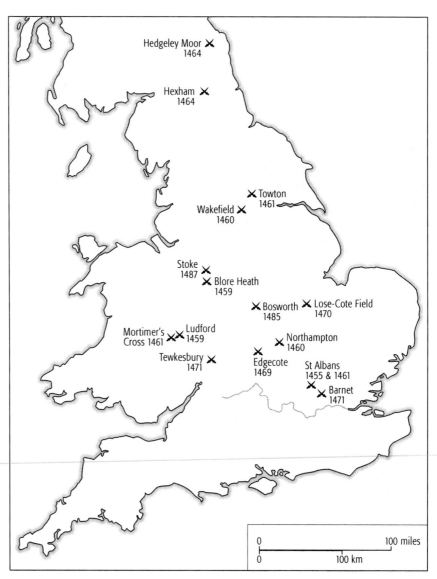

The major battles of the Wars of the Roses.

24 March, when members of the rival factions walked into St Paul's Cathedral arm-in-arm. In reality, the rift was anything but healed. While York was away carrying out his duties in Dublin, the feud between York and Lancaster revolved mainly around Warwick and Margaret of Anjou, who tried to have Warwick arrested for alleged crimes of piracy and inciting a riot at court.

By 1459 Margaret of Anjou and the duke of Buckingham appear to have convinced the king that Richard, and his ally, the earl of Warwick, intended to seize the throne. In June 1459 the Lancastrians decided the time had come to crush the Yorkist opposition by force. Indicted for treason, York and his supporters mobilised their forces once again. A small Yorkist army led by the earl of Salisbury defeated a larger Lancastrian force in September at Blore Heath, in Shropshire. A game of cat and mouse followed as the bulk of the king's army, together with the king, pursued York to his base at Ludlow. The subsequent desertion of Yorkist troops, however, following the king's promise of a pardon, put paid, for the time being, to the Yorkist cause. Duke Richard, leaving his remaining commanders arrayed for battle in the field, fled to Ireland while Salisbury and Warwick fled to Calais. York left his wife, his two young sons and 13-year-old daughter behind at Ludlow. The duchess was taken into captivity and Ludlow was ransacked by the Lancastrian soldiers.

What role did Margaret of Anjou play in the disputes between Lancaster and York?

The Parliament of Devils

From this point on, the position of the Yorkists, and other malcontents, was markedly different. The leaders of the Yorkist party were declared rebels at the 'Parliament of Devils' in Coventry in November 1459 and their lands and goods forfeited to the crown. The harsh treatment of the rebels and the disinheritance of their innocent heirs shocked other members of the nobility, who otherwise might have stayed loyal to Henry. Meanwhile, Warwick and Salisbury in Calais prepared for their next campaign, Warwick funding it through piracy against the French, which had the added value of making good nationalist propaganda for the Yorkist cause.

The Yorkist invasion, 1460

In June 1460 Warwick and York's son, Edward, the earl of March, returned to England, landing with 2,000 men at Sandwich. Declaring his intent to relieve the king of evil counsellors, Warwick was admitted into Canterbury with the blessing of the archbishop and then marched towards London, gathering support as he went. The lord mayor of London was persuaded by popular feeling and the Yorkist sympathies of certain resident magnates to open the capital's gates to Warwick's now vast army of around 40,000. A number of Lancastrian nobles meanwhile took refuge in the Tower of London.

The inevitable engagement between the Yorkists and King Henry took place at Northampton on 10 July 1460. Outnumbered, the Lancastrians were soundly defeated in the space of half-an-hour. Between 300 and 400 soldiers were killed out of 50,000 or so involved and, among them, lay the duke of Buckingham. The king, on Warwick's orders, was taken alive. The day was a wet one, so wet that the king's army was unable to fire its batteries of guns on Warwick's soldiers as they marched towards Northampton along the London road. The hero of the day was York's son, Edward, soon to become Edward IV. Richard himself was still in Ireland.

A parliament was called with a view to revoking the Parliament of Devil's attainder of 1459. Only when York returned in September was a Yorkist claim made to the throne of England. This appears to have been on York's own initiative, unexpected by his supporters and resisted by his ally, Warwick, who feared the fury such a claim would unleash. A fifteenth-century chronicler, Whethamstede, recorded York's arrogant behaviour when he arrived at Westminster in October 1460:

> On entering the palace he marched straight through the great hall until he came to the solemn chamber where the king is wont to hold his parliament with his Commons. And when he came there he walked up to the king's throne and putting his hand on the cushion, as a man taking possession of his own, and kept it there for a short space. At length withdrawing it he turned his face towards the people and, standing quietly under the royal cloth of state, awaited the applause of the onlookers. While he stood, Master Thomas Bourchier, Archbishop of Canterbury, approached him, and with due reverence asked him whether he wished to come and see the lord king. To which he answered thus: 'I mind me of no one in this kingdom to whom it is not more fitting that he should come to see me than I to him.' Then the duke withdrew to the principal chambers in the whole palace (as the king occupied the queen's apartment), and the bolts having been broken and the doors forcibly opened, he took up his abode there for some time in the manner of a king rather than of a duke.

York did not succeed in persuading the lords to depose the king in his favour but they did agree that York and his heirs should inherit on Henry's death. An Act of Settlement, the 'Act of Accord', was drawn up to this effect on 24 October 1460, becoming law by regal and parliamentary agreement four days later. In the same month the attainders against York and his followers were reversed. Charles Ross in *The Wars of the Roses* (1976) has described the years 1460 to 1487 as 'the first truly revolutionary period in English history'. As often as not, after 1460 the king himself, in addition to his 'evil counsellors', became the target of opposition bent on overthrowing the governments of the day. As a result, the crown changed hands six times in just 25 years.

The Battle of Towton, March 1461

Incensed by the Act of Accord, which had turned a struggle for governmental reform into a dynastic one, the Lancastrians rallied under Queen Margaret at Hull. In November 1460 they marched south, determined to free the king in London from his captors. The speed with which the Lancastrians responded to recent developments and their decision to wage war so late in the campaigning season appear to have taken York by surprise. Leaving Warwick to safeguard London, York marched north with a small army of around 4,000 to meet the 20,000 or so Lancastrians. Although he recruited as he marched, York finally confronted Queen Margaret with no more than about 12,000 soldiers. York's final battle was fought outside his castle at Sandal, near Wakefield, on 30 December. His army, depleted while soldiers were out foraging for provisions, was overwhelmed by the larger Lancastrian force and both he and his second son, the young earl of Salisbury, were killed. Their heads, the duke's adorned with a paper crown, were impaled on Micklegate, an entrance into the city of York.

Margaret then marched south, her forces ravaging the towns and villages through which they passed, 'just like so many locusts' according to one contemporary chronicler. The disreputable and the impoverished joined them for no better reason than seizing booty from the villages, manor houses and monasteries which were plundered as they passed. Whole towns, including Coventry, switched allegiances from Lancaster to York as news of the northerners' atrocities reached them. Queen Margaret enjoyed a second victory at St Albans on 17 February 1461, when Warwick's army was overwhelmed. Warwick had taken Henry VI with him, who, it is said, passed the battle a mile away, sitting under an oak tree, laughing and singing. Warwick fled and Henry was reunited with his wife.

Margaret now looked set to recapture London but the reputation of her army went before it. The city prepared to defend itself against Lancastrian butchery, by now perceiving the Wars of the Roses as a struggle between the north and the south. According to some historians, it was her genuine desire to protect the interests of Londoners that inspired Margaret to withdraw and so allow the Yorkists under Edward, earl of March, to enter the capital on 27 February.

Fresh from his victory against a Lancastrian army at the Battle of Mortimer's Cross, fought in the Cotswolds a few weeks earlier, 18-year-old Edward now proclaimed himself king. The Lords in parliament declared his claim superior to that of Henry VI and he received the rapturous support of crowds of ordinary Londoners.

The greatest and bloodiest battle of the Wars of the Roses was fought days later at Towton in Yorkshire where, on 29 March, Palm Sunday, Edward IV caught up with the Lancastrians who had regrouped around the city of York with a view to organising a decisive strike on the south. Between 60,000 and 100,000 men met at Towton, around 2 per cent of the total population. The Lancastrian army was made up of mainly northerners, the Yorkist army of southerners. The battle was exceptionally long, lasting from 11 a.m. to about 9 p.m. in an era when most battles were over within three or four hours. The weather was vile, the wind driving snow into the soldiers' faces. The fight had started badly for Edward when, on the previous day, an advance force was

Henry VI painted in a pose that emphasises his piety. This was thought to be a worthy but not necessarily the most valuable kingly attribute. He cut a very different figure from both his father, Henry V, and his usurper, Edward IV.

ambushed by a contingent of cavalry led by Lord Clifford and massacred. He raised the morale of his army at this point by slaying his horse in front of them and declaring his intent to fight with the army on foot, to the end.

The Yorkists won the day and the enemy force was shattered with the killing of 6 Lancastrian peers and more than 40 knights. Thousands more died, many drowned in the river or were cut down as they fled the battlefield. It is likely as many as 9,000 perished during and directly after the battle. One contemporary commented: 'so many dead bodies were seen as to cover an area six miles long by three broad', and modern historians, like Alison Weir in *Lancaster and York* (1995), consider it 'probably the bloodiest battle ever to take place on English soil'. At York, Queen Margaret and Henry VI received news of the defeat and promptly fled to Scotland, narrowly avoiding capture by those in pursuit. According to the fifteenth-century chronicler, Waurin, the house of Lancaster had received its just deserts:

King Henry and his wife Queen Margaret were overthrown and lost that crown which his grandfather Henry IV had violently usurped and taken from King Richard II, his first cousin, whom he caused to be wretchedly murdered . . . Men say that ill-gotten gains cannot last.

Edward entered York in triumph. Passing through Micklegate he was greeted by the dismal sight of the rotting heads of his father and brother. These he had removed and buried with the other remains at Pontefract. In their place were now impaled the heads of the earl of Devon and two other leading Lancastrians who had also taken refuge in York.

Historical interpretation: the long-term and short-term causes of the Wars of the Roses

Long-term causes

As historians explore the reasons why major historical events occurred, they often order their conclusions into long-term and short-term causes. One of the debates surrounding the origins of the Wars of the Roses concerns how far back the historian should look for explanations. The struggle between two dynasties that partly gave rise to the wars stemmed from at least as early as the unfortunate reign of Richard II. This was ended by his cousin, Henry Bolingbroke, the dispossessed duke of Lancaster. However justified Bolingbroke, now Henry IV, had been in usurping his vengeful, profligate and predatory cousin, the doubtful claim of the Lancastrians to rule would trouble the closing years of the reign of Henry's grandson, Henry VI. From the earliest Tudor times, historians held that Henry VI merely reaped the sins of his fathers.

Short-term causes

Some historians, however, view the causes of the civil wars in the shorter term. According to one, B. P. Wolffe in 'The personal rule of Henry VI', in S. B. Chrimes, C. D. Ross and R. A. Griffiths (eds.), *Fifteenth-century England 1399–1509* (1972), 'it is unnecessary to look back beyond the period of Henry VI's personal rule.' Just as Richard II had been the author of his own downfall, it is claimed by Henry's latest biographers that his incompetence alone explains the conflict that led to his overthrow. Wolffe even frees the government of the 'protector' during Henry's minority, from all blame. Indeed, most authorities now consider England was ruled well until Henry VI was old enough to take over.

Other views

Both perspectives are equally credible. Alison Weir, in her highly readable account of the wars, *Lancaster and York: the Wars of the Roses* (1995), has combined the short-term and long-term causes of conflict:

> At the centre of this bloody faction fight was the pathetic figure of the mentally unstable Henry VI, whose ineptitude in government and mental incapacity gave rise to political instability, public discontent, and dissensions between the great landed magnates that in turn led ultimately to war and a bitter battle over the throne itself. Henry's chief rival was Richard Plantagenet, duke of York, the man who should have been king, according to the law of primogeniture as it was then understood.

Furthermore, she takes the roots of the conflict back even further to the reign of the prolific Edward III (1327–77), who helped establish a history of rivalry among those of royal blood by producing a brood of 13 princes and princesses.

> The kingdom of England was not an island in the first half of the fourteenth century. The claim of English kings to territories in France and the wars they fought, first to seize and then to protect them, have a place in any explanation of the origins of the Wars of the Roses. Henry V, victorious at Agincourt, immortalised by Shakespeare, has long been held to be the greatest of the English kings of the middle ages. However, his enthusiasm for campaigning resulted in his early death and, therefore, the first potential disaster of Henry VI's reign: accession at the age of nine months. Furthermore, as Charles Ross has observed in *The Wars of the Roses* (1976), while beacons, lit on English hilltops to celebrate and spread the news of victory over the French, made good royal propaganda at the time, the French wars saddled the English crown with a heavy burden of debt. This debt was to increase steadily 'under the crippling strain of another 22 years of campaigning; and Henry's preoccupation with France effectively prevented him from tackling the urgent problems of lawlessness and disorder which afflicted his realm of England.'

Thus the debate, in part, revolves around the controversial issue of how far Henry VI really was to blame for the misfortunes of his reign and how far he was the victim of his inheritance and other circumstances beyond his control. In a recent account of Henry VI's rule, *Henry VI and the politics of kingship* (1996), John Watts reached the conclusion that those who were behind the conflicts that eventually erupted into civil war were themselves 'victims, driven by the hideous logic of a dysfunctional system to the fruitless creation and defence of an authority which could not be exercised'. According to Watts, the fault lay not with any overmighty subject or dynastic faction, defeat in foreign wars or the misapplication of patronage, but a constitution which relied too much on the personality of the king. In the hands of a Henry V or an Edward IV, the monarchy was relatively secure, but with a man like Henry VI at the helm, the system was almost bound to fail.

Summary questions

1 Identify and explain the difficulties confronting Henry VI in his government of England between 1450 and 1455.

2 Explain why Henry VI was usurped in 1461.

3 Explain the reasons for the insurrections of Richard, duke of York.

4 Compare the importance of at least three of the reasons why English territories in France were lost during the reign of Henry VI.

2 The Wars of the Roses and the first reign of Edward IV

Significant dates

1461 *February* Edward IV's first reign begins.
March The Yorkists are victorious at the Battle of Towton.

1462 Queen Margaret, with French support, attacks the north of England from Scotland.

1463 Edward IV secures a truce with France. The French promise to withdraw support from the Lancastrians.

1464 Edward IV marries Elizabeth Woodville.
The Battle of Hexham takes place.

1465 Henry VI is captured.

1466 Elizabeth Woodville's father, Earl Rivers, is made treasurer of England.

1469 A rebellion led by Robin of Redesdale breaks out.
The Battle of Edgecote takes place.
Edward IV is held prisoner by Warwick.

1470 *February* The Lincolnshire rising occurs.
March Warwick is defeated at the Battle of Empingham.
September Warwick invades England and Edward IV flees.
October The readeption (restoration) of Henry VI takes place.

1471 *March* Edward IV returns to England.
April Warwick is defeated and killed at the Battle of Barnet.
May Prince Edward is killed at the Battle of Tewkesbury. His mother, Queen Margaret, is captured.
Henry VI is put to death in the Tower of London.

Overview

Edward IV was a very different kind of king from the pious, schizophrenic and generally unheroic Henry VI. The new king was 18 and handsome, unusually tall, lean and athletic. Edward was usually good-natured and approachable; his appetite for food and women was excessive: he was known to make himself vomit in order to enjoy the pleasure of filling his stomach again, and he seduced women of all rank, married and unmarried. He spent considerable sums of money on a luxurious lifestyle and he loved hunting. This king made

A portrait of Edward IV, who possessed all the valued qualities of the archetypical medieval king.

every effort to look the part, wearing his crown whenever making a public appearance, enforcing strict rules of etiquette on his courtiers, dressing in fine and lavish costumes. A visiting dignitary from Bohemia described his as 'the most splendid court that one could find in all Christendom'. Edward IV took a personal interest in the details of government and he worked hard at establishing a personal rapport with the mightiest of his subjects. Furthermore, although he had no interest in promoting an imperialist foreign policy, Edward had proved himself to be dynamic and relentless in war. He was victorious in his first command at the Battle of Mortimer's Cross and it was he who had steered the Yorkists into the triumph at Towton.

The decade of Edward's first reign was a turbulent one which saw further civil war, betrayal by his closest friends and relatives, capture, defeat and flight. His success in holding on to power for so long, given the circumstances of his accession, is as remarkable as the speed with which he regained it in 1471.

For a long time it was assumed that the battles Edward fought for the throne were disastrous for the people and economy at large. This view was most forcibly put by the early Tudor chronicler, Polydore Vergil, in his *Anglica historia*, completed in 1537:

> ...while one [faction] sought by any manner to subdue the other, and raged in revenge upon the subdued, many men were utterly destroyed, and the whole realm brought to ruin and decay.

In more recent times, however, historians have questioned the extent to which the wars represented catastrophe and widespread anarchy (see Chapter 6).

How was Yorkist power consolidated following the Battle of Towton?

Edward IV's position in 1461 was tenuous to say the least. Many families in the north, secure in their great fortress castles, remained staunchly loyal to the Lancastrian cause. The house of Lancaster had two figureheads with which rebels in England or invaders from abroad might find common cause: King Henry in the north and young Prince Edward in Scotland.

Warwick, to whom Edward IV gave full responsibility for military affairs, was successful in the first months of the reign in taking rebel fortresses in the north of England, which included the castles of Bamburgh, Alnwick and Dunstanburgh. After the slaughter of Towton, Edward was remarkably lenient during the 1460s in his dealings with the leaders of pro-Lancastrian families and both Henry Beaufort, duke of Somerset, and Sir Ralph Percy were forgiven and their castles restored to them. Such generosity did not pay off: by

Following his defeat at the battle of Hexham in 1464, the duke of Somerset was executed.

1462 Percy was back in league with the rebels, and was eventually killed on the battlefield of Hedgeley Moor in 1464. The duke of Somerset, despite being shown real friendship by Edward, which included the rare privilege of occasionally sharing his bed, led the resistance of 1464 which ended in defeat at Hexham in May.

In November 1462 Queen Margaret reopened hostilities by invading the north from Scotland with the support of a small army provided, with the French king's approval, by the grand seneschal of Normandy. Her reliance on French support made her cause all the more unpopular in England. Worse still, she had promised Louis XI Calais in return for his help. Although the castles of Alnwick, Bamburgh and Dunstanburgh admitted her, she was unable to raise a force capable of withstanding the massive army Edward launched against her. She fled by sea, having narrowly escaped capture, further north.

In October 1463, Edward secured a truce with the French King Louis XI by which it was agreed that France would cease funding the Lancastrian cause. Warwick began to seek a suitable French bride for Edward in order to strengthen the new Anglo-French rapport. In December a similar agreement was reached with the Scottish government and Henry VI was obliged to leave Edinburgh and seek the refuge of Bamburgh Castle from which to rule his small kingdom. This was now made up of only a handful of Northumbrian castles.

Why was Edward's truce with Louis XI so important?

In the spring of 1464 the duke of Somerset launched one last desperate attempt to revive the house of Lancaster by trying to inspire rebellion in Wales, Cheshire and Lancashire. The Lancastrians were defeated at the skirmish of Hedgeley Moor and, decisively, at the Battle of Hexham by Warwick's brother, John Neville. Although Henry VI escaped, the most prominent Lancastrian leaders, including Somerset, were either killed in the fighting or executed shortly afterwards. A few pockets of resistance remained but the Lancastrian cause as a whole was shattered. Henry spent over a year in Yorkshire, Lancashire and the Lake District on the run with a single companion, his chamberlain, Sir Richard Tunstall. He was finally captured in July 1465 and brought to London, lashed to his horse and wearing an undignified straw hat. As he rode through the streets on his way to the Tower, he was abused and even pelted with rubbish by onlookers as he passed.

Having suppressed the Northumbrian revolt in 1464 and finally taken Henry into captivity, Edward's position was relatively secure so long as his Yorkist sympathisers stayed loyal. The next crisis of the reign would come from an unexpected quarter – the rebellion of his former ally, the earl of Warwick.

Why did Warwick turn against Edward IV?

Warwick's rebellion

Warwick has been labelled by tradition with the epithet **'Kingmaker'** for his part in championing and fighting for the Yorkist cause. In fact, it was an even alliance and the victories were Edward's own, Warwick proving less adept in battle. Edward was neither 'made' by Warwick nor controlled by him. Warwick was rewarded for his support with territories and titles such as captain of Calais, admiral of England and constable of Dover Castle. This mightiest of subjects, however, was denied a complete monopoly of power as royal patronage extended to other faithful pro-Yorkists. This was particularly true in the case of Lord Hastings, who was given Warwick's stewardship of the duchy of

'Kingmaker' The nickname 'Kingmaker' came to be attached to the earl of Warwick in the sixteenth century, and with some justification, although other factors also need to be taken into consideration. Warwick's support of the Yorkists was instrumental in securing victory at the Battle of Towton and thus establishing Edward IV on the throne. The support of this mightiest of nobles was the foundation on which the Yorkist invasion of 1460 had rested. Ten years later his rebellion against Edward IV was the most important element in the readeption of Henry VI. Warwick's irrepressible ambition made the Wars of the Roses and the bloody rivalries between those that fought them much worse.

The earl of
Warwick's badge:
a chained bear.

**Elizabeth Woodville
(c. 1437–1492)** Edward
married Elizabeth
Woodville on 1 May 1464.
It is evident from the
circumstances of the
ceremony that he
appreciated the dismay
with which his action
would be received. On his
way north to confront the
remaining Lancastrian
opposition he arose before
dawn on May Day and
rode to Grafton in
Northamptonshire, the seat
of the Woodvilles, on the
pretext of going hunting. In
the early morning, in a
small chapel at Grafton
called the Hermitage, his
marriage to Elizabeth was
witnessed by just the priest
and his helper, the bride's
mother and two
gentlemen. That night the
new queen was smuggled
into his bedchamber at
nearby Stony Stratford by
her mother. A little over a
week later Edward rode on
alone to meet his army at
Leicester.
Edward's marriage
provoked an ultimately
fatal rift in the house of
York. Warwick and other
magnates were alienated
by this elevation of a 'low'
family with previous
Lancastrian sympathies
(Elizabeth's father, brother
and first husband had
fought on 'the other side').
Edward's two brothers and
mother were equally
outraged.

Lancaster, and Sir William Herbert, who was elevated to the lieutenancy of South Wales in place of the earl. To add insult to injury, Edward secretly married **Elizabeth Woodville** just as Warwick was close to concluding a political marriage alliance with the French royal family. Edward's marriage appears to have been a purely romantic affair – unlike other women moving in court circles, the beautiful and manipulative Elizabeth refused to let the king sleep with her unless wed. Politically, the marriage, and Edward knew it, was utterly irresponsible at a time when the young king's hand could have been used to great national advantage. Edward was the first English monarch to marry a commoner since before the Norman Conquest. Furthermore, their union went against royal marital convention because she could not protest her virginity – she had had two sons by a previous marriage to Sir John Grey. He had died at the Second Battle of St Albans in 1461, fighting with Edward's enemies, the Lancastrians.

On 14 September 1464, while under pressure from Warwick to conclude a French marriage alliance, Edward confessed to the council he was already wed. The assembled magnates were horrified as the Woodville family was thus suddenly and unexpectedly raised to the upper echelons of the English aristocracy. The further marriages in quick succession of Elizabeth's several siblings linked the family to some of the greatest houses in the kingdom. Warwick's own daughters were usurped as Elizabeth's sisters secured the most eligible bachelors in the kingdom, including the heir of Lord Herbert and the 11-year-old duke of Buckingham. Her brother John, at the age of 20, was married off to a rich heiress, the duchess of Norfolk, who was approaching her eightieth birthday! Members of the Woodville clan acquired some of the highest positions in the land: one of Elizabeth's brothers was made bishop of Salisbury, another admiral of the fleet. In 1466 Earl Rivers, her father, became treasurer of England in place of Lord Mountjoy, Warwick's uncle.

The wedding of Edward IV and Elizabeth Woodville. This marriage was to have a profound effect on Edward's reign.

George Neville During celebrations for Warwick's brother's appointment as archbishop of York, more than 4,000 sheep, 500 stags, 100 oxen and 13,000 puddings were consumed, washed down with a 105 gallons of spiced wine and 300 casks of ale. Warwick was the 'steward of the feast' but, ominously, the king was absent.

As the Woodvilles rose, Warwick's influence over the king declined. His family remained powerful, indeed his brother, **George Neville**, was enthroned as archbishop of York in September 1465 but, increasingly, Edward failed to act on his advice. Family matters aside, the king and his hitherto first minister were divided over foreign policy. Edward moved towards Burgundy, while Warwick believed that England's best interests lay in permanent alliance with the traditional enemy of England, and present enemy of Burgundy, France. As early as 1467, Louis was contemplating the possibility of bringing Queen Margaret and the earl of Warwick together in an attempt to overthrow the increasingly pro-Burgundian English king.

At much the same time, Warwick began to engineer the marriage, against the king's wishes, of his daughter, Isabel, to the king's ambitious brother and heir presumptive, George, duke of Clarence. When Edward became aware of

Warwick's overtures, he was furious and regarded the earl's plans as a blatant attempt to make himself more powerful and to challenge the Woodvilles. When, in June 1467, he heard that George Neville, archbishop of York, was seeking dispensation from the pope to marry his niece to Clarence, Edward dismissed him from his office as lord chancellor, to the approval of the Woodvilles. This last insult seems to have determined the final collapse in the once close friendship between Warwick and Edward. The ensuing alliance with Burgundy, applauded by London's merchants and consolidated by Edward's sister's marriage to the duke of Burgundy's eldest son in 1468, marked the beginning of Warwick's personal alliance with King Louis of France. Jean de Waurin, a contemporary chronicler, writes:

> He [Louis XI] had done his utmost to make an alliance with the English in order to destroy the duke of Burgundy, so it was generally said, and he had succeeded in winning over the earl of Warwick to his side, and with him almost the whole commons of England.

According to the chronicler of the Abbey of Crowland, this marriage, rather than that of Edward to Elizabeth Woodville, was the principal reason for the conflict between the king and the earl of Warwick. Deeply alarmed by the resurrection of the Anglo-Burgundian alliance, Louis cultivated the rift between Edward and Warwick and even offered the earl a principality forged out of Holland and Zeeland as an incentive for dismantling the Edward–Woodville regime.

What were the causes of the rift between Warwick and the king?

By the spring of 1469 Warwick was in league with Clarence in seeking to undermine the Woodvilles, the one with a view to controlling the king himself, the other contemplating taking his brother's place on the throne. Clarence encouraged Warwick to turn against the king and helped spread the rumour that his brother was not Duke Richard's son but the bastard of an archer called Blaybourne.

In July 1469 at Calais, Clarence defied his brother by marrying Warwick's daughter, Isabel. The marriage coincided with a pro-Warwick rebellion in the north led by Robin of Redesdale, almost certainly instigated by the earl himself. Edward commanded Warwick, who was part of the wedding party in Calais, to return to England and lend his support but Warwick refused. Instead, on 12 July, he issued a manifesto declaring his intent to relieve England from the tyranny of poor government, high taxes and lawlessness by petitioning the king to dispense with his corrupt and inept councillors. If he failed to do so he would deserve deposition, like unreliable kings before him. Warwick invited his supporters to meet him in three days at Canterbury, while his ally, Sir John Conyers, marched a large army from Yorkshire towards the Midlands.

Warwick arrived at Canterbury on 16 July. With an army made up of men of Kent and soldiers from the Calais garrison he then rode north to join the northern army and do battle with the loyalists, led by the earl of Pembroke. They met and fought a ferocious battle at Edgecote Hill, ten kilometres north of Banbury, on 26 July. Pembroke was defeated and, without justification, beheaded for treason on Warwick's orders.

Edward IV received news of Pembroke's defeat three days later while camped a few kilometres away at the village of Olney near Coventry. Knowing he was now at Warwick's mercy with his main army shattered, he allowed his supporters to disperse and remained at Olney, awaiting the arrival of Warwick's soldiers.

With Edward held in custody, first in Warwick Castle and then Middleham, Warwick, with Clarence's support, attempted to rule in his name. The Woodville dynasty now suffered the retribution of the Nevilles: following their capture in the Forest of Dean, Earl Rivers and Sir John Woodville were beheaded on 12 August and Rivers' wife shortly after was accused of witchcraft and arrested, though later released.

Anarchy in parts of the realm, including London, and a Lancastrian rising in the north, forced Warwick to release the king in mid-September, for, without him, Warwick was unable to gain the support of the lords or command the loyalty of Yorkist soldiers. Warwick gave Edward his liberty in return for the support of the loyal northern magnates, who provided him with an army which rapidly suppressed the rebellion.

Edward, reinstated, returned to London where, in December, he was publicly reconciled with his brother and Warwick. Despite their recent antics, neither was punished and those who had fought for them in the summer were pardoned – Edward could ill afford to maintain old enmities but, equally, Warwick no longer could expect any further royal favour.

A rebellion in Lincolnshire in the spring of 1470, largely engineered by Clarence, presented Warwick with another chance to achieve his objectives, this time throwing in his lot with the king's brother in a bid for the crown. The swift defeat of the Lincolnshire rebels, crushed by Edward at the Battle of Empingham (Lose-Cote Field) before Warwick could provide reinforcements, put paid to their attempts to extend rebellion into the north and west. The traitors fled to France and the protection of Louis XI. Men seized from ships at Southampton belonging to the earl, one of which had been destined to carry Warwick and Clarence to safety, were less fortunate. According to Dr John Warkworth of Cambridge University, a contemporary chronicler, writing about 12 years later in his *Chronicle of the first thirteen years of the reign of King Edward the Fourth*, they received the full force of Edward's violent retribution:

King Edward then came to Southampton and commanded the **earl of Worcester** to sit in judgement of the men who had been captured in the ships: and so 20 gentlemen and yeomen were hanged, drawn and quartered, and then beheaded, after which they were hung up by their legs and a stake was sharpened at both ends; one end of this stake was pushed in between their buttocks, and their heads were stuck on the other. This angered the people of the land and, forever afterwards, the earl of Worcester was greatly hated by them, for the irregular and unlawful manner of execution he had inflicted upon his captives.

Why did Edward IV lose the throne in 1470 and how did he recover it in 1471?

The restoration of Henry VI

In France, Warwick enacted a startling change of heart in seeking the forgiveness of Margaret of Anjou and promising to support the Lancastrian cause in the hope of redeeming his position in England. In this grand project, Warwick had the full support of the French king, who promised to aid their cause with money, ships and soldiers. In return, Louis would receive English support in the campaign he planned to launch against Burgundy. After lengthy talks with King Louis and uncomfortable audiences with her old enemy, Warwick, Queen Margaret was eventually persuaded to accept the earl as her ally. The alliance was sealed by the marriage of Prince Edward to Warwick's daughter, Anne Neville, but only after Warwick had agreed to withdraw all allegations he had previously made regarding his new son-in-law's paternity. Margaret meanwhile accepted the fact that her husband was incapable of ever ruling his kingdom alone again, and promised to make Warwick Henry's regent and governor of England. Clarence was not entirely neglected in these proceedings: he was promised the crown in the event of Prince Edward dying without issue.

As other members of the Neville family rose in the north, distracting the king from possible invasion in the south, Warwick and Clarence returned in force. They landed in Devon, a Lancastrian stronghold, in September 1470 when King Edward was away in Yorkshire concerned with the northern rebels. Warwick marched north to do battle with Edward and the king headed south. However, while Warwick gathered support along the way from his own admirers and supporters of the house of Lancaster, Edward's followers began to desert him, most crucially the marquess of Montague, who had raised an army ostensibly intended for the suppression of the northern rebels but was now urging his troops to join Warwick. Edward was obliged to abandon

earl of Worcester
(1427–70) Nicknamed 'the Butcher of England', John Tiptoft, earl of Worcester, became the most hated of Edward IV's councillors. Highly educated and cultured, Tiptoft married Warwick's sister, Cecily Neville and, in 1452, was made the realm's treasurer at the age of 24. As constable of England for the most of the 1460s, he played a central role in establishing Edward's regime but became very unpopular because of the severity of his methods. According to pro-Lancastrian chroniclers, these included particularly cruel executions. Some methods were of his own invention, some imported from abroad.
When the earl of Oxford was found guilty of involvement in a Lancastrian conspiracy to depose Edward IV in 1462, Tiptoft had him condemned to death: he was disembowelled, castrated and, still conscious, burned alive. When Henry VI was readepted (restored), Tiptoft, alone among the Yorkist nobility, was arrested and beheaded for treason. Tiptoft's translations of Cicero were among the first works to be printed by a later admirer, William Caxton.

thoughts of defeating Warwick in a last heroic battle in the Midlands and instead fled east with a small entourage, boarded a ship at King's Lynn on 2 October and sailed for Holland and the protection of Burgundy.

On 3 October 1470 Henry VI was released from captivity in the Tower of London and formally readepted (restored) to the English throne. Warwick, who had played such an important part in his overthrow, now made him king once again and carried his train in St Paul's Cathedral in a formal thanksgiving ceremony. The contemporary chronicler, John Warkworth, explained the reasons why Edward failed to keep his throne in 1470 in his *Chronicle of the first thirteen years of the reign of King Edward the Fourth*:

> They [Edward's supporters] had expected prosperity and peace from Edward IV, but it was not to be. One battle followed another, and there was widespread disorder, and the common people lost much of their money and goods. Firstly, a tax of a fifteenth part of all their property was levied, and then another fifteenth to pay for the fighting. These and many other factors had reduced England to the direst poverty. Many people thought, moreover, that King Edward was to blame for harming the reputation and esteem of the merchants for, at that time, both in England and abroad, these were not as great as they had been before.

The return of Edward IV

The readeption of Henry brought with it war with Burgundy: the condition on which Louis XI of France had supported Warwick's campaign of 1470. France opened the hostilities in December of the same year and England followed suit in February. England's merchant community was horrified as the loss of the wool trade's chief markets loomed. For Warwick, the support of France was a political disaster for it pushed Duke Charles of Burgundy into close alliance with England's fugitive King Edward. With 50,000 crowns donated by Duke Charles, Edward IV was able to start planning his own restoration. Once again, the attitude and involvement of foreign powers would determine English history.

Why did the war with Burgundy lose Henry VI so much support?

England had entered the war without the consent of parliament and against the wishes of the London merchants. When Edward set sail for England in March at the head of a tiny army, Warwick could no longer rely on widespread public support.

Edward landed at Ravenspur in Yorkshire on 14 March 1471. Although he expressed his determination to succeed by giving orders for the ship he had sailed in to be burned, there was no certainty that the country at large would rise in his support. While Edward made his way to York, Warwick desperately tried to assemble an army to defeat him. Initially neither party was particularly successful in its recruiting drive: Hull barred its gates to Edward and a number of magnates ignored Warwick's pleas for help. Defiantly, Edward headed south with a couple of thousand men preparing to challenge the might of Warwick's much larger conscript army (according to one contemporary chronicle his soldiers were enlisted 'on pain of death'). By the time he confronted Warwick, camped behind Coventry's city walls with perhaps as many as 7,000 men, Edward's army was at least 5,000 strong and led by a king who had never yet lost a battle. According to the chroniclers, some of those who lent him their support did so because he owed them money, others because their wives, with whom he had been secretly acquainted, urged them into the field! Warwick wisely stayed put and awaited reinforcements while Edward occupied the earl's castle at nearby Warwick.

At Banbury, on 3 April, Clarence, with a host of 12,000, joined forces with his brother, Edward, who forgave him and promised the full restoration of his estates. Together they now marched on London, taking care to guard their rear with seasoned troops against an attack from Warwick. Meanwhile Warwick's brother and archbishop of York, George Neville, prepared to defend London, parading his liege, Henry VI, through London's streets in the hope of securing public support and confidence. He gained neither, for when the mayor and aldermen of the capital were made aware of the size of the army descending upon them they decided not to resist. Even Neville himself abandoned his brother at this point and sent messages to Edward declaring his readiness to open London's gates. On 11 April Edward and Clarence entered the city, received by cheering crowds and formal greetings from its mayor and other dignitaries. Having confined Henry VI to the Tower, Edward was reunited with his wife, Elizabeth, and their two daughters. Here too Edward met, for the first time, his five-month-old son – the hope and future of the Yorkist dynasty.

Rather than await Warwick's arrival, Edward next decided to ride out of London and meet the duke's pursuing force some distance away from the capital. They met at Barnet, 16 kilometres out of London, and fought a fierce battle on Easter Sunday, 14 April. Warwick had the larger force – possibly twice the size of Edward's, which numbered around 10,000. Both Edward and Warwick were engaged in the thickest of the fighting, choosing, as was then the custom, to lead their armies from the front. Confusion in Warwick's ranks, which began when a body of archers mistook some of their own for the enemy and fired on them, gave Edward a hard-earned victory. The Yorkists lost 500 men and around 1,000 of Warwick's men were slain. The earl himself was killed as he tried to escape from the battlefield. His body was brought to London and displayed for three days in St Paul's Cathedral for public viewing, in order to scotch any rumours that he had survived.

A contemporary illustration of the battle of Tewkesbury. This may show the death of Prince Edward, who was killed when he and the remains of the division under his command had been routed by the Yorkist troops and were fleeing northwards towards the town.

Jasper Tudor
(**c. 1431–95**) Created earl of Pembroke in 1452, Jasper Tudor was a prominent supporter of the house of Lancaster. He went into exile following his defeat at the Battle of Mortimer's Cross in 1461, and championed his nephew, Henry Tudor, the future Henry VII. In 1485 Henry made him duke of Bedford.

The day before the battle, Henry's queen, Margaret of Anjou, and son, Prince Edward, had sailed into Weymouth to raise an army in the south and west against Edward. Margaret heard the news of Warwick's defeat while resident at Cerne Abbey in Dorset. Initially she abandoned all hope of defeating her husband's usurper but, as her army swelled with Lancastrian supporters from the southern counties joining her at Cerne, her resolve strengthened. A plan of campaign was developed in which **Jasper Tudor** would ride ahead and set about raising an army in Wales and she would follow, heading north to Lancashire via Bristol, Gloucester and Chester.

On 23 April, a week after hearing of Margaret's landing, Edward left London, at the head of a small army, in an attempt to engage Margaret before she was able to join forces with Jasper Tudor. As Margaret headed north through Exeter, Glastonbury and Wells, recruiting as she marched, Edward moved west to Cirencester and then went south to Malmesbury, hoping to block her advance. However, Margaret was already in Bath and, instead of veering north-east towards Edward's waiting army, she chose to go further west to Bristol, arriving there on May Day. With Edward in pursuit, Margaret continued north and rested at Berkeley Castle, a little way south of Gloucester, with Edward camped some miles behind at Chipping Sodbury.

The Lancastrian army then continued to Tewkesbury, intending to cross the Severn, but here Edward finally caught up with Queen Margaret and the prince. Margaret's army outnumbered Edward IV's but his was more experienced and better equipped. The Battle of Tewkesbury was fought on 3 May 1471 and, for the second time in three weeks, Edward was victorious. In the carnage Prince Edward, together with many other Lancastrian magnates, was killed and, a few days later, Queen Margaret was captured. Although Warwick's cousin, the Bastard of Fauconberg, launched an unsuccessful assault on London, Edward was triumphant and arrived back in the capital on 21 May to great public acclaim. Towards midnight on the same day the 50-year-old King Henry VI was put to death in the Tower, presumably on Edward's orders. This monumental event was recounted by John Warkworth about 12 years later, in his *Chronicle of the first thirteen years of the reign of King Edward the Fourth*:

> And the same night that King Edward came to London, King Harry, being in ward in prison in the Tower of London was put to death the 21st day of May on a Tuesday night between eleven and twelve of the clock, being then at the Tower the duke of Gloucester, brother to King Edward, and many other; and on the morrow he was chested and brought to Paul's and his face was open there that every man might see him. And in his lying he bled on the pavement there; and afterwards at the Black Friars was brought, and there he bled new and fresh; and from thence he was carried to Chertsey Abbey in a boat and buried there in Our Lady's Chapel.

It is interesting to note that in this account, which almost certainly predates his reign, Richard III (the duke of Gloucester) is implicated in the martyred king's murder.

His queen, Margaret, was spared and, after some years of benevolent captivity in England, she was permitted to return to France where she died in poverty in 1482. Jasper Tudor, with whom, fatally, she had failed to meet in May 1471, fled to France, eventually to return with his nephew, Henry Tudor, the future Henry VII, in 1485.

What was the nature of war during the Wars of the Roses and how did it affect the participants?

The military historian trying to investigate the Wars of the Roses has little detailed, reliable evidence from which to draw conclusions. Few accounts of the conflicts were ever written down: of the 13 battles fought, a total of just four provide eye-witness versions of these momentous events that determined dynastic history. Unreliable and often conflicting chronicles, written some time after the events described, provide the 'history' of the rest.

The nature of warfare in the middle years of the fifteenth century was quite unlike that of earlier times. The outcome of the fighting was more likely to be determined by unarmoured foot soldiers rather than mounted knights; artillery, particularly in siege scenarios, began to play a crucial role. On the other hand, the traditional long bow retained, for the time being, its importance as the preferred projectile weapon of English commanders. The primitive hand guns familiar to German mercenaries were virtually absent on England's fifteenth-century battlefields, although Edward IV brought with him a contingent of Flemish hand-gunners when he returned from Burgundy in 1471. The infantry were armed with billhooks and bows. The long bow forced cavalrymen to dismount and fight on foot to preserve their horses. For their own protection they wore heavy fluted armour, capable of deflecting arrows and blades. Quality mid-fifteenth-century armour was more vulnerable to bludgeoning, and maces and flails (spiked iron balls on chains) were widely employed. A popular weapon among men of rank, such as the duke of Gloucester (later Richard III) at Barnet, was the poleaxe: an axe mounted on a metal-studded, five-foot long pole, designed to crush and rip open armour. The weight of their arms and armour, perhaps as much as 50 kilograms, rapidly exhausted the combatants and thus most engagements were of no more than a couple of hours' duration. The unmounted men-at-arms and infantry determined the outcome in battles that, after an initial exchange of arrows and cannon fire, dissolved into a mêlée of ferocious hand-to-hand fighting, in which the long bow no longer played a decisive part. Under such circumstances, skill, weaponry and armour were critical, and the extent of participation by the nobility, their retainers and hired professional mercenaries was all-important. Lords and kings, with the exception of Henry VI, fought, and sometimes fell, in the thickest of the fighting; 12 noblemen were killed in the fighting between 1459 and 1461 and 10 between 1469 and 1471. Such 'leadership from the front' virtually eliminated the chance of tactical warfare once the enemy was engaged at close quarters. The survival of the leaders would help determine whether or not their followers fought on.

Why was the role of the foot soldiers so important in fifteenth-century battles?

In their defence against an attacker, armies used caltraps and pavises. The caltrap was made up of a number of small metal spikes forged together, each pointing in a different direction. A precursor of twentieth-century tank traps, it was designed to bring down the heavy cavalryman whose mount had the misfortune to tread on one of the caltraps littering the ground. The pavise was a wooden screen protecting an archer, with windows cut into it through which he could shoot. This, too, might be spiked with nails protruding from one side so it could be laid on the ground to further hinder the enemy as the archer withdrew.

The number of soldiers involved in any of these pitched battles can only be guessed at. Certainly the figures provided by the chroniclers and eye-witnesses are notoriously inaccurate. William Gregory claimed for example that 200,000 fought for the Yorkists against an even larger Lancastrian force at Towton. This simply does not tally with modern demographers' calculations of a total of just 600,000 men of fighting age living in the whole of England at that time. In most cases the soldiers were local men fighting as an obligation to their lords. Paid professionals could be relied upon to undertake extensive campaigns over considerable distances, but not the unpaid amateurs who had fields to tend and more peaceful trades to pursue. Only the biggest engagements, such as Towton (1461) and the Second Battle of St Albans (1461), were anything more than local conflicts grounded in local feuds and loyalties. At Towton, however, no less than 75 per cent of the surviving adult peers participated and this exceptional battle probably involved over 50,000 – less than the 500,000 or so implied by William Gregory but still a colossal encounter by contemporary standards. This was far and away the greatest battle in numerical terms; even the decisive Battle of Bosworth in 1485 was fought out by fewer than 25,000 men. Many were a good deal smaller still. There were, for example, just 5,000 or so men at the First Battle of St Albans.

Overgenerous estimates for the numbers involved inevitably mean the casualty totals were exaggerated. Towton was an unusually large battle, of uniquely long duration, and exceptionally bloody. Thousands were killed: contemporary sources range from almost 40,000 to a more credible 9,000.

The high proportion of nobility killed in the wars reflects both the number involved and their personal contribution in hand-to-hand combat. Participation, and every great family in England participated, provided opportunities for reward and the chance to defeat a rival in some private vendetta. Old rivalries polarised allegiances: as one family sided with York or Lancaster another supported the opposition. Gentry retainers, however, were not always willing to follow the example of their turn-coat lords, as the duke of Clarence found in 1469.

Self-interest motivated many of those involved and determined the sides on which they fought, which might well change between battles. For others, honour and kinship were the decisive factors and some pursued lost causes to their own ruination. The duke of Exeter lost everything in 1461 and went into exile in France where he was reduced to walking barefoot, begging for food from house to house while taking care not to reveal his identity.

Most of the lords, in fact, remained loyal to their feeble king, Henry VI, until his defeat at Towton in 1461. Edward IV effectively created a new Yorkist nobility by reviving old titles and making new ones. In 22 years he added to their ranks 35 'new' peers. For the remainder of the conflict between York and Lancaster, therefore, the peerage was more evenly divided between the two sides. Lands forfeited to the king by the vanquished provided endowments for some of these additional lords. Edward's growing reliance on these jumped-up gentry, to the detriment of established peers, has been shown as a political blunder by historians, and the main cause of Warwick's change of allegiance and rebellion in 1469.

Some historians have depicted the elevation of such peers as Rivers and Stafford as too radical a break with tradition for the longer-established magnate families to tolerate. Furthermore, Warwick's defeat of this new aristocracy proved how unsubstantial this power could be; the Woodvilles and their allies lacked the loyalties that, after generations of service, bound together the older lords and the gentry.

The greatest magnates, such as Warwick, had a substantial retinue made up of retainers who held their estates as the feudal tenants of their lord. In 1448 the duke of Buckingham, for example, numbered among his retinue 10 knights and 27 esquires, many in receipt of valuable annuities, and numerous paid servants and officials managing his estates across 22 counties. Consequently, Buckingham probably had the capacity for creating the largest private army in England. His decision to abandon a neutral stance in 1459, and to support Margaret of Anjou's cause, provided her with the resources to challenge the Yorkist protectorate and so provoke further civil war. The initial rout of the enemy after Blore Heath brought rewards for Buckingham in the form of forfeited Yorkist lands and goods. A few months later he was killed when Warwick and the future Edward IV defeated the Lancastrians at Northampton. Typical of his caste, he had been driven by a combination of loyalty to his anointed king and the prospect of material gain.

What factors played a part in determining the side on which each magnate chose to fight?

Summary questions

1 Why did Edward IV face difficulties in his first reign?

2 How important were the threats to Edward IV's maintenance of authority in the period to 1471?

3 Explain the reasons why Warwick turned against Edward IV.

4 Compare the importance of at least three significant events in the first reign of Edward IV.

3

The end of the Yorkists, 1471–85

Focus questions

- ◆ To what extent was Edward IV's foreign policy a failure?
- ◆ How effectively did Edward IV manage his financial affairs?
- ◆ Did Edward IV create a 'new monarchy'?
- ◆ Why, and with what consequences, did Richard, duke of Gloucester, make himself king of England?
- ◆ Why was Richard III overthrown by Henry Tudor?

Significant dates

1452 Richard III is born at Fotheringay castle; a frail child considered unlikely to survive infancy.

1460 Richard's father and brother are killed at the Battle of Wakefield.

1461 Richard III's brother, Edward, is crowned Edward IV; Richard is made duke of Gloucester.

1470 Edward IV and Richard, duke of Gloucester, go into exile following the readeption of Henry VI.

1471 The Battles of Barnet and Tewkesbury take place. Edward IV is restored as king and Henry VI is murdered in the Tower of London.

1478 George Plantagenet, duke of Clarence, is put to death in the Tower of London.

1483 *April* Edward IV dies.
June Edward V is usurped as king of England by the duke of Gloucester, now Richard III. The two young princes in the Tower disappear.
October–November Buckingham's rebellion occurs.

1484 Richard III's only legitimate son dies.

1485 *March* Anne Neville, Richard III's wife, dies. Rumours spread that she was murdered so that the king could marry his niece.
August Henry Tudor defeats and kills Richard III at Bosworth; Henry VII's reign begins.

Yorkist foreign policy, 1471–85

1475 Edward IV invades France in alliance with Burgundy and Brittany, but fails to secure the French crown.
The Treaty of Picquigny is signed.

1477 Louis XI invades Burgundy.

1480 Edward pledges support to the Burgundian cause which is now taken up by Maximilian of Austria, who is married to Mary of Burgundy.
The Scots, perhaps encouraged by the French king, begin making raids on English border territory.

1482 England invades Scotland. Berwick upon Tweed is regained. The Burgundian conflict ends with the Treaty of Arras.

1483 Edward IV and Louis XI die.
Richard III's reign begins. Alexander, duke of Albany, brother of James III of Scotland, launches an abortive, English-sponsored, attack on Scotland.
Henry Tudor attempts an invasion of England, supported by the duke of Brittany.

1484 A three-year truce between England and Scotland, backed by a marriage alliance, is signed.

1485 Henry Tudor invades England with French assistance; Richard III dies at the Battle of Bosworth.

Overview

The second reign of Edward IV

After the drama of the first, the second decade of Edward IV's reign might seem a little dull. There were no further crises after 1471 to compare with Warwick's rebellion. Moreover, the campaigns Edward launched against France and Scotland lack the drama of the string of bloody 'all or nothing' battles fought on English soil in 1460 and 1461, when he first secured the throne. Nevertheless, the second reign was not uneventful: he was threatened by a rebellious brother, his invasion of France brought to mind Henry V's empire-building and, on the eve of his death in 1483, English armies ravaged the lowlands of Scotland. For a time, Scotland's king and his seat of Edinburgh were held captive. Edward was barely 40 when he died of an illness allegedly brought on as a result of a dissolute lifestyle. His early death, leaving a child as heir, was the one great disaster of his reign. Had he lived long enough to see his son grow into adulthood, the history of the turbulent 1480s would have been very different indeed.

The reign of Richard III

> Richard III has divided opinion for five hundred years. To many he has always been a villain, a bloody tyrant and detestable child-murderer deservedly overthrown. To others he was and remains a hero, a noble prince and enlightened statesman tragically slain.
>
> A. J. Pollard, *Richard III and the princes in the Tower*, Stroud, 1991, p. 1

Richard, duke of Gloucester, was Richard of York's son and the youngest brother of Edward IV. When Edward died in 1483 he was the only surviving brother – four of York's sons died in childhood, Edmund, earl of Rutland, was killed with his father almost a quarter of a century earlier at the Battle of

Edward IV is presented with a book by leading members of the Woodville family. To his left stand his queen, Elizabeth Woodville, and their son, Prince Edward.

Wakefield and George, duke of Clarence, was put to death in the Tower of London in 1478. Unlike Clarence, Richard had been entirely loyal to his brother and was rewarded accordingly. His marriage to the widowed Anne Neville, Warwick's daughter, resulted in his inheriting the earl's great northern estates. He was entrusted with the defence of the realm in the north, with full authority to cede to his territories anything he could conquer across the border in Scotland.

When Edward died, his 13-year-old son became Edward V. Before his coronation, however, Richard took the boy into custody, first declaring himself protector and then the rightful king of England. The prince and his younger brother disappeared some time in the summer of 1483, probably murdered in the Tower, and members of the Woodville faction were put to death. His enemies now rallied around the hitherto insignificant figure of the exiled Henry Tudor, who, in 1485 at the Battle of Bosworth Field, defeated and killed the usurper and made himself King Henry VII, the first of the mighty **Tudor dynasty**.

Yorkist foreign policy, 1471–85

Edward IV

Edward IV's foreign policy was characteristic of kings throughout the fifteenth century. He was preoccupied with French relations, France being the 'traditional enemy' of England and the natural ally of an independent Scotland (in what was known as the 'Auld Alliance'). Like his predecessors, Edward laid claim to the French crown. Although he probably believed it was beyond his grasp, this was the ultimate objective of his invasion of France in 1475.

Obviously Edward had enough to occupy him in securing his position at home without becoming entangled in dynastic struggles abroad. In fact, foreign policy was intimately wrapped up in domestic matters since the French king, Louis XI, was likely to do all he could to undermine the English crown and to keep England at bay while he pursued his own continental objectives. Furthermore, Louis was sympathetic to the Lancastrian cause, as he was related to Margaret of Anjou, Henry VI's queen. Louis' obvious ally in this was Scotland, who was fiercely determined to remain independent of England, while Edward's continental allies, who wished to be independent of France, were the duchies of Burgundy and Brittany.

Edward organised two major campaigns abroad – one in France, the other in Scotland. A huge army was landed in France in July 1475, partly paid for by a **benevolence**. The duke of Burgundy failed to provide much support, however, and, within weeks of landing, the campaign was terminated by the Treaty of Picquigny in August 1475.

Tudor dynasty The reason the name Tudor became synonymous with the English monarchy of the sixteenth century is because, according to one chronicler, Catherine of Valois could not 'curb her carnal passions'! After the death of Henry V in 1422, when she was just 21, the prospect of her remarriage became a major political issue since her new husband would be stepfather to her baby son, Henry VI. In 1428 parliament passed a statute forbidding her to marry without the permission of the king, once he had come of age. In 1429, after meeting at a ball where he fell drunkenly into her lap, she married Owen Tudor in secret. By choosing a commoner, who had no part in the faction struggles of the day, she side-stepped the controversy that a marriage to a more significant player would have unleashed. Few would have envisaged a time when the children of her second marriage would determine England's dynastic future and furnish England with five monarchs.

benevolence This was an obligatory 'gift' of money which the king demanded from the great families. It had to be paid in order to retain the favour of the king.

Louis XI of France, who was a formidable enemy of Edward IV. The 'Auld Alliance' between France and Scotland posed a serious threat to the security of the realm.

This temporary restoration of good relations would be wrecked by England's involvement in the French–Burgundian conflict that erupted in 1477. With the guarantee from Burgundy's ally, Maximilian of Austria, that he would pay the Picquigny pension (see pp. 53–54) in the event of war between England and France, in 1480 Edward prepared to launch a further campaign.

Any plans Edward laid were stalled by Scottish incursions into English territory in the same year. The resulting English invasion of Scotland started well with the capture of Edinburgh and James III, but bad planning and poor leadership left just Berwick upon Tweed in English hands.

Meanwhile Louis had greatly diminished the independent status of Burgundy and, in the Treaty of Arras (1482), Maximilian was forced to concede territory, and his daughter was promised to the **dauphin**, Louis' son. By the time Edward died, he had lost his French pension and the alliances upon which the successful outcome of his continental policy depended.

dauphin Dauphin was the title of the eldest son of the king of France, in use from 1349 to 1830.

Richard III

Richard III's foreign policy was also determined by relations with France and Brittany, and concern to prevent an alternative claimant to the throne gaining foreign support. In this he was clearly, and fatally, unsuccessful. He appears, however, to have came close to removing the threat of Henry Tudor by eventually persuading the Bretons, after they had attempted to invade England in support of Henry in 1483, that they had more to gain by backing him. In return for handing over Henry, it was promised that Duke Francis of Brittany would receive the earldom of Richmond, English ships would cease to harass Breton merchants, and that England might support the duchy in another campaign against France. A timely flight to France, advised by fellow exile, John Morton, bishop of Ely, saved Henry and paved the way for his victory in 1485.

To what extent was Edward IV's foreign policy a failure?
Foreign relations and the renewal of war with France

Edward had been restored to the throne at least in part because of the support of Burgundy. Drawn together by a mutual and traditional antipathy for France, some form of retaliation for French interference in English affairs would have seemed likely after Edward's victory in 1471. The young king had earned for himself a formidable reputation as a warrior and might reasonably have been considered a new Henry V, destined to rebuild his great predecessor's French kingdom, so ignominiously lost during the reign of Henry VI. At the very least, Edward could be expected to commit England to the defence of Calais, the obvious target of French aggression. In fact, although not necessarily by intent, Edward's second reign saw no major continental campaign. The absence of such a campaign greatly contributed to Edward's success in financial terms: despite the cost of winning the throne and the general turbulence of civil war, helping to provoke the economic crisis he inherited in 1471, he was the first king of England in two hundred years to leave the crown solvent on his death.

Edward, born in Normandy, certainly envisaged war with France and inherited the traditional ambition of English kings to wear the French crown. He was sufficiently the realist to know that a full reconquest was out of the question but he relished the prospect of glory abroad and limited territorial gains. At the very least, he could hope to prevent Louis XI of France from lending further support to the Lancastrians. In this he had the support of parliament. Lengthy negotiations with potential allies in a continental campaign resulted in 1475 in a tripartite alliance between England, Burgundy and Brittany. A large army, consisting of 12,000 troops and almost the entire English nobility, was raised, paid for by additional taxes and a benevolence. In the summer of 1475, Edward invaded France. One chronicler on the French side, Philippe de Commynes, later wrote in his *Mémoires*:

Charles the Bold, duke of Burgundy. During the fifteenth century English kings tended to ally with Burgundy against France, their traditional enemy.

> ... this army was the largest that a king of England had ever brought over, and all the men were mounted and were better armed than any that had ever come to France, and nearly all the lords of England were there ...

This, however, did not mark the beginning of a glorious campaign and within a few weeks it was over, concluded by the terms of the Treaty of Picquigny of August 1475. An Anglo-French war would have been cripplingly expensive and unlikely to achieve the ultimate objective. Charles Ross, in *Fifteenth-century England 1399–1509* (1995), is of the opinion that Edward was inadvertently saved from his own misadventure by the actions of the duke of Burgundy: 'It is hard to say exactly what Edward's plans entailed but it is fairly certain he hoped to achieve something more glorious, and probably less bloodless, than the final outcome.' Ross has argued that his invasion of France was not an impromptu decision but a scheme for which Edward had been preparing, diplomatically and militarily, during the preceding three-and-a-half years.

If, in fact, Edward merely intended to intimidate France and wrest from the French king some compensation for his interference in recent English affairs then the campaign was a great success. By the terms of the treaty, Edward secured an immediate 'tribute' of around £15,000, on condition he withdraw

The historic meeting of Louis XI and Edward IV at Picquigny is the subject of this carving in St George's Chapel, Windsor.

his army, and a further annual 'pension' of £10,000 to prevent his returning. This arrangement, designed to last for seven years, was to be reinforced by the intended marriage of Edward's daughter to the French dauphin. The English king and his whole army had been lavishly fêted by the French at Amiens as a satisfactory settlement was being agreed. After Edward had departed from Calais, Louis is said to have joked, 'I chased the English out of France far more easily than my father did – he had to do so by force of arms, but I simply used meat pies and good wine.'

Despite continued tension between the two countries and the implicit support that Louis XI gave to the troublesome James III of Scotland, the truce ran its course and Edward continued to receive his valuable French pension until Burgundy and France made their own truce – the Treaty of Arras in December 1482.

In the same year, Edward launched a punitive invasion of Scotland against James who, encouraged by Louis, continued to condone border raids on the north of England. Supporting James's brother's claim to the Scottish throne, Edward's army, led by Richard of Gloucester, seized Edinburgh and captured the king. When his brother, the duke of Albany, suddenly renounced his claim, there was no longer any reason for the invasion and Gloucester withdrew, retaining for England the border fortress town of Berwick-upon-Tweed. The exercise had been very costly, provoking riots in southern England, and could be said to have been quite unnecessary. It is true that, for a short while, Gloucester's exploits made good royal and English nationalist propaganda: celebratory bonfires were lit and cannons fired all over England when the duke entered Edinburgh. The string of minor victories on land against the Scots, and the devastation of James III's fleet in the Firth of Forth in May 1482, was some consolation for the lacklustre campaign in France seven years earlier.

Edward's foreign policy was unspectacular during his second reign and doubtless he did not live up to the expectations of those contemporaries who

James III of Scotland and his heir, the future James IV. James III's hostility caused Edward IV much trouble and expense throughout his reign.

had seen him triumphant in 1471. The Treaty of Arras was a bitter blow that, it has been suggested, hastened his death in 1483. It might have been prevented had he concentrated on preserving the old animosity between France and Burgundy instead of undertaking the venture in Scotland. Some historians have painted a very negative picture of Edward IV's foreign undertakings. The Treaty of Arras is highlighted as his greatest failure. He was, it is claimed, out-manoeuvered by Louis XI and he failed, through lack of resources, to take full advantage of the rivalry between France and Burgundy.

A more sympathetic assessment might highlight the huge financial burden a more 'heroic' policy would have represented, and point to the peace with France, the payment of the French pension, the humiliation of James III and the acquisition of Berwick as modest successes.

What were the successes and failures of Edward IV's dealings with France and Scotland?

How effectively did Edward IV manage his financial affairs?

It is likely that Edward IV's personal excesses contributed to his early death. This was the result of a stroke, brought on in the opinion of Charles Ross by excessive, relentless gluttony. He was renowned for his splendid costume and once impressive figure, but infamous for his overindulgence. In the words of the chronicler, Dominic Mancini, an Italian cleric resident in London in 1482–83:

> In food and drink he was most immoderate: it was his habit, so I have learned, to take an emetic for the delight of gorging his stomach once more. For this reason and for the ease, which was especially dear to him after his recovery of the crown, he had grown fat in the loins, whereas previously he had been not only tall but rather lean and active.

Edward's luxurious court, the lavish gifts to his favourites and kin, as well as the cost of maintaining the royal castles, conducting foreign campaigns and paying the salaries of certain officials, placed a substantial financial burden upon the royal shoulders. His ordinary income derived from the crown lands (spectacularly increased by the attainders of 113 of his enemies after 1461), **feudal dues** (including **wardships** involving the juvenile heirs of nobility killed in the wars), customs duties and fines. Any 'extraordinary' income to meet extraordinary expenditure, that associated with a military campaign for example, could be raised as a tax introduced by parliamentary consent. Corruption, reluctance to pay additional taxes and general bureaucratic inefficiency obliged Edward to rely in part upon the 'voluntary' payment of benevolences. His need for cash in order to fund his invasion of France in 1475 led him into one of his many 'perambulations' around the kingdom, as he cajoled nobles, mayors, aldermen and rich widows into making donations. 'And thus', reads *The great chronicle of London*, 'by his own labour and other solicitors . . . he gathered notable sums of money with the which all provision was made in all goodly haste for the said voyage.' The campaign provided Edward with a welcome additional income by the terms of the Treaty of Picquigny. By such means Edward was able to 'live of his own' without having to rely too heavily upon unpopular taxation. Claims that he promoted a more lucrative, reformed management of the crown estates have, however, been challenged by some historians who have identified many estates in which there was no significant increase in yield across the years of Edward's second reign.

Under Edward the handling of **royal finances** became more efficient, with the king himself at the centre of affairs. Many of the financial responsibilities of the heavily bureaucratised Westminster-based Exchequer were transferred to the Chamber; royal funds were now housed in the king's personal apartments and he scrutinised spending. The Chamber clerks thus held some of the

feudal dues In return for land, rent was paid by the tenant in the form of services of various kinds which were known as feudal dues.

wardships In the event of a minor inheriting an estate, the landlord could make the heir his ward and take control of the estate until the ward came of age. This was known as wardship. The lord might claim the right to arrange his ward's marriage.

royal finances When he first came to the throne, Edward IV faced the challenge of royal insolvency. Despite his personal extravagances and the keeping of a lavish court, he was successful in steering the crown away from bankruptcy. Several Acts of Resumption ended many grants and pensions made during Henry VI's highest posts in the kingdom. The lord chamberlain had to be a most trusted servant.

Although Edward, by 1478, was solvent, it would be inappropriate to consider him as financially astute as the greatest royal economist of the fifteenth century, Henry VII. Inheritance, attainders and luck, as much as, perhaps more than, careful financial administration, accounted for his success in this particular area.

The monk, Ingulf, wrote in the *Chronicle of the Abbey of Crowland*:

> He dared not from now on demand subsidies from the English people ... he bent all his thoughts towards gathering together a treasure worthy of his royal estate from his own substance and by his own industry ... He appointed surveyors of the customs in every port of the kingdom, the most prying of men, and, by all accounts, excessively hard on the merchants. The king himself procured merchants' ships, loaded them with the finest wool, cloths, tin and other commodities of the kingdom and, just like any man living by trade, exchanged merchandise for merchandise ... He would only part with the revenues of vacant prelacies [bishoprics], which according to **Magna Carta** cannot be sold, for sums which he had determined on, and on no other terms. He scrutinised the registers and the rolls of Chancery and exacted heavy fines from those heirs whom he found to have intruded themselves without due process of law, as recompense for the issues which they had enjoyed in the meantime ... Within a few years he had made himself into a most opulent prince so that none of his predecessors could have equalled him in collecting vessels of gold and silver, tapestries and precious ornaments for his palaces and churches, in building castles, colleges and other fine places and in acquiring new lands and possessions.

Did Edward IV create a 'new monarchy'?

Edward has been more admired for the strength of his rule in England than for his foreign policy. Claims that he reduced the autonomy of the nobles, that he centralised power and made the process of government more efficient, have inspired historians, notably J. R. Green (1837–83), to describe Edward's as a 'new monarchy', the model his successors would fashion into Tudor '**despotism**'. Such commentators regarded the civil and dynastic wars as the principal means by which fifteenth-century monarchs broke the might of 'overpowerful' noble families.

Recent examinations of the relationship between the crown and nobility conclude that, in fact, there was no significant change under Edward IV.

reign, spending in the royal household was more carefully monitored, he acquired the wealth of a number of estates confiscated from defeated Lancastrians and the officials running his estates were made more accountable. In 1465 parliament was persuaded to grant him, for life, the monies raised by customs duties at England's ports. His wealthier subjects were required to offer benevolences –'gifts' of money to their monarch from time to time as a gesture of loyalty. Unlike Henry VI, he was careful to repay loans, thus making the crown more creditworthy. This helped whenever he needed to borrow money. Furthermore, his reign coincided with a general improvement in trade with continental Europe as the economic depression lifted in the later 1460s.

Magna Carta The Magna Carta, or Great Charter, was sealed by King John at Runnymede in 1215, at the insistence of rebellious barons. It came to be regarded as the fundamental statement of English liberties, including the principles that freemen should be judged by their peers and 'to no one will we sell, to no one will we deny or delay right or justice'.

despotism A despot is a ruler with absolute power and despotism is the word used to describe the rule of a despot.

Although he just about managed to keep control over them during his second reign, Edward continued the tradition of allowing great magnates to rule more or less independently, on his behalf, in peripheral regions. However, in this reign he proved less tolerant of those who might seek to usurp him a second time; Henry VI was murdered on 21 April 1471, and Edward's brother, Clarence, who had conspired with Warwick in 1469, was finally arrested in 1477 and placed in the Tower, accused of further treasonable activities. He was killed there in February 1478.

On the other hand, the king was a generous patron of his supporters and allowed some particularly close family members, notably his brother, the duke of Gloucester, the future Richard III, to become very powerful indeed. He permitted them to retain their private armies of retainers, relying on mutual interests to curb any inclination to use them against him. Old opponents were given the opportunity to redeem themselves and, between 1472 and 1475, 30 attainders were reversed. Meanwhile old feuds between great families, such as the one between the Harringtons and Stanleys, continued unabated. Full-scale civil war was temporarily ended, but regular bouts of localised provincial lawlessness, violence and bloodshed remained.

> What evidence is there that Edward IV did not significantly challenge the power of the nobles?

Historical sources

A 'new monarchy'?

1 Edward revitalises government

He [Edward IV] did much to consolidate the monarchy, to rehabilitate its finances, and to restore its prestige. He stopped the process of decay in monarchy and government . . . The foundations of what has commonly been called the 'new monarchy' were laid not by Henry VII, but by Edward IV.

Source: S. B. Chrimes, *Lancastrians, Yorkists and Henry VII*, Basingstoke, 1964, pp. 124–25

2 Edward fails to restrain the aristocracy

king's council The council, to an extent, was reformed under Edward IV. Where in the past it was made up of members of the aristocracy and a high proportion of churchmen, in the 1460s it became more secularised and promotion to and within the council became dependent on ability as much as birth. Some of its 12 or so members were mere gentlemen.

The **king's council** retained its importance and its functions changed little. There is no doubt that many of Edward's personal servants were capable and effective, but he did lack a strong personal following in the provinces, such as that built up by Richard of Gloucester in the north, and there was always suspicion and jealousy of the Woodvilles. Edward made no consistent effort to restrain the power of the aristocracy. He still relied on the support of the great families in the shires, such as the Stanleys in Lancashire and Cheshire.

His failure to restrain aristocratic power can be contrasted unfavourably with the far more assertive Henry VII. If the country was not as lawless as in the reign of Henry VI, this simply reflected Edward's more powerful personality.

Source: David Grossel, in John Lotherington (ed.), *The Tudor years*, London, 1994, p. 21

3 Law and order

The crux of the problem [maintaining law and order] lay in the immunity of the powerful offender, especially those who had the king's support. There was an inherent conflict between repeated demands for impartial justice and the king's committed support of the great men to whom he had given rule of the shires. Bitter complaints against their excesses run through the reign. The Commons in 1467 were particularly outspoken in linking a rising crime rate with the 'heavy lordship' of men in standing with the king, against whom redress could not be obtained . . . Edward was extraordinarily lavish in delegating local power and influence to his supporters. No man had ever enjoyed the power in south Wales wielded by Lord Herbert in the 1460s. The same is true of Richard of Gloucester in the north in the 1470s. Professor Chrimes would have us believe that by 1483 'there was no over-mighty subject left in England.' But was not Gloucester [later Richard III] the mightiest of over-mighty subjects? And was not his great north-country connection, built up with active royal encouragement, a major factor in enabling him to consolidate his hold on the throne? This was part of the price that Edward IV paid for effective political control during his lifetime.

Source: C. D. Ross, 'The reign of Edward IV', in S. B. Chrimes, C. D. Ross and R. A. Griffiths (eds.), *Fifteenth-century England 1399–1509*, Stroud, 1972, 1995, pp. 62–63

4 Edward and the nobles

Rather than centralising power, he [Edward] took the traditional course of relying on the nobility as his agent in the localities. The great nobles retained their independence and freedom of manoeuvre. It was Henry VII who succeeded in making service at court, rather than extensive lands and local authority, the benchmark of status for a noble. Edward IV made no such attempt. Granted, he did choose to exploit the increasing education of the lesser nobility by employing them in such roles as receivers: granted also that he elevated others to the dignity of magnate. But this does not amount to a policy of supplanting the **old nobility** with 'new men' of markedly lower social status. Nor does it mean that the power of the king increased at the expense of the nobility – another supposed characteristic of new monarchy.

. . . When J. R. Green wrote *A short history of the English people* in the 1870s, he not only argued that Edward IV was the founder of the new monarchy, but also that he was despotic: in fact, despotism, or the exercise of an

old nobility During Edward IV's reign, the phrase 'old nobility' covers the aristocratic opponents of the Woodvilles and Greys. Not all were 'old' at all: Edward created a new Yorkist peerage during his reign consisting of no less than four dukes, two marquesses, eleven earls, two viscounts and six barons.

unconstrained, absolute authority, was supposed to be part and parcel of new monarchy itself. Was Edward IV a despot? Some contemporary chroniclers clearly thought that he had that tendency and intention. The judicial execution of his dangerous brother, the duke of Clarence, in 1478 was cited as an example . . . Also, Edward's use of benevolences – in effect, 'gifts' extracted from the nobility, supposedly as an alternative to military service – might be taken as further proof of creeping despotism. But the overall case is not a strong one. The benevolences were never intended as a permanent system of taxation . . . And it could be argued that Clarence brought about his own doom.

Source: John Warren, *The Wars of the Roses and the Yorkist kings*, London, 1995, pp. 141–42

Historical-source question

1   Read all the sources carefully. How far do you think Edward was responsible for establishing a 'new monarchy'?

George, duke of Clarence (1449–78)

George Plantagenet had much in common with his older brother, Edward IV; he was tall and good looking, charming and crafty, but also fatally ambitious and jealous of power. In 1467 he was just 17 when he became embroiled in the rift between the earl of Warwick and Edward IV following the king's ill-advised marriage to Elizabeth Woodville. Warwick at this had made overtures to both Clarence and his younger brother, Richard, duke of Gloucester, regarding their marriage to his daughters, Isabel and Anne. Edward, when he realised what was being hatched, was furious. He summoned his brothers and commanded them to abandon the scheme; a York–Neville marriage would greatly strengthen Warwick and possibly inspire treason. Warwick, however, continued to work towards a marriage alliance and found in Clarence a willing participant. Clarence was a headstrong youth who did not like being told what to do by his older brother. Furthermore, like Warwick, he believed his right to a position of real power had been eclipsed by the rise of the Woodvilles. Easily led, he married Isabel in 1469 and joined Warwick in the coup, which resulted in the readeption of Henry VI.

By 1471 Edward IV had recovered the throne, Warwick, Henry VI and his son were all dead and Clarence was reconciled to his brother. That Clarence should then contemplate treason a second time around the year 1477, this time from a much weaker position, is remarkable, perhaps an act of insanity. Once again rumours began to circulate, as they had in 1470, regarding Edward IV's legitimacy. Clarence, who may have initiated the current notion that his brother was born out of wedlock, rarely visited the court and when he did so refused to eat or drink anything, the implication being that he feared his brother wished to have him poisoned. Worse still, he accused the queen of witchcraft! Even after two of his associates, Dr John Stacey and John Burdett, were executed for treason – a final warning to Clarence – he remained outspoken and critical of the king. On 18 February he was put to death in the Tower of London.

His mother protested against a public execution and, according to legend, he was 'drowned in a butt of malmsey' – a barrel of wine. Various explanations have been provided for this unusual fate: it has been suggested that Clarence, as a joke, requested it himself; one intriguing theory proposes he was drowned in his bath, for baths commonly were made from sawn-down wine butts. Some historians have rejected it outright as a colourful fiction while others accept it as a literal, and telling, truth.

> To what extent did George, duke of Clarence, bring about his own downfall?

Why, and with what consequences, did Richard, duke of Gloucester, make himself king of England?

> Every tale condemns me for a villain
>
> William Shakespeare, *Richard III*, Act I, Scene i

Richard, duke of Gloucester, was greatly empowered by his marriage to Anne Neville, heir to much of Warwick's estate, and had been rewarded with *Successes* Scottish territory by his brother, Edward IV, for the recapture of Berwick from the Scots in 1483. He, in what one of his recent biographers, Desmond Seward, has described as 'one of the most brilliant double coup d'états in history', seized the throne shortly after his brother's untimely death at the age of 42, in April 1483.

Edward IV's immediate successor was his 12-year-old son, who reigned until June as Edward V. In a battle for survival, Richard found himself, after years of loyalty to his brother, facing a desperate struggle against the ambitions of the Woodville family, elevated to greatness by Edward IV's irresponsible marriage to Elizabeth Woodville. Indeed, his defenders cite a Woodville attempt to usurp Richard from his rightful place (according to the terms of Edward IV's will) as regent as the fundamental cause of his determination to shatter Woodville aspirations and, ultimately, to remove Elizabeth Woodville's son, the uncrowned Edward V, from the scene altogether.

Initially, at least, Richard could count on the support of those courtiers who considered themselves undermined by the Woodvilles' meteoric rise. Most importantly he had the backing of William, Lord Hastings, and Henry Stafford, duke of Buckingham, the greatest magnate among the old nobility.

Richard III and his queen in her coronation robes. As duke of Gloucester, Richard had greatly added to his personal fortune by marrying Anne Neville.

Tower of London When the princes were imprisoned in the Tower of London it was still a palace with apartments and a banqueting hall sufficiently luxurious to contain the king and his court in an emergency. Confinement in the Tower of London did not, at the time, have the same dread significance it would acquire under the Tudors.

royal progress In a reign that lasted just 26 months, Richard III was in London for only 6. He undertook a great progress of central England following his coronation in the summer of 1483, which was followed by the campaign against Buckingham and his fellow rebels in the autumn. He spent much of 1484 in the north visiting his estates and planning a major invasion of Scotland, although this was abandoned because of the cost and the threat of Henry Tudor. After returning to London a final royal progress was made eastwards to Canterbury. In the summer of 1485 the king marched north for the last time – a journey that terminated at Bosworth Field.

Three weeks after his father's death, his uncle, Richard of Gloucester, took Edward V into his custody and made himself protector for the duration of the boy king's minority. Meanwhile, Richard's supporter, Henry Stafford, duke of Buckingham, challenged the legitimacy of Edward V's reign by claiming that Edward IV was already contracted to marry Lady Eleanor Butler when he married Elizabeth Woodville. Richard and his faction doubtless feared the consequences of Woodville revenge in the event of Edward V coming of age and reinstating his mother's family. Furthermore, Richard's supporters wished for rewards that only a king could grant. Some historians, therefore, consider his removal of Edward V as a historical inevitability.

On 26 June Edward was dethroned and the duke of Gloucester became King Richard III. Edward and his younger brother, Richard, were held in the **Tower of London**. By the autumn of 1483, they had disappeared from public view, almost certainly murdered, very likely on their uncle's instruction. Richard's ostentatious coronation in mid-July was followed by an extensive **royal progress** around his kingdom, reaching York in triumphant procession in August. By September, however, he was on his way back to London as discontent swelled in the southern and western counties.

Edward V

Prince Edward, Edward IV's son and heir, was 12 years old when his father died in April 1483. Immediately the Woodville-dominated royal council began preparations for the boy's coronation. Earl Rivers made preparations to bring the child from Ludlow to London. The royal party was intercepted by Richard, duke of Gloucester, the boy's uncle, at Stony Stratford in May and taken into Gloucester's custody. According to the Italian chronicler, Mancini, Gloucester, in so doing, was safeguarding the terms of Edward's will, which declared his brother should become protector during the child's minority. This cannot be corroborated since the will has not survived. As protector, Gloucester would be far more powerful than as the mere figurehead of a royal council.

Gloucester now entered London as protector and the coronation was postponed until the end of June. By the beginning of that month, it is clear that Richard of Gloucester was already making arrangements for the purge of the council which began with the execution of Lord Hastings, a loyal servant of Edward IV and, hitherto, Gloucester's friend, but one certain to resist any attempts on Gloucester's behalf to depose the heir. Gloucester again raised the spectre of Edward IV's supposed illegitimacy, and introduced a new notion that his marriage to Elizabeth Woodville was illegitimate, because he had been precontracted to Lady Eleanor Butler (hence bastardising all of their children). Justifying his actions in this way, he had himself crowned king on 26 June.

By the end of the summer, rumours were spreading that the children had been done away with in the Tower and Richard III made no effort to quell them. Edward V had been king in name only, although until 16 June government was carried out in his name. A contemporary illustration of a fair-haired boy, the subject of numerous later romantic paintings, has survived, but little is known of his personality or potential. John Russell, the *Crowland chronicle* continuator, wrote a brief sketch, probably designed to highlight for his readers the iniquity of Richard III's conduct:

> To King Edward IV succeeded, but for a lamentably short time, his son King Edward V, who was residing at Ludlow at the time of his father's death; the boy was thirteen and a half, or thereabouts. He was brought up virtuously by virtuous men, remarkably gifted, and very well advanced in learning for his years.

What motives might Richard III have had for taking over the throne himself?

Buckingham's rebellion

During October and November 1483, the new king faced rebellion in the south from certain members of Edward IV's entourage, including Henry Stafford, duke of Buckingham, after whom this rebellion was named.

Buckingham had been Richard's greatest ally in the usurpation, but now, like Warwick the Kingmaker before him, enacted a startling turn around, quite possibly inspired by the Woodville faction, to save the princes before it was too late. Rumour at the time had that he was making a bid for the throne himself, to which he had a very remote claim. Buckingham and the countess of Richmond were the only peers involved. The other leaders were gentlemen loyal to Edward IV and his sons.

As rumours of the murder of the princes spread, the rebels began to champion the doubtful regal claim of Henry Tudor, grandson of Henry V's queen, Catherine of Valois, by her second marriage, to Owen Tudor. Buckingham invited Henry back to England from exile in Brittany and a plan was hatched to reinforce his claim by marrying him to Elizabeth, Edward IV's eldest daughter. Richard's royal progress through central England immediately after his coronation probably helped him secure the loyalty of the Midlands when his tour was interrupted by the rebellion in October.

Richard raised an impressive army and marched south to Exeter. The revolt was suppressed without a fight following the arrest or flight of its perpetrators. The estates of Buckingham and other 'traitors' were seized by the king and given to his supporters even before such actions could be legalised by parliamentary Acts of Attainder. A wave of these followed in the parliamentary sittings of January 1484. This intrusion of newly rewarded loyal nobility from the north and elsewhere into the lives of the southern gentry was deeply resented. Two years later, and shortly after Richard's defeat at Bosworth, the Crowland chronicler made the following remarks:

> What great numbers of estates and inheritances were amassed in the king's treasury in consequence! He distributed all these amongst his northerners whom he planted in every part of his dominions, to the shame of all the southern people who murmured ceaselessly and longed more each day for the return of their old lords in place of the tyranny of the present ones.

More than ever before, the conflicts of the second half of the fifteenth century had taken on a regional character – the north versus the south.

Buckingham was executed without trial at Salisbury on 2 November. Meanwhile, Henry Tudor, who had sailed to the south-west on Buckingham's invitation but not participated, retreated back into exile, followed to Brittany by a number of rebel members of the southern gentry.

The victory over Buckingham, however, had not come cheaply, as the Crowland chronicler a while later recorded:

> After these events, the king gradually reduced the size of his army, discharging those whom he had summoned to the expedition from

the distant northern Marches, and came to London having triumphed over his enemies without going to war, though at no less cost than if the two armies had fought it out hand-to-hand. In this way all that very great treasure and wealth which King Edward had thought he was leaving behind him for very different purposes began rapidly to be used up.

Why did Richard face rebellion so early in his reign?

Richard's attempts to retain power

In stark contrast to his overindulgent brother, Richard III cultivated his image as a pious, God-fearing and just monarch. Legislation was passed by parliament outlawing benevolences – the much despised obligatory 'gifts' upon which Edward IV had relied; another new law protected accused felons from losing their goods before conviction. Despite this, his unpopularity, even before posterity turned history into legend, cannot be denied. The death of his son in 1484 was followed by the death of his wife in March 1485. Richard now made known his plan to marry Edward's daughter, Elizabeth, himself. Not only did this expose him to accusations of incest but also it alienated the enemies of the Woodvilles and those who had benefited from their recent fall; inevitably there would have been some restoration of Woodville influence if the king married his niece, the daughter of Elizabeth Woodville. Malicious rumours were spread through London that Richard had his wife poisoned because of, in the words of a contemporary chronicler, his 'incestuous passion'. In a scene reminiscent of impeachment proceedings against late-twentieth-century heads of state, Richard felt obliged to make a public statement of denial before a special congregation of lords, aldermen and the mayor of London. Meanwhile the removal of benevolences forced him to resort to the equally unpopular device of forced loans to pay for his preparations against the anticipated invasion of Henry Tudor.

The history of Richard's usurpation and the popular assumption that he had done away with the princes in the Tower tarnished his reputation for ever. He tried to undermine the authority of the mighty, but unreliable, earl of Northumberland by instituting a Council of the North under his supporter, John Howard, duke of Norfolk. Even so, when Henry Tudor launched his assault in 1485, the extent of Richard's authority proved fatally inadequate. Unable to secure the loans from his greater subjects necessary to protect his realm, he died defeated on Bosworth Field in 1485.

Richard III's short reign was plagued by the consequences of his usurpation and he never had much of an opportunity to demonstrate fully his capacity for kingship. Had he survived the first few years, as had the usurpers Henry IV and Edward IV before him, history might have remembered him rather differently. After a brief respite of three and a half weeks following a spectacular coronation, his troubles began. The first and only parliament of his reign had to be postponed in the autumn of 1483 because of risings in the south and west. When finally it met in December, its main business concerned the forming of legislation designed to confirm Richard's right to the throne. The Act which followed, the *Titulus Regius*, was designed for public consumption; it proclaimed his nephews' illegitimacy and contrasted the corruption of the previous reign with the glorious epoch now looming as England's rightful heir to the throne took the stage. In February most of the lords were requested to take an oath of loyalty to Richard's son, Edward – a safeguard against the possibility of the king's early death.

Despite his difficulties, perhaps because of them, during the reign there were several economic and legal reforms. These included protection of English producers and traders against foreign imports, a commitment to the principle of bail for suspected felons, and the abolition of benevolences. It is difficult to determine the extent to which these were initiated by parliament and how much by the king himself. Where he does appear to have played a central role in promoting justice, the principle to which he had committed himself on making his coronation oath, it is hard to tell how far this was prompted by a sense of social responsibility and how far by a self-interested desire to cultivate personal popularity.

The confiscation of rebel estates after the October 1483 rebellion enabled him to expand his power base by rewarding his followers. Much of the property and the titles taken from the hundred or so attainted rebels fell into the hands of Richard's supporters, several of whom came from the north of England – a fact of course which contributed nothing to promoting his popularity in the south. But not all beneficiaries of the rebellion were from the north, and some of the rebels themselves were forgiven and welcomed into Richard's fold. Nevertheless, Richard's own household was dominated by northerners.

Richard had been the archetypal 'overmighty noble' who had relied on his power base in the north as the means of asserting his claim to the throne in 1483. It is not surprising, therefore, that he took measures to try to prevent any one magnate from becoming too powerful in his own reign. Instead of handing over authority in the north to his principal advocates in 1483, the earls of Northumberland and Westmorland, he established a new Council of the North, a number of northern peers ruling directly on his behalf.

The rebellion of 1483, war with Scotland in 1484 and preparations for facing Tudor's invasion in 1485 made huge demands on the **royal purse**. Sir Thomas More's later allegations of extravagance and excessive generosity to his friends and supporters were unfounded. Even so he had to rely on loans once again in 1485 and what reputation he had cultivated for 'living off his

royal purse Although Edward IV had added the wealth of the estates of Henry VI and other defeated Lancastrians to his own in 1461, he was still short of money. This was in spite of other sources of royal income, which included the very valuable customs duties. Consequently he was obliged to borrow from London merchants and foreign bankers. He also devalued the coinage and burdened the nobility with benevolences. The more efficient management of his estates, which were controlled directly from the royal chamber, checks on corruption and the exploitation of old feudal dues and rights enabled him, however, to balance the books and pay his debts. Unusually among England's medieval kings, he died solvent.

own' was moribund by the time of his destruction at Bosworth. According to the Crowland chronicler, these loans were not freely given:

> He resorted to the demands of King Edward IV which he had condemned in parliament – although he spurned entirely the use of his brother's word 'benevolence' – sending out hand-picked men to extract the greatest possible sums of money from the coffers of almost all the estates of the kingdom by pleas and threats, by fair means or foul.

Richard's decision to continue the campaign against Scotland, which had begun in the previous reign, was probably motivated by his wish to be revealed as a conquering hero and worthy king of England. That the planned assault largely fizzled out in the early summer of 1484 is explained perhaps by the fact of his son and heir's death in April, an event which, declare the chronicles, traumatised both parents. The less ambitious programme which followed was inglorious, culminating in the defeat of a small English army at Lochmaben in July and a three-year truce concluded in September. By this time, the border struggle had paled into insignificance in the face of the greater threat of invasion from Brittany or France by Henry Tudor.

In addition to diplomacy Richard used propaganda widely in his struggle with Henry. He took the controversial decision to associate himself with the Woodville clan, posing as their friend and benefactor so that, in the public imagination, they might seem reconciled to the new regime rather than allied to Tudor's cause. The Crowland chronicler commented on the exchange of clothes, during the Christmas festivities of 1484 to 1485, by Queen Anne and Queen Elizabeth Woodville's daughter, Elizabeth. According to the chronicler, Richard was already planning to marry Princess Elizabeth:

> . . . after the death of the queen – for which he was waiting – or through a divorce for which he considered he had sufficient grounds. He could see no other way of confirming his position nor of depriving his rival of hope.

Another propagandist device was the promotion by Richard's regime of the cult of King Henry VI. In August 1484 Henry VI's remains were exhumed from Chertsey Abbey and reburied in St George's Chapel, Windsor, and Richard began, publicly, to patronise Henry's foundation of King's College, Cambridge. By such means he endeavoured to make his claim to the Lancastrian inheritance stronger than that of Henry Tudor.

By the time Henry was ready to invade England in the summer of 1485, Richard III was still far from secure within his realm. Powerful forces were arrayed against him as the usurper, a supposed child-killer, an ungenerous friend to those who had helped him, a Woodville-sympathiser, possibly a wife-killer, and an insolvent. Propaganda and reformism had proved inadequate foes of history and circumstance.

Henry Stafford, duke of Buckingham

One of the most enigmatic characters of the period, Buckingham was instrumental in Richard III's usurpation of power and yet gave his name a few weeks later to the futile rebellion that cost him his life. This was despite having been massively rewarded by Richard with offices in Wales and the Marches. Buckingham had served Edward IV faithfully and, as steward at the time, pronounced the duke of Clarence's death sentence in 1478. His support for Edward IV's remaining brother, Richard, immediately after the former's death is indisputable – he promoted the idea of Edward V's bastardy, and some maintained that he initiated, even carried out, the murder of the princes in the Tower. His loyalty to Richard, according to one contemporary, the Italian, Dominic Mancini, was important in persuading other magnates to support the usurper:

> . . . the lords were mindful of the fate which had befallen Hastings and were well aware that the alliance of these two dukes, of Gloucester and Buckingham, who had such vast armed forces at their disposal, would be difficult and dangerous to r sist. Fearing for their own safety, they decided to declare Richard king and request him to assume the duties of government.

According to the Crowland chronicler, Buckingham's change of heart, which led him into rebellion, was a matter of personal conscience:

> It was publicly proclaimed that Henry, duke of Buckingham, who had supported Richard III and was then living in Wales at Brecon, was repentant of what had happened and was to lead the enterprise against the king. After this, it was widely believed that Edward's two sons must have met their fate by some unspecified act of violence.

The contemporary chronicler and Warwickshire antiquary, John Rous, accredits Buckingham with hatching the plot to put forward Henry Tudor, hitherto floundering in exile abroad and the political backwater, as the new candidate for the throne. According to Rous it was also Buckingham's idea to wed Henry Tudor to Elizabeth of York, Edward IV's daughter, in order to make his claim more credible. Buckingham, it seems, was quite as much the 'kingmaker' as the earl of Warwick in the reign of Henry VI.

Richard III's spies unearthed the plot before it came to fruition and Buckingham was tracked down in hiding. Apparently he had sought refuge in the hut of 'a poor man' and was given away by 'the unusually abundant supply of food that had been brought there'. He was executed on 2 November 1483 in the market place at Salisbury. His fellow conspirators and other rebels fled abroad, some to join Henry Tudor in his invasion some 18 months later.

Why did the duke of Buckingham turn against Richard III?

Historical interpretation: Richard III – hero or villain?

> ... close and secret, a deep dissembler, lowly of countenance, arrogant of heart, outwardly companionable where he inwardly hated, not hesitating to kiss whom he thought to kill, pitiless and cruel, not for evil will always but oftener for ambition and either for the surety or increase of his position.
>
> Source: Thomas More, *History of King Richard the Third, c.*1540

Shakespeare's portrayal of Richard III as a deformed, scheming, cold-hearted murderer shattered any reputation for good his acolytes once tried to establish. Just as his former supporters changed sides in the rebellion of 1483 and, later, at Bosworth, so too did the chronicler of his reign. The contemporary chronicler, John Rous, in *History of the earls of Warwick*, originally described Richard as a model king, 'most mighty', appointed 'by the grace of God', a selfless and just king loved by his subjects and admired by 'the people of all other lands about him'. Once Henry Tudor was king, however, Rous rewrote his version of the history, now describing Richard as some kind of freak, 'retained within his mother's womb for two years

A self-portrait by the late Yorkist and early Tudor chronicler John Rous. His verdict on the reign of Richard III changed after Henry's seizure of power.

An early Tudor portrait of Richard III probably based on an earlier depiction. Unlike the other portraits of the king, this one does not show Richard with a hunched back.

Richard III Society The Fellowship of the White Boar, later the Richard III Society, was founded in 1924. Its members have promoted a great deal of research into the reign of Richard III and seek to exonerate Richard of the guilt with which, traditionally, he has been associated.

and emerging with teeth and hair to his shoulder', a cruel master of deception, 'like a scorpion he combined a smooth front with a stinging tail'. He, not Edward IV, was now found guilty of causing the murder of the deposed Lancastrian, Henry VI, after his final defeat at the Battle of Tewkesbury in 1471. He also had on his hands the blood of the princes in the Tower and his own wife, Queen Anne, whom, allegedly he had poisoned. John Rous also helped establish the tradition, so central to Shakespeare's characterisation, that Richard III was a hunchback: 'He was small of stature, with a short face and unequal shoulders, the right higher and the left lower.'

Richard has his defenders too, notably members of the **Richard III Society**, who seek the restoration of Richard's reputation. Attempts have been made to portray him as a deeply religious man driven to usurpation by the shock discovery of the illegitimacy of Edward V's claim to the throne, and the case for his innocence in the princes in the Tower affair has often been proclaimed. Either way, by anyone's criteria, his reign was a

In the work of Victorian artists, such as this painting by J. E. Millais, the princes were romanticised and the pathos of their situation was accentuated.

failure, the disastrous outcome of a desperate coup that resulted in the accession of the Tudors.

Much of what we know, or might think we know, of the personality and deeds of Richard III comes from Thomas More's *History of King Richard the Third*, which first appeared in the 1540s, although he started work on it many years earlier, probably in 1513. The work is written on the epic scale and it has been criticised as both propagandist and melodramatic. On the other hand, More probably based his narrative, in part at least, on the accounts of those who had been witnesses to the events it describes. As Desmond Seward, in *Richard III: England's black legend* (1997), has pointed out, More was 'a man famous for plain dealing and love of truth – he paid for it with his life' when he ran into trouble with his master, Henry VIII, concerning the latter's claim to supremacy over the church in England. More's assumption that Richard III was a murderer was certainly

realpolitik This is a term usually associated with late-nineteenth-century government and diplomacy, particularly that of the German statesman, Bismarck. Brewer's *Twentieth-century dictionary of phrase and fable* (1991) defines it as 'Practical politics, political realism; politics based on national interests or material considerations as distinct from moral objectives'.

one shared by many who lived during his reign. Some historians, however, regard More's work as a political treatise, designed on the one hand to gratify the Tudors, and on the other to illustrate the horrors of *realpolitik*, the 'ends justifies the means' approach to politics, which was taking root in parts of Europe at the time. The later Tudor historian, Edward Hall, who provided Shakespeare with his version of the legend, painted More's picture of the king even blacker.

It has been said many times that history is written by the victors and, for Richard III's apologists, this is an essential consideration in forming any verdict on his reign. The remarkable evidence of John Rous, who attempted, but failed, to destroy his first, pro-Richard, account of the reign, stands testimony to the unreliability of the early chronicles. At worst, Richard's supporters portray him as a man of his times, at best he is seen as a well-meaning and capable, even great, king who was cruelly betrayed and prevented from fulfilling his potential.

Students of history are taught to question the evidence and perceived truths. The highly influential and highly controversial English historian, A. J. P. Taylor, carved a reputation for himself by questioning the received wisdom on such sensitive issues as the origins of the Second World War. This principle of 'playing the Devil's advocate' in order to reopen the debate and shake other, more conservative, historians out of their complacency was nothing new when Taylor was rocking the boat in the 1960s. The first great historian-iconoclast was Horace Walpole (1717–97). Walpole wrote a book entitled *Historic doubts* (1768) in which he refuted tradition by trying to prove that Richard did not kill Henry VI or the princes. This was the first, and one of the least convincing, of many books and papers defending Richard III. Even so, to the dismay of Richard's supporters, the version of the story popularised by More, Hall and Shakespeare continues to dominate. In the opinion of Paul Murray Kendall in *Richard the Third* (1955): 'What a tribute this is to art; what a misfortune this is for history.'

Did Richard III murder the princes in the Tower?

Much near-contemporary comment indicted Richard III for the murder of his nephews and this tradition, despite brave attempts to detract from it, has endured. The assumption that they had been killed appears in contemporary records by the end of the summer of 1483. For example, Robert Ricard wrote in his *Kalendar* for 1483 'in this year the two sons of King Edward were put to death in the Tower of London.'

The birth of the legend of Richard as murderer coincided with the disappearance of the princes who, in the early stages of their captivity, it appears, were seen frequently at play about the Tower. Certainly a rumour of their murder was in circulation by the early years of Henry VII's reign and, in 1488, in *Historical notes of a London citizen*, Richard's henchman, the exceptionally powerful duke of Buckingham, was implicated:

> Item: this year King Edward V, late called Prince of Wales, and Richard, duke of York, his brother, King Edward IV's sons, were put to death in the Tower of London on the instruction of the duke of Buckingham.

Attempts have been made in recent times to find Buckingham the initiator of, rather than an accessory to, the supposed crime. The most popular alternative solution, however, to the disappearance of the princes which absolves Richard from any blame, is that 'the other side' was guilty, that Henry VII, not Richard III, was the murderer. It has been suggested, most colourfully perhaps in Josephine Tey's detective 'docu-novel', *The daughter of time* (1951), that the princes survived Richard's reign but were dispatched at the start of Henry's. The evidence is flimsy to say the least. The only 'proof' that the children enjoyed Richard's protection are a couple of contemporary records regarding provision for children in the king's household in 1484 and 1485 but very likely they refer to other children, possibly including Richard's own illegitimate son, John. It is quite reasonable to assume that, had they been found alive, Henry VII would have done away with the boys for the very same reasons that Richard probably had them murdered.

A more popular, and politically charged, third explanation at the time for the fate of the children was that they survived both Richard's reign and Henry Tudor's usurpation. Thus Henry VII was plagued by pretenders during the first half of his reign. However, the shift of the opposition's focus away from the princes and towards Henry Tudor, even by the end of 1483, implies that, long before the invention of new identities for the pretenders Lambert Simnel and Perkin Warbeck, Richard's enemies had abandoned hope of ever again seeing Edward V and his brother alive. The fact that Richard III made no real attempt to deny his guilt, or to give them any sign that the children lived still, would have confirmed their suspicions.

Without doubt, Richard's reputation was damaged as a result of the disappearance of the princes and it was a factor in the continued opposition to his reign. The killing of innocent children, and one's own flesh and blood, was then, as now, regarded as the most loathsome of acts. His 'northerness' and 'plantation' of northerners into the great estates of the south and high offices (half his council were northerners), however, was a greater cause of discontent. If indeed he did arrange for their murder, it was a measured step and one

Why did both Richard III and Henry VII have cause for doing away with the princes in the Tower?

political expedient A political expedient is an act which, although distasteful, is performed in order to keep a ruler in power. Richard III's rule has often been likened to the political principles embodied in *The prince*, a hugely influential treatise written by an Italian, Niccolò Machiavelli, in 1513. This work considers strategies for the seizure of power and the means by which it can be successfully exercised. It anticipates nineteenth-century *realpolitik* by separating the concept of successful government from any moral or religious principles; the end, perhaps, justifying the means. Some commentators have described Richard III's activities in 1483 as 'Machiavellian' in that he perpetrated 'wicked' deeds for, what he considered, the greater good. In so doing, such opinion might cast Richard as the archetypal Renaissance prince.

that he would have considered a necessary, if distasteful, **political expedient**. He was not the first, nor would he be the last, to consolidate his position by such means.

Why was Richard III overthrown by Henry Tudor?

Henry Tudor's exile began in 1471 when he fled from England with his Lancastrian uncle and guardian, Jasper Tudor, following the collapse of Henry VI's regime. His mother, Margaret Beaufort, is accredited with being a prime mover in promoting his claim after the disappearance of the princes in the Tower. In 1472, Margaret Beaufort had married Edward IV's councillor and steward, Thomas, Lord Stanley, Richard III's constable of England. The wife of one of the most powerful men in England, Margaret was in a strong position to shape peoples' loyalties, not least her husband's. The possibility of a Stanley-backed rebellion did not pass Richard III by – when he marched to Bosworth he took with him, effectively as a hostage, Stanley's son and heir, Lord Strange.

Having promised to marry Princess Elizabeth on securing the throne, Henry Tudor's credibility was further strengthened when he won the financial and military backing and general hospitality of the government of Charles VIII, France's child king, late in 1484. Henry Tudor had spent most of his exile in Brittany but, by 1484, his position there had become extremely insecure. This was because Richard III negotiated a deal with his hosts whereby England would supply the Bretons with a company of archers, for their struggle for independence against France, in return for Henry's arrest. In the nick of time, Tudor learned of the plan and, in September, escaped to France. The French were now only too willing to strike back at an English king prepared to ally with rebel Bretons.

In the summer of 1485, Henry began to assemble an army and invasion fleet at the port of Le Havre. Richard had been preparing for the now inevitable invasion since December 1484. In June he established his headquarters at Nottingham, a central position from which he could respond equally fast to an invasion at any port in the kingdom.

On 7 August Henry Tudor with a French army and other English exiles landed at Milford Haven in south Wales and marched north through Wales and into Shropshire. The king knew of his arrival by 11 August and began mobilising his army and summoning further support. Henry now headed east towards London and Richard left Leicester to intercept him. They met just outside Market Bosworth on 22 August. As he had feared, Stanley proved unfaithful to Richard and his assault at the rear of the king's army helps account for his stepson Henry's swift victory. Although Richard's army

Why do you think Henry Tudor chose south Wales as a landing point?

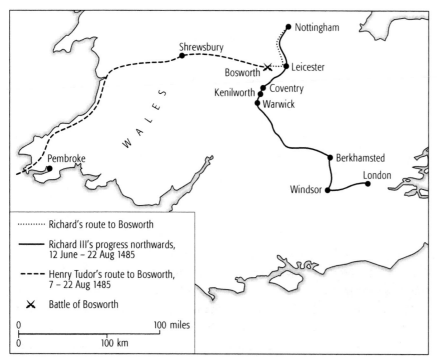

The routes taken by Richard III and Henry Tudor to Bosworth.

outnumbered Tudor's, he was further let down by the failure of the earl of Northumberland to engage his force, which was large and well equipped. The lack of support at the critical hour reflected his mismanagement of patronage earlier in the reign. His favouritism towards the few when it came to distributing offices and attainted lands resulted in his having to rely on a small powerful clique of nobles. Had he spread the fruits of his usurpation wider, he might have enjoyed broader-based support. These factors, combined with a reckless charge led by the king, resulted in Richard's defeat and death in the fighting. As Rous reports:

> King Richard, after receiving many mortal wounds, died a fearless and most courageous death, fighting on the battlefield, not in flight. His body ... after suffering many humiliations ... was taken to Leicester in an inhuman manner, with a rope around its neck, while the new king also was proceeded to Leicester wearing the crown he had so conspicuously won.

Richard III, killed at the age of 32 after a brief but dramatic reign, was buried with little ceremony in the choir of a Franciscan friary in Leicester. Rous concludes that 'Although Richard III's days were short, they were ended with no lamentation from his groaning subjects.'

The Stanleys

The support of the Stanleys at Bosworth was a, probably the, decisive factor in Henry Tudor's victory. From the start, Richard III had relied on the support of four overmighty magnates: the duke of Buckingham, Lord Stanley, the earl of Northumberland and the duke of Norfolk. Only the last mentioned remained true to his cause. Buckingham gave his name to the revolt of 1483 and Stanley and Northumberland abandoned Richard at the critical hour in 1485. After Buckingham's death, the power base was contracted, with Buckingham's lands and titles being shared out among his remaining supporters. The fact that Stanley's wife, Margaret Beaufort, mother of Henry Tudor, had helped instigate the conspiracy should perhaps have given Richard III sufficient cause to restrict the power of her husband. Instead, having proclaimed his loyalty, Stanley replaced Buckingham as lord great chamberlain of England.

As Henry Tudor's invasion loomed in 1485, it is clear Richard III had no doubts regarding the danger of relying upon the loyalty of Lord Stanley and his brother, Sir William. Consequently Stanley's son was in the king's custody as he marched to Bosworth. Although Stanley's support of Henry Tudor by this stage is indisputable, he was held back from fully committing himself to his stepson by the precarious situation of his son, particularly after the latter's failed attempt to escape from his captivity at Nottingham Castle, where the royal army was encamped in August. Richard could at least feel reasonably assured of Stanley's neutrality and Henry, without the earl's support, faced almost certain defeat.

At Bosworth both Richard and Henry sent messages to the Stanleys, who had brought their vast army to the field, imploring them to lend their support. Richard's army numbered around 12,000, Henry's 5,000 and the Stanleys' 3,000–8,000. They remained undecided, even when Richard ordered the immediate execution of Stanley's son, Lord Strange, (which his captains refused to carry out). Only when Richard launched and led a foolhardy charge against Henry and his bodyguard, resulting in a mêlée in which quite possibly he exchanged blows with Tudor himself, did William Stanley act, seizing the moment to take advantage of the king's rash and impetuous move to enter the fray. The chroniclers record how Richard fought like a cornered and ferocious wolf to the last, crying 'Treason! Treason! Treason!' as he succumbed to the innumerable blows raining down on him.

Why was Stanley's support at Bosworth so important to Henry VII?

1 Identify and explain the reasons why Richard III faced opposition during his short reign.

2 Assess the problems which confronted Richard III before he was defeated at Bosworth.

3 Explain why Richard, duke of Gloucester, became king.

4 Assess at least three reasons for Richard III's defeat in 1485.

4 Henry VII and the establishment of the Tudor dynasty

Focus questions

- How did Henry Tudor consolidate his position as king of England?
- How successfully did Henry VII deal with opposition to his rule?
- To what extent did domestic crises determine Henry VII's continental policy?
- To what extent was Henry VII more successful than his predecessors in containing and pacifying the Scots?

Significant dates

1485 Henry VII's reign begins.

1486 A truce is signed between England and Scotland.

1487 The pretender, Lambert Simnel, invades England, supported by German mercenaries. His forces are defeated at the Battle of Stoke.

1489 The Treaty of Redon is signed by Brittany and England. The Treaty of Medina del Campo between England and Spain, which includes a marriage alliance between Prince Arthur Tudor and Catherine of Aragon, is agreed.

1491 The pretender, Perkin Warbeck, appears in Cork, Ireland.

1492 The English invade France; the Treaty of Etaples is signed by Henry VII and Charles VIII of France.

1493 The Austrian Emperor, Maximilian, supports Warbeck's claim and gives him protection. Henry VII ends English trade with Antwerp and the Low Countries in retaliation.

1494 The Irish parliament passes Poynings' Law.

1495 Warbeck launches an unsuccessful invasion of England and flees to the Scottish court.

1496 A trade treaty is signed with Burgundy, Warbeck's native country.

1497 Warbeck lands in Cornwall; the Anglo-Scottish truce prevents a simultaneous invasion in the north; Warbeck is captured.

1501 The marriage between Prince Arthur and Catherine of Aragon takes place.

1502 The Treaty of Perpetual Peace is made between England and Scotland; it is confirmed that James IV of Scotland should marry Princess Margaret Tudor.

1506 A trade and defence treaty is signed with Burgundy.

Overview

The year 1485 is one of the great landmarks in British dynastic and constitutional history. In that year Richard III was defeated in the field at Bosworth, Henry VII's reign began, and a new dynasty, which would last for more than a century, was founded. Its longevity alone contrasts markedly with the turbulent decades before Henry's accession, as the houses of York and Lancaster wrestled over possession of the throne, which changed hands no less than five times between 1461 and 1485.

History has treated Henry VII well. He has been celebrated as the individual who, after years of disorder, secured the peace and stability that would continue until the outbreak of a new civil war in 1642. This led his biographers into an assumption that Henry brought to the throne a unique and 'modern' approach to government and in so doing played a leading role in hauling England out of its 'middle ages'. Modern historians, however, wary of the dangers of oversimplifying the past, are less inclined to see the year of his accession, 1485, as such a watershed.

The son of Edmund Tudor, half-brother of Henry VI, Henry Tudor, the earl of Richmond, became head of the house of Lancaster in 1471 after Henry VI was put to death following his defeat by Edward IV at the Battle of Tewkesbury. With the crown back in the hands of the Yorkists, Henry's own life was in jeopardy and a childhood that had begun in Pembroke, Wales, in 1457 was now continued in exile in Brittany with his uncle, and guardian, Jasper Tudor. King Edward was eager to lay hands on 'the only imp now left of Henry VI's brood' and nearly succeeded when he almost lured Henry back to England in the mid-1470s with the offer of his daughter's hand in marriage. Henry was warned of Edward IV's true intention and stayed in Brittany under the protection of Francis II. However, it was only after Richard III's usurpation and the supposed murder of Edward IV's sons that Henry Tudor became a credible contender for the crown.

His triumphant return in 1485 was the result of many factors, including the support of the French king, the efforts of his mother, Margaret Beaufort, to steer the champions of the princes in the Tower in his direction, the aid of the Stanleys, and a measure of good fortune. He displayed that remarkable capacity of late-fifteenth-century kings, kingmakers and pretenders alike, of gambling all in desperate bids for power which had anything but a certain outcome.

When, at the age of 28, he became king he had little familiarity with his new kingdom and none of the grounding in, or experience of, the world of government that a young prince growing up at court would have received.

Despite such inauspicious beginnings, Henry proved both an able administrator and a shrewd politician. His reputation for austerity might be deserved in some respects but he could be indulgent, establishing a lavish court, investing in exotic wild animals, housed in the Tower, and patronising fools, jesters and troupes of actors. He had a passion for hunting, he commissioned several major palatial building works, added considerably to the stock of the royal library, and promoted all kinds of artistic enterprise. Assessments of his reign, in part, revolve around the question whether this energetic and talented prince was the archetypal Renaissance man, establishing a 'new monarchy', or a king in the more traditional medieval mould.

How did Henry Tudor consolidate his position as king of England?

When Henry became king he was faced with a number of potential challenges to his authority. The danger of a Yorkist uprising was considerable, other claimants to the throne might (and did) appear, and some form of foreign invasion was always a possibility. This insecurity, in fact, was a feature of most of Henry's reign, at least until the early years of the sixteenth century.

Just over a fortnight after defeating Richard at the Battle of Bosworth, Henry was proclaimed king on 7 September 1485, and subsequently crowned at the end of October. His coronation was further strengthened by a parliamentary bill in November, designed to uphold Henry's authority in the courts and to ensure he had full possession of crown lands. This read:

> To the pleasure of almighty God, the wealth, prosperity and surety of this realm of England, to the singular comfort of all the king's subjects of the same, and in avoiding all ambiguities and questions, be it ordained, established and enacted by authority of this present parliament that the inheritance of the crowns of the realms of England and of France ... be, rest, remain and abide in the most royal person of our now sovereign lord King Harry the VIIth and in the heirs of his body lawfully coming, perpetually with the grace of God so to endure, and in no other.

Why were the new king and parliament so keen to eliminate 'all ambiguities and questions' at this time?

By having his coronation before parliament sat in November, Henry made sure that parliament could never claim to have made him king, a claim which would have set a very dangerous precedent for the present and future rulers. The Tudor dynasty was careful to maintain the ancient assumption that God made kings, that theirs was a monarchy established by divine and ancestral right. As Henry VIII's chronicler, Edward Hall, wrote:

> King Henry obtained and enjoyed the kingdom as a thing elected and provided by God, and encompassed and achieved by his special favour and gracious aspect. For men commonly report that 797 years ago it was revealed by a heavenly voice to Cadwallader, last king of the Britons, that his stock and progeny should reign and have dominion in this land again. Most men were convinced that by this heavenly voice Henry VII was provided and ordained long ago to enjoy and obtain this kingdom, which Henry VI also claimed. Wherefore Henry VII was by right and just title of inheritance, and by divine providence, thus crowned and proclaimed king.

Officially the reign was said to have begun on 21 August 1485, the day before Bosworth. Thus Richard and his supporters were declared traitors and their lives and property forfeit. In one fell swoop Henry was now able to rid himself of potential opponents and strengthen his position by seizing their lands or encourage their loyalty with the threat of such retribution.

Henry proved decisive in the opening weeks of his reign, though more inclined to forgive than condemn. True, certain powerful individuals who had survived the wars were promptly gaoled until such time as they ceased to pose a threat; these included the earl of Surrey and the duke of Northumberland. The strongest claimant to the throne by blood lineage on Richard's side, his ten-year-old nephew, the earl of Warwick, was confined, in some comfort, in the Tower of London. Another nephew, however, the earl of Lincoln, was asked to join the king's council, having declared his loyalty to Henry despite being Richard's chosen heir. Freedom was granted to other Yorkist magnates in return for their promises of good and loyal behaviour. His supporters, needless to say, were rewarded: Jasper Tudor, his uncle, was made duke of Bedford and Thomas Stanley received the earldom of Derby. Other followers, such as Bishop Morton and Richard Fox, were awarded high offices in his council.

The new king's approach to the consolidation of his position is summarised in this contemporary letter to Rome from John de Giglis, one of the pope's ambassadors and the papal collector of taxes in England. It is dated 6 December 1485.

> Most blessed father, after most humble commendation and kisses of thy most blessed feet. Since the last letters which I wrote to you, most Holy Father, little or nothing new has occurred in the state of these affairs. Certainly a new public assembly of the kingdom, which they call parliament, is being held for the information of the kingdom,

and in this some Acts have been passed, the chief of which is a general pardon of all offence committed against the king. The earl of Northumberland, who has been captured and imprisoned, has been set at liberty, but on security from all the prelates, temporal lords, and also the Commons. The earl of Surrey is still kept in prison: but I hear that he will be released. The eldest daughter of King Edward has been declared duchess of York. There are persistent rumours that the king is about to marry her, a thing which all consider will be most beneficial for the kingdom. The king himself is considered most prudent and also very merciful: all things seem disposed towards peace if only men's minds remain constant. For there is nothing more harmful to this kingdom than ambition and insatiable greed, the mother of all faithlessness and inconstancy: and if God will preserve us from this, the condition of this kingdom will be peaceful . . .

Why should Henry's marriage to Elizabeth of York be 'a thing . . . most beneficial for the kingdom'?

Henry's marriage to Elizabeth of York was a powerful means of legitimising his claim to the throne in both Lancastrian and Yorkist eyes. The marriage had

Elizabeth of York. The hand of Edward's daughter in marriage was a powerful means of legitimising a usurper's place on the throne, a fact appreciated by both Richard III and Henry VII.

been proposed by Henry's shrewd mother, **Margaret Beaufort**, back in 1483. Elizabeth was the eldest daughter of Edward IV and Henry publicly promised in a ceremony at Rennes Cathedral, while in exile, that he would make her his queen should he succeed in wresting the throne from Richard. In so doing he could rely on the support of those disaffected Yorkists who loathed Richard III's usurpation. They were finally married on 18 January 1486, having secured special dispensation from the pope since, as descendants of Edward III, they were distant cousins.

The significance of this marriage was not lost on Polydore Vergil in *Anglica historia* (1537):

> It is legitimate to attribute this to divine intervention, for plainly by it all things which nourished the most ruinous factions were utterly removed, by it the two houses of Lancaster and York were united, and from this union the true and established royal line emerged which now reigns.

In March 1486 Henry VII's claim to the throne was confirmed by a papal bull 'by reason of his highest and undoubted title of successor as by the right of his most noble victory, and by election of the lords spiritual and temporal and other nobles of this realm, and by the act, ordinance, and authority of Parliament . . .' For his and his queen's personal security he surrounded himself with a troop of hand-picked men, including a number of good archers, whom he named the 'Yeomen of his Guard'. In so doing he adopted a French custom and a wise defence against court intrigue.

How successfully did Henry VII deal with opposition to his rule?

Throughout this period Henry was troubled by challenges to his authority. These included risings led by Yorkist lords (Lord Lovell in Yorkshire, Thomas and Humphrey Stafford in the west in 1486 and Sir John Egremont in Yorkshire in 1489), a popular protest against taxes for a war on Scotland (the Cornish rebellion of 1497), and the phenomenon of 'pretenders', conspiracies in support of fake claimants to the throne (Lambert Simnel during 1486 and 1487, and Perkin Warbeck between 1491 and 1499).

The rising of Lord Lovell and the Staffords, 1485–86

Richard Grafton, a mid-sixteenth-century chronicler, writes that, in 1486, having settled his affairs in London, Henry set out on a 'progress' of his realm 'so that he might weed and root out and purge the minds of men tainted and defiled with the contagious smoke of dissension and privy factions, especially

Margaret Beaufort (1443–1509) Margaret Beaufort, countess of Richmond and Derby, might have been as young as 13 when she gave birth to her only child, Henry Tudor, in 1457, son of her recently deceased second husband, Edmund Tudor, earl of Richmond and half-brother of Henry VI. She was descended from Edward III through John of Gaunt, duke of Lancaster. She married John de la Pole in around her eighth year, a marriage that was dissolved in 1453. She played an important part in promoting Henry's claim to the throne, narrowly escaping execution for her role in the rebellion of 1483, and providing Henry with money to help finance his campaign of 1485 and, most usefully, encouraging her fourth husband, Sir Thomas Stanley, to support Henry Tudor's cause.

She was deeply religious and the benefactor of many ecclesiastical houses. She translated the fourth book of Thomas à Kempis' *Imitation of Christ* from French into English, as well as commissioning a number of other devout works. She is also associated with the world of learning by founding Christ's College, Cambridge, and through the patronage she gave to William Caxton.

in the county of York, which were secret favourers and comforters of his opponents'. Shortly after Easter, Henry arrived in York, only to be warned of an impending assault on the city by Francis, Lord Lovell, which was to coincide with an attack in the Midlands on the city of Worcester, launched by Humphrey Stafford. The king promptly instructed the duke of Bedford and other magnates to organise armies with which to confront any encamped rebels. They were to offer free pardons to all who would submit and to take every measure necessary to avoid bloodshed. The rebellion was successfully pre-empted: Lovell deserted his army in the middle of the night and fled to Lancashire and from thence to Flanders. Hearing this news, Humphrey Stafford also took fright and moved east towards Oxford, near where he was taken prisoner, conveyed to London and executed at Tyburn. His brother and co-conspirator, however, was forgiven for having made the mistake of following an evil older brother's malignant advice.

The crisis passed, the king returned to London. Shortly afterwards, in September, his queen, Elizabeth of York, gave birth to their first child – a boy, destined, they hoped, to become the future king of England. He was named Arthur. Henry Tudor thus set a Tudor precedent at this point by associating the dynasty with England's most revered and ancient of kings.

Lambert Simnel

Arguably Lovell's and Stafford's was a lost cause. Without a legitimate Yorkist claimant to the throne, their gesture had been an empty one, destined to be defeated by a 'rightful' king who, furthermore, had reunited the houses of Lancaster and York. History now took a surprising turn as Henry's diehard opponents backed the claims of impostor princes.

Richard Symonds Little is known of the man who engineered Lambert Simnel's scheme to take the throne. According to one contemporary chronicler, this Oxford priest was driven by malice and the expectation that success would lead to his own promotion to an archbishopric or other high office. Symonds instructed the boy in the art of 'princely behaviour' and Lambert proved an avid learner. He was well able, by the time he arrived in Ireland, to speak convincingly of his royal pedigree and noble upbringing.

The first pretender to challenge Henry was a ten-year-old boy from Oxford, the son of an organ maker. His resemblance to Richard of York, the youngest of Edward IV's sons, the princes presumed to have been murdered in the Tower, caused him to become the pawn of Yorkist supporters around Oxford. When it began to be rumoured that Edward IV's nephew, the earl of Warwick, also detained in the Tower, had died, Simnel's advocate, an Oxford priest named **Richard Symonds**, decided to change the boy's supposed identity to that of Warwick. He was subsequently taken to Ireland and, in May 1487, crowned King Edward VI in Dublin, another centre of Yorkist sympathy.

Once more Henry VII tried to pre-empt war by offering those who had supported the impostor king a free pardon if they admitted their mistake. This time, however, he was less successful. Simnel provided the cause that the aborted rebellion of 1486 had lacked. With the backing of such powerful supporters as the earl of Kildare and the archbishop of Dublin, the boy's

Arthur, prince of Wales. The Tudors' claim to be descended from King Arthur was a central element in royal propaganda.

new-found 'aunt', Margaret of Burgundy, sister of Edward IV and Richard III, co-ordinated the insurrection.

Despite Henry's parading of the real earl of Warwick in London, an invasion led by **John de la Pole**, the earl of Lincoln, and Lord Lovell, supported by 2,000 German mercenaries, was staged in the summer of 1487. Landing in Furness, Lancashire, the predominantly Irish army met Henry's at Stoke, near Newark, on 16 June and, outnumbered, was decisively defeated. The earl of Lincoln had not met with the support of his fellow English nobles he had hoped for but, hoping to defeat the king's larger army, as Henry himself had done at Bosworth, he did not shy from an engagement. Henry, however, had had plenty of time to prepare for the invasion and his well-organised and well-armed force was more than a match for the poorly equipped Irish retainers under the command of Kildare, although the presence of hardened German mercenaries helped prolong the fight.

The Battle of Stoke was the last battle of the Wars of the Roses. Lovell was never heard of again and probably died on the battlefield along with Lincoln. The pretender and his creator were both captured but, characteristically, Henry spared them both – partly for purely propagandist reasons but also perhaps because one an innocent child and the other was a priest. Richard Symonds was sentenced to life imprisonment and Simnel was found employment in the king's kitchen.

John de la Pole (?1464–87) A principal supporter of Lambert Simnel, John de la Pole, earl of Lincoln, was a genuine Yorkist prince and the Yorkist heir-presumptive from 1486, his mother being Edward IV's sister. Although John had been a supporter of Richard III, Henry VII had cultivated his loyalty and made him, in 1486, lord lieutenant of Ireland. His decision to abandon Henry's court in 1487 turned him into Henry VII's deadliest enemy and led him to his death on the battlefield at Stoke.

John Guy has declared this to have been one of the most serious revolts faced by Henry VII since it had 'dynastic intentions'. It was all the more worrying to the security of the new regime since it came so soon after the Battle of Bosworth.

Of the lenient way in which the surviving conspirators were treated, G. R. Elton remarked, 'Henry proved merciful in a politic manner': instead of unleashing bloody vengeance, such as his royal descendants would upon their opponents in the sixteenth century, he proved magnanimous. Simnel eventually became one of the king's falconers. Henry VII successfully played down the Simnel conspiracy whereas a less shrewd statesman would have martyred those responsible.

What reasons lay behind HenryVII's leniency towards conspirators?

Sir John Egremont and the northern tax rebellion of 1489

Henry VII broke with tradition early in his reign by making the same tax demands on northerners as on southerners. Custom appears to have excused the north from raising certain monies for the defence of England and ventures abroad, on the grounds that they tended to foot the bill for defending the border country from the ravages of Scottish raiding parties. When Henry declared in 1489 that every man, including those in the north of the realm, should pay a tenth penny of his goods towards the cost of a campaign in Brittany, people in Yorkshire and in the bishopric of Durham refused. The earl of Northumberland, entrusted with enforcing payment by any means, was attacked and murdered, together with a number of his household servants. A small army of defiant non-taxpayers and, doubtless, some sympathisers of Richard III, was formed under the leadership of Sir John Egremont. They openly defied the king and declared they would fight if necessary to retain their liberty and rights. Henry VII himself joined the earl of Surrey in an expedition to the north to impose his will upon the rebels. The ringleader, John Chamber, together with his accomplices, was hanged at York. The majority of those who had resisted paying their dues, however, were spared. Egremont meanwhile had escaped and joined fellow malcontents gathered around Margaret of Burgundy in Flanders.

Perkin Warbeck

The other great pretender to challenge Henry VII was the mysterious Perkin Warbeck. He began to cultivate the rumour, started when he was in Cork in Ireland in 1491, that he was in fact Richard, the younger of the murdered princes in the Tower. For the rest of the nineties he would cause trouble for Henry through his habit of making alliances with the king's foreign enemies in Ireland, Scotland and France. He led a forlorn invasion of England in 1497, but survived until the end of November 1499, when he was hanged

Perkin Warbeck.
His false claim to be
Edward IV's second son,
Richard, gained him
many supporters.

after being found guilty of plotting to escape from captivity in the Tower of London.

The Henrician chronicler, Edward Hall, catalogued reasons for the considerable support this new pretender attracted:

> ... many ... who had fallen into debt and feared to be brought into captivity and bondage assembled together in a company and crossed over the sea to Flanders, to their counterfeit Richard son of King Edward IV, otherwise named Perkin Warbeck. After this many noblemen conspired together, some induced by rashness and temerity, some so earnestly persuaded of their own conceit as if they knew perfectly that this Perkin was undoubtedly the son of King Edward IV ... Others joined them through indignation, envy and greed, ever judging and thinking they were not suitably rewarded for their pains taken on the king's behalf in his quarrels. Others who it grieved and vexed to see the world stand still in security and all men living in peace and tranquility, desirous for some change, ran headlong into that fury, madness and sedition.

The narrative of events in Warbeck's career is summarised in the chronology on pages 88–89. What motivated this young Fleming from Tournai is less

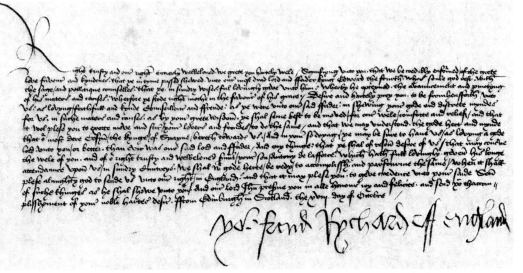

Perkin Warbeck's signature as Richard of England on a letter sent from Scotland in 1496. Warbeck made Scotland, rather than Ireland, his base after 1495.

certain and is certainly intriguing, although his own account given on the scaffold shortly before his execution in 1499 provides some clues:

> Now when we were there arrived in the town of Cork . . . [there] came unto me an Englishman and said to me . . . that they knew that I was King Richard's bastard son . . . They advised me not to be afeared but that I should take it upon me boldly . . . so that they might be revenged on the king of England, and so against my will made me learn English and taught me what I should do and say. And after this they called me the duke of York, second son to King Edward IV, because King Richard's bastard son was in the hands of the King of England . . .

Controversy remains over whether, in J. D. Mackie's words, he was merely 'a conceited, ambitious youth with an engaging address' who stumbled by chance upon Yorkist opportunists in Cork, or whether, as claimed by Henry VII's biographer, S. B. Chrimes, this was in fact 'the first overt action in the unfolding of a definite plan'.

Warbeck and rebellion, chronology of events

1489   The temporary truce with France made during conflict over English and French claims to Brittany comes to an end.

1491   Warbeck arrives in Cork, Ireland; and, possibly inspired by the agents of Charles VIII of France and Margaret of Burgundy, claims to be Richard, duke of York.

1492   Warbeck is made welcome in the court of Charles VIII and is joined in Paris by around 100 English Yorkists.
October The English invade France and lay siege to Boulogne.
November The Treaty of Etaples is made between Henry and Charles; a clause is included stating the French king will no longer support Warbeck or English rebels. Warbeck flees to the court of his 'aunt', Margaret of Burgundy, in Flanders.

1493   Henry breaks off all trade with Flanders.
Warbeck is recognised as Richard IV by the new Holy Roman Emperor, Maximilian (Margaret of Burgundy's son-in-law).

1495   Sir William Stanley (chamberlain of the king's household) and Lord Fitzwalter (royal steward) are executed for alleged conspiracy.
July Warbeck lands with supporters at Deal, Kent; lack of local support results in his fleeing to Ireland. He lays siege to Waterford for 11 days, without success, departs for Scotland and is given refuge by James IV. He receives James' cousin's hand in marriage and an annual pension of £1,200. The Scots invade England, headed by Warbeck, which proves disastrous, the northern counties failing to rise in support of the pretender. James IV subsequently signs lasting truce with Henry.

1497   The Cornish rebellion breaks out. Warbeck returns to Ireland before sailing to Cornwall in search of support. Another fiasco occurs and Warbeck surrenders to Henry who generously keeps him, and his young Scottish wife, in his custody at court.

1498   Warbeck escapes, is captured, publicly humiliated in the stocks, and sent to the Tower.

1499   Allegations of further conspiratorial behaviour surface which result in Warbeck's execution by hanging. The earl of Warwick, nephew of Edward IV and imprisoned in the Tower since the beginning of Henry's reign, is implicated in the conspiracy. Although probably entirely innocent, he is beheaded a week later.

Sir William Stanley's 'conspiracy'

The highest profile victim, after Warwick, of the Warbeck years was Sir William Stanley. The younger brother of Henry VII's stepfather, Thomas Stanley, first earl of Derby, William Stanley had played a crucial role at Bosworth where he turned his army of 3,000–8,000 against Richard III. His assistance at Bosworth was amply rewarded for he was appointed chamberlain of the royal household and came to be considered the richest commoner in England.

He was beheaded in 1495 on the grounds that, ostensibly, he was in league with Margaret of Burgundy and her 'puppet', Perkin Warbeck. Allegedly he had remarked, perhaps in a moment of humour, that he would not resist Warbeck if indeed he really was Prince Richard. It is possible that he was in contact and conspiring with Margaret through Sir Robert Clifford, who returned from her court in January 1495. This was Clifford's own claim and, while he was not indicted (was he a 'double agent' working for the king as well as Stanley?), the chamberlain, who had turned coat at a critical hour once before, was found guilty of treason and executed.

Quite likely Stanley, guilty or not, was killed in order to deter anyone from even contemplating lending their support to the pretender, who was expected to launch an invasion in the near future. It seems unlikely that a man as successful as Stanley would see anything to gain in support of such a spurious claimant. Moreover, Henry VII had shown on a number of occasions that he had capacity for mercy even when dealing with the most treasonable of offenders. Cynical *realpolitik* as opposed to genuine conspiracy or kingly paranoia might well explain Sir William Stanley's fate.

Stanley's motives, if indeed he was guilty, have always mystified historians as this extract from Edward Hall's *The union of the two noble and illustre families of Lancaster and York* (1548) testifies:

> What caused the sincere and faithful mind which Sir William Stanley always bore to King Henry to turn into cankered hatred and spite, and why the special favour the king bore him was changed to disdain and displeasure, different men have different explanations. Some say that … he remembered more the benefit he had done to the king than the rewards and gifts he received … Some say he desired to be earl of Chester and being denied that began to bear a grudge and to disdain his high friend the king … When the king perceived that his stomach began to canker and grow rusty he was not a little displeased with him, and so when both their hearts were inflamed with melancholy both lost the fruit of their long-continued friendship and favour …
> At this time the king thought it best to use some sharp punishment and correction for the offences of his subjects, so that the lately begun sedition might sooner be oppressed. When knowledge of the slanderous and opprobrious words concerning the expected arrival of the feigned Richard, duke of York, came to the king's ears, he caused several people to suffer punishment for their heinous offences.

To what extent can Henry VII's treatment of William Stanley be regarded as atypical?

Opposition in Ireland and Poynings' Law

Though considered a part of the kingdom by English kings, much of Ireland remained in cultural and political isolation throughout the period. As G. R. Elton wrote in *England under the Tudors* (1974): 'The better part of the wild, wooded, boggy, and hilly country of the north and west had never so much as seen an English soldier or administrator.' No Tudor monarch visited Ireland and, in 1485, only the 80 kilometre strip extending northwards from Dublin, known as the Pale, was securely held by the crown. Elsewhere the greater

Anglo-Irish families, notably the Geraldines and Butlers, and the Irish chieftains held sway.

In Ireland rebellions were fermented: Lambert Simnel's invasion of England was launched from Ireland, and Perkin Warbeck first appeared in the southern Irish port of Cork in 1491. Initially, as elsewhere, Henry relied upon local magnates to impose his authority. In 1485 the post of lord deputy was held by a Fitzgerald, the earl of Kildare. When Lambert Simnel was brought to Ireland and, posing as the earl of Warwick, crowned in Dublin in 1487, Kildare, eager to undermine English authority in Ireland, was among those to recognise him as King Edward VI.

Following Simnel's defeat at the Battle of Stoke, Kildare gave himself up, admitted his mistake in supporting the boy's claim, and was forgiven.

In 1491 Kildare expressed support for a second pretender, Perkin Warbeck, and this time Henry was less forgiving. Kildare was dismissed in 1492. In his place in 1494, Henry, breaking with tradition, chose an Englishman, Sir Edward Poynings. Poynings bought off potential rebels in the northern province of Ulster and assembled a parliament, passing laws designed to reduce Irish independence. By the terms of Poynings' Law, no laws could be passed in Ireland without the English king's approval, and any new English legislation would automatically apply to Ireland as well. The first parliament attainted the earl of Kildare, had him arrested and sent to the Tower of London. This apparent destruction of Ireland's most powerful leader was impressive indeed. In 1495 Perkin Warbeck was driven out of Ireland into a Scottish exile.

The cost of controlling Ireland and trying to impose English Law outside the Pale proved great, and in 1496 Henry reverted to the tradition of relying on the Irish nobility to manage Irish affairs. Characteristically, Henry forgave Kildare his earlier indiscretions and he was reappointed lord deputy. The show of strength between 1492 and 1496 helped establish the authority of Henry VII. The country furnished no more pretenders and, from this point on, Henry was largely untroubled by Irish affairs. Kildare, now married to the king's cousin, denied Warbeck further support in 1497, and remained in post as deputy until the end of the reign.

The Cornish rebellion, 1497

Described by John Guy as 'the most important revolt in Henry's reign' this rebellion was provoked by the demand for additional taxes needed to raise revenue with which to pay for a projected invasion of Scotland, part of an ages-old conflict that had been made worse by Perkin Warbeck's recent activities. According to Raphael Holinshed's *Chronicle* (1571), the rebel leaders promised 'not to hurt any living creature' but to punish those of the king's ministers, including the archbishop of Canterbury, who were associated with the imposition of the unwanted tax. The 15,000 Cornish rebels marched on London before being defeated on 17 June 1497. The *Registrum Annalium Collegii Mertonensis* for the year 1497 gives an account of the events:

> Memorandum, in this year about the beginning of May, a great rising of the people occurred in the kingdom beginning in Cornwall where the ringleader was a smith named Michael Joseph. A great multitude of people supported him, but there was none of noble blood except Lord Audley. Crossing the counties of Devon, Somerset, Wiltshire, Southampton, they came at length to Blackheath on 16th June, where they pitched their camp for the night. On the morrow, 17th June, Henry VII met them with a great multitude of nobles. He gained the victory without great slaughter on either side and the said captain and Lord Audley with others were captured and committed in chains to the Tower for their deeds. From there on the 27th of the month the said Michael and one Flammok, a lawyer, were drawn through the places of the city to Tyburn and there were hanged. Their bodies were taken down quartered, and by the king's orders were hanged in various cities and places in the kingdom. On the next day, the 28th, the said Lord Audley was drawn from Newgate through the places of the city to the place of punishment near the Tower, and there his head was struck off. His body was, by the king's grace, buried in the Preachers, but his head was fixed on London Bridge.

According to John Stow in his *Annals of England* (1592), both the king and the rebels lost about 300 men, and about 1,500 were captured following the battle. More recently, it has been estimated that around 1,000 rebels were killed at Blackheath. A number of important families in the south and west were accused of connections with the rebellion and fined accordingly; in Somerset alone the charged included three members of parliament and four sheriffs. Those who rallied around Warbeck later in the year, when he arrived in the south-west, might have done so because of the severity with which the Cornish rebels were treated.

The *Registrum Annalium Collegii Mertonensis* for 1497 reads:

> Memorandum, in that year on 7th September, one Perkin, by nationality a Fleming, pretending that he was the second son of Edward IV, and calling himself Richard, duke of York, landed at the port of St Ives in Cornwall and proclaimed himself king of England. About 10,000 Cornishmen who hated Henry VII on account of their defeat at Blackheath on the previous 17th June, and who wished to avenge themselves on the king joined him, and they set out towards the east in battle array.

Why did so many Cornishmen support Perkin Warbeck?

Henry abandoned the Scottish campaign and, instead, took a conciliatory line with James IV in which he was successful.

The threat of 'The White Rose'

Even after the executions of Warbeck and Warwick and the start of a new century, Henry VII continued to be plagued by conspirators and would-be rebels. One such was another Yorkist heir, Edmund de la Pole, the duke of Suffolk, nicknamed 'The White Rose'. Suffolk was the nephew of Edward IV and Richard III, and the brother of the earl of Lincoln who had been slain in 1487 at the Battle of Stoke for his part in supporting Lambert Simnel's insurrection.

Alarmed no doubt by the fate of Stanley and Warwick, Suffolk fled England in July 1499 and took refuge in France, near Calais. After a brief reconciliation with the king he took flight again, this time joining other Yorkist exiles in Flanders. Suffolk became more of a threat after the deaths of Henry's infant son, Edmund, in 1500 and his heir, Arthur, in 1502, the succession now passing to Arthur's younger brother, ten-year-old Henry.

In 1504 Suffolk's family, together with other associates tarnished by previous Yorkist/Ricardian sympathies, was ruthlessly purged. The chronicler, Richard Grafton, writing around 1550, explained the rationale behind Henry's actions at this time:

> King Henry now [1504] growing old, before this time had always been vexed and provoked by the scrupulous stings of sedition and civil commotion, so that he detested and abhorred internal and private war more than death or anything more terrible. Therefore he determined to provide so prudently that all causes of such unquietness and mischief to come should be rooted out and banished ... remembering the old proverb that men through abundance of riches grow more insolent and headstrong ...

A total of 51 men were attainted by parliament, their coffers, according to the chroniclers, being emptied into the king's purse. Chief among those who carried out Henry's vengeful work, indicting men for transgressing previously neglected penal laws, were Sir Richard Empson and Edmund Dudley. Both of these men would pay dearly for their activities early in the reign of Henry VIII. Some in the process were condemned to death, most famously Sir James Tyrell, who was made to confess that, during his tenure of the office of constable of the Tower, he had murdered Edward's sons at the start of Richard III's reign. In so doing, Henry and his fellow accusers could hope to eliminate the possibility of further pretenders posing as the troublesome princes now grown to adulthood. On the eve of his execution, with nothing personally to gain in so doing, Edmund Dudley admitted that some of what he had been instructed to do by his royal master amounted to extortion. Henry VII himself effectively admitted the dubious nature of his money-raising schemes in the last years of his reign when, in his will, he instructed the setting-up of a committee to investigate claims by individuals who had been wronged under his administration.

In 1506 he finally wrested Suffolk from the protection of Philip of Burgundy on the condition that he spare his life. This he did, but kept Suffolk captive in the Tower until he was executed in 1513 in the reign of Henry VIII. At last, for the first time in more than 20 years, with most of his potential dynastic rivals buried or imprisoned, Henry could feel reasonably secure, but the future of his own dynasty rested precariously with the life of his surviving son, Henry.

Why did Henry VII treat the Suffolk family so harshly?

Margaret, duchess of Burgundy, 1446–1503

> ... this diabolical duchess ... she always cared nothing for peace and tranquility and desired nothing more than dissension, civil war and the destruction of Henry.
>
> Edward Hall, *The union of the two noble and illustre families of Lancaster and York*, 1548 (enlarged by Richard Grafton, 1550), Charles Whitby (ed.), 1904

Sister of Edward IV and Richard III, Margaret of Burgundy ruled the Low Countries for the first part of Henry's reign. She was the widow of Charles the Bold, duke of Burgundy, who died in 1477. She became heavily involved in various conspiracies against Henry during the first half of his reign. Yorkist supporters flocked to her court, including Francis, Lovell Lord and John de la Pole, the earl of Lincoln. Here too she gave shelter to Lambert Simnel, possibly from as early as 1486. She used her position and wealth to support his campaign by providing him with 2,000 German mercenaries and a fleet to carry them to Ireland.

Following Simnel's defeat she became involved in the activities of Perkin Warbeck. Accepting Warbeck's claims, she publicly acknowledged him as her nephew. Once more, she used her wealth to assist a pretender as indicated by a document from 1494, in which Warbeck acknowledged to her a debt of 800,000 florins. In Holinshed's *Chronicle*, published in 1571, he wrote:

> Also they sent unto Flanders to the Lady Margaret, sister to King Edward and late wife to Charles, duke of Burgoyne [Burgundy], to purchase aid and help at her hands. This Lady Margaret bore no small rule in the Low Countries, and in very deed sore grudged in her heart that King Henry (being descended of the house of Lancaster) should reign and govern of the realm of England, and ... though she well understood that this was but a coloured matter, yet

to work her malicious intention against King Henry, she was glad to have so fit an occasion, and . . . promised the messengers all the aid she should be able to make . . . and also to procure all the friends she could . . .

What is Holinshed's explanation for Margaret of Burgundy's support of Henry's opponents? Can you think of any other reason for her behaviour?

Is Holinshed unbiased in his account of Margaret of Burgundy?

At one stage Warbeck claimed to be the son of Margaret and the bishop of Cambrai. (Historians since have been intrigued by the fact that, when visiting London in 1498, the bishop specifically asked to see the pretender.) As Warbeck's fortunes declined, Margaret disassociated herself from him and, in 1498, sent Henry VII a formal apology for her previous involvement.

To what extent did domestic crises determine Henry VII's continental policy?

. . . the English are great lovers of themselves and of everything English. They think there are no other men worth considering and no other part of the world either.

Venetian envoy to England, c.1500

Yorkist and early Tudor foreign policy was determined by the need to secure the throne in England, to safeguard trade interests and to maintain English aspirations in continental Europe. These objectives could be achieved by either diplomacy or war. England's population during the sixteenth century was at best half that of Spain and only one third that of France. The income of English kings was smaller than that of their immediate neighbours and involvement abroad represented the additional cost of transporting armies abroad. Henry VII's fleet was insignificant – a total of seven royal ships on his inheritance and just five by the time he died. In armed diplomacy England was seriously disadvantaged.

Henry's position in 1485 in relation to continental powers was the reverse of his predecessors. The Yorkist policy was anti-French and pro-Burgundian. France, since 1330, had been regarded as a legitimate claim of English kings and Burgundy, the bitter enemy of France ever since she had gained her independence earlier in the century, was an obvious ally. Henry had, however, attained the throne by enlisting French support, and Burgundy, with Margaret of Burgundy sponsoring pretenders to engineer his downfall, was his enemy. After her husband, Charles the Bold, died in 1477, the dukedom was inherited by Maximilian of Habsburg, who became the Holy Roman Emperor in 1493. He was the husband of Charles the Bold's daughter by a former marriage. Thus England was potentially embroiled in the bitter conflict between the French house of Valois and the Austrian Habsburg dynasty.

Once again, events in Brittany turned things around. English kings had long sought the preservation of Burgundian and Breton independence, a vital counter-balance to the might of France. France of course aspired to a full absorption of these provinces into the kingdom, and when duke Francis of Brittany died in 1488, leaving as heir a minor, his daughter Anne, Charles VIII exerted his feudal right of wardship which, effectively, would place the duchy in French hands.

The Treaty of Redon in 1489 brought England into an alliance with Brittany in defiance of French interests and Henry put further pressure on France by making the **Treaty of Medina del Campo** with her southern neighbour, Spain. Despite this, Charles had no intention of backing down and proceeded to marry Anne of Brittany in December 1491, thus reuniting Brittany with the French crown.

Henry, troubled by Perkin Warbeck at home, was in no position to wage a major war and, instead, launched a short campaign, reasserting English claims to France, in October of 1492. A short siege of Boulogne was ended by the Treaty of Etaples, from which Henry secured a pension of 50,000 crowns a year, payable until the agreed total of 745,000 crowns had been met. In addition, Charles promised to cease supporting English rebels.

The support Perkin Warbeck received from Burgundy continued until 1496. The damage done to Anglo-Burgundian trade due to the embargo Henry placed on all trade with the Low Countries in 1493, coupled with Emperor Maximilian's desire to enlist English support for his campaign against France, led to a truce. As a result, Margaret of Burgundy, Maximilian's mother-in-law, was obliged to abandon Warbeck and his supporters. Although England joined Maximilian's **Holy League**, Henry had no intention of being drawn into the Habsburg–Valois conflict and the peace with France remained intact.

At the turn of the century, therefore, Henry's foreign relations could not have been better: he had made his peace with France, he was the ally of Spain, he had the support of the Emperor, and the rapprochement with Burgundy had begun. Just as his victory at Stoke had marked his acceptance as king at home, the Treaty of Medina del Campo represented recognition abroad.

The alliance with Spain, however, guaranteed by the marriage of first Prince Arthur and then Prince Henry to Catherine of Aragon, began to founder after 1504. The relationship with Ferdinand, king of Aragon, turned sour when his wife, Isabella, queen of Castile, died. Instead of supporting Ferdinand's claims to his deceased wife's kingdom, Henry decided to back the claims of Isabella's mad daughter, Joanna, who was married to Emperor Maximilian's son, Philip the Handsome of Burgundy. In October 1505 Ferdinand signed the Treaty of Blois with France and married Louis XII's niece the following March. The ruination of Henry's Spanish policy was amplified when, in 1508, Ferdinand joined France in the League of Cambrai. France and Spain were thus aligned together against Henry and his unreliable allies.

How did Henry VII's relationship with France fluctuate during his reign?

To what extent was Henry VII more successful than his predecessors in containing and pacifying the Scots?

During the fifteenth century, English kings effectively abandoned their claims to overlordship in Scotland. After years of intermittent skirmishes in the border regions and at sea, English kings after 1461 sought an ending to this 'cold war' with Scotland. So long as English interests were threatened by France, Scotland was a dangerous enemy, gravitating towards anti-English alliances with France.

In June 1463 Edward IV, fearing a Lancastrian invasion from the north, secured a 15-year truce with James III of Scotland. Further Scottish raids across the border in the early 1480s, however, inspired Edward's decision to capitalise on the conflicts between James and his brother, Alexander, the duke of Albany. Richard of Gloucester organised a campaign headed by Albany in 1482. When Albany regained his former positions, however, he abandoned his claim. Gloucester then released the recently captured James and withdrew his army from Edinburgh. After Albany was charged with treason by the Scottish parliament in 1483, Gloucester, now Richard III, pursued the cause of the duke, now fugitive in England. This led to a second, unsuccessful invasion and Albany was forced to flee to France. In 1484 a three-year truce was agreed between Richard and James. The 'Auld Alliance' between Scotland and France, however, remained and Scottish troops would soon fight with the French-backed invasion that led to Richard's destruction on Bosworth Field.

Why did Scotland and France share an 'Auld Alliance'?

Henry VII tried to secure a lasting peace with Scotland and made a new truce, with James IV, when he became king in 1488. Despite this, relations deteriorated to such an extent that James married his cousin, Lady Catherine Gordon, to the pretender to the English throne, Perkin Warbeck, in 1495. In the event of Warbeck achieving his objectives, it was agreed that Scotland should take back Berwick, lost to the English in 1482. Warbeck's subsequent invasion from Scotland, in 1496, was a fiasco, his Scottish troops retreating back across the border once it became apparent that the north would not rally to his cause. It was in retaliation to this that Henry attempted to raise the subsidy to wage a war against Scotland that resulted in the Cornish rebellion. The revolt was quelled, though not before the rebels reached Blackheath in their march on London. Meanwhile James IV's troops made another incursion into England but were pushed back by an army under the command of the earl of Surrey.

Why was a policy of peace regarding Scotland more advisable in 1497 than a policy of punishment?

Henry reverted to a policy of peace rather than punishment and, in September 1497, signed the Truce of Ayton with James IV. This was extended by the Treaty of Perpetual Peace in 1502, reinforced by the marriage of James to Henry's daughter, Margaret, in 1503. This peace proved a lasting one and Henry enjoyed good relations with Scotland for the remaining half-decade of his reign.

James IV of Scotland and Henry VII of England

James III, who was murdered in 1488, had been a weak and feeble king. His son and heir to the Scottish throne, James IV, was of a different breed. A Spanish visitor to Scotland from 1496 to 1497 wrote that James was:

> . . . of noble stature, neither tall nor short, and as handsome in complexion and shape as a man can be . . . He speaks the following foreign languages: Latin, very well; French, German, Flemish, Italian and Spanish . . . He is courageous, even more so than a king should be.

Renaissance
Renaissance means literally 'rebirth'. The Renaissance, which began in fourteenth-century Italy, was an artistic and cultural revival which spread throughout Europe.

He promised to be a formidable foe should the new English king endeavour to pursue claims to lordship over Scotland, revived by Henry's Yorkist predecessors, Edward IV and his brother, Richard III. James shared many of those qualities of the archetypal **Renaissance** prince that some have identified with Henry VII. An extract from Henry VII's funeral oration in 1509 states:

> His politic wisdom in governance was singular, his wit was always quick and ready, his reason pithy and substantial, his memory fresh and holding, his experience notable, his counsels fortunate and taken by wise deliberation, his speech gracious in diverse languages, his person goodly and amiable, his natural complexion of the purest mixture, his issue fair and in good number; leagues and confederacies he had with all Christian princes, his mighty power was dreaded everywhere . . .

However, in one respect they seem to have been very different. The chronicler, Polydore Vergil, in *Anglica historia* (1537), declared that Henry was 'constitutionally more inclined to peace than war', and another early commentator, Bernard Andreas, stated, in his *Life of Henry VII*, 'without doubt, he first of all the kings to come in future years, deserves to be crowned with the title of the "peacemaking king."' According to one contemporary observer quoted in the *Calendar of state papers Venetian, 1202–1509*, his was very much a defensive and cautious policy:

> He garrisons two or three fortresses, contrary to the custom of his predecessors, who garrisoned no place. He has neither ordnance nor munitions of war, and his body guard is supposed not to amount to one hundred men.

James IV on the other hand was a dedicated and reckless warrior. Given his limited resources, his expenditure on weaponry was remarkable. He was a great enthusiast for artillery and established, at vast cost, a huge and up-to-date arsenal. He deluded himself into believing that he could be a major player in European affairs and the politics of armed diplomacy. Scotland, ultimately, paid the price, with defeat on **Flodden Field** in 1513. He also, unwisely, took the offensive against England in the 1490s when Henry VII appears to have been content to play down English aspirations beyond the border.

By 1497 Henry VII was assembling the largest army of his reign in order to punish James for lending support to Warbeck. Scotland never felt the full force of Henry VII's retribution; the taxation imposed to raise this army helped spark the Cornish rebellion which diverted Henry from his Scottish campaign and used up some of the resources upon which it relied. According to G. R. Elton, in *England under the Tudors* (1974), it was a lucky escape for James IV:

> The story of Scotland's share in Warbeck's Odyssey has already been told. At one time, in 1497, it looked as though Henry VII would accept the challenge and attempt serious war in the north, but the Cornish rebellion came just in time to save James IV from his ill-regulated combativeness. If one may judge from later events in Henry VIII's reign, the Scottish army would have stood but a poor chance against the forces which the earl of Surrey was marshalling on the border.
>
> As it was, Henry VII preserved his peaceful reputation unsullied, to prove once more how well he could exploit difficult situations without precipitating war. Surrey did cross the border once to teach James a sharp lesson, incidentally refusing a typically chivalrous but unrealistic offer of single combat. The end of Warbeck left James rather at a loss, and his own position in a country where some of whose chief lords were ready to throw in their lot with the enemy was none too comfortable. Henry even hinted that two could play at the game of supporting pretenders and showed signs of adopting the cause of a Stuart claimant, the duke of Albany, then living in France. All these things working together, and Henry still continuing to offer real peace, an agreement was arrived at in December 1497.

The ensuing Treaty of Ayton of 1497, as we have seen, resulted in harmonious relationships with Scotland for the rest of Henry's reign.

Flodden Field James IV's support for Louis XII of France resulted in a disastrous defeat at Flodden at the hands of the earl of Surrey. James, along with 10,000 other Scots, was killed.

Why was Scotland such a threat to the English kings during this period?

For what reasons was England unable to impose its authority over Scotland between 1461 and 1509?

> ... if any Parliament be held in the land hereafter, contrary to the form and provision aforesaid, it be deemed void and of no effect in law.
>
> Source: Poynings' Law, 1494

Traditionally English kings had administered Ireland through the Anglo-Irish nobility. The lord deputy in Dublin enjoyed a good deal of autonomy and distance from the king's government in England. When Henry VII acquired the throne in 1485, Dublin and its Pale remained staunchly loyal to the Yorkist cause. In 1487 the pretender, Lambert Simnel, was crowned king in Dublin, much to Henry VII's irritation. However, not wishing to jeopardise his position in England by getting embroiled in a conflict in Ireland, Henry proved remarkably lenient in pardoning those involved in promoting Simnel's unsuccessful coup. In return for a mere oath of allegiance the lord deputy, the earl of Kildare, and the other great Anglo-Irish magnates were left to run Ireland as before.

When, in 1491, a second pretender, Perkin Warbeck, arrived in Ireland, posing as the younger of the princes in the Tower, Richard, Henry VII's patience was stretched too far. Kildare was dismissed, a small English army was landed in Ireland, and Warbeck fled to France. In 1494, to quell continuing Irish troubles and prevent Warbeck using Ireland as a base a second time, Henry sent over another small army and a governor, Sir Edward Poynings. The English governor brought with him a package of proposals, subsequently passed by Ireland's parliament, which undermined Irish autonomy by preventing the Anglo-Irish nobility, likes the Kildares, from holding parliamentary sessions and legislating without the English government's approval. During the brief spell of his governorship (he returned to England in December 1495) he crushed a major rebellion organised by Kildare's brother, captured Kildare and sent him to England as a prisoner, and he once more dispersed another attempt by Perkin Warbeck to gain a footing in Ireland.

In 1496, however, Henry VII reverted to the old policy of governing Ireland through that country's own nobility and he reinstated Kildare as lord deputy. Kildare's son stayed at the English king's court in England: a surety for his father's good behaviour.

Historians are divided over the success of Poynings' governorship and the reasons for Henry VII's reinstatement of Kildare. The lack of support for Warbeck in Ireland compared to that he found in Scotland, and compared to that enjoyed by Simnel in Ireland some years earlier, has been cited as evidence for a generally successful colonial policy. His recall of Poynings and restoration of authority in the hands of Irish nobles, according to some, was the decision of a strong and confident king who had quelled the Irish. Roger Lockyer writes in *Henry VII* (1983):

> By the end of 1495 Ireland had been pacified, and Poynings returned to England. Henry, who needed money and men for operations against Scotland, now disentangled himself from his Irish involvement and returned to the practice of ruling through the Irish magnates. He had been impressed by Kildare, and when it was pointed out to him that 'All England cannot rule yonder gentleman', he replied 'No? Then it is mete to rule all Ireland'. Kildare was therefore reinstated as Deputy, having abandoned his Yorkist inclinations, and Ireland ceased to be a major problem for Henry.

Other historians, like G. R. Elton in *England under the Tudors* (1974), have been less generous to Henry VII and have questioned the success of his Irish policy:

> In effect Henry despaired of the success of the measures initiated in 1494 when ... he recalled Poynings and restored Kildare to favour ... The problem of Ireland had turned out to be too big for solution; the return of Kildare meant the end of effective English control, despite the operation of Poynings' laws ... There were no claimants about to disturb the peace from Ireland; why, then, waste good money on a probably futile policy of direct rule? Henry VII was lucky to die before the Irish problem revived, but revive it did – and largely because he gave up the fight.

According to S. J. Gunn in *Early Tudor government* (1995), Henry, like his predecessors and successors, was dogged by old problems in Ireland which Poynings' Law manifestly had failed to resolve:

> In the years 1470–1534, the Fitzgeralds [earls of Kildare] were repeatedly appointed as governors, removed for misgovernance or political disloyalty, and then reappointed, often when the local followers through whom they ruled refused to co-operate with any alternative regime. Only when they overstepped the mark totally in the revolt of 1534 did Henry VIII turn to direct rule by an English governor with a subsidised garrison.

Edward Hall, the early Tudor historian, implied Henry's Irish policy in the mid-1490s was only ever intended as a temporary measure, 'to purge all the towns and places where Perkin was received, relieved or favoured'. Certainly Poynings succeeded in quelling the pro-Warbeck movement in Ireland through negotiation with the Irish lords and swift retribution where treason was encountered. His recall coincides exactly with Warbeck's arrival in Scotland in November 1495. Henry VII's policy in Ireland should only be considered a failure if he had any genuine intention of achieving more than the assertion of his authority in the face of Warbeck's posturing.

Summary questions

1 Identify and explain how Henry VII consolidated his position after 1485.

2 How successful was Henry VII in facing problems from pretenders during his reign?

3 Identify and explain any two successes in Henry VII's foreign policy.

4 Compare the importance of at least three military campaigns associated with Henry VII between 1485 and 1509.

5 Henry VII and the government of England

Focus questions

- ◆ How well did Henry VII manage his financial affairs?
- ◆ What was Henry VII's relationship with the English nobility?
- ◆ How was England governed during the reign of Henry VII?
- ◆ What place did the church have in the government of the realm?

Significant dates

1485 Henry VII's reign begins.
Henry VII holds his first parliament.
The first Navigation Act is passed.

1486 A commercial treaty is made with France.

1487 Henry VII's holds his second parliament.

1488 Henry VII's famous ship, *Great Harry*, is constructed.

1489 Henry VII holds his third parliament.
The second Navigation Act is passed.

1490 The commercial treaty with Denmark is renewed.
A commercial treaty is made with Florence.

1491 Henry VII holds his fourth parliament.

1493 An embargo is placed by Henry VII on Anglo-Flemish trade.

1494 The Irish parliament passes Poynings' Law.

1495 Henry VII holds his fifth parliament.
A new Statute of Treasons is passed.
A dry dock is constructed at Portsmouth.

1496 Jesus College, Cambridge, is founded.
John Cabot and his son, Sebastian, are commissioned by Henry VII to find a new trade route to Asia.
Weights and measures are standardised.
A trade agreement, the *Magnus Intercursus*, is signed.

1497 Henry VII holds his sixth parliament.
A commercial treaty is made with France.

1499 A commercial treaty is made with Riga.

1501	Henry VII declines the pope's request to lead a crusade against the Turks. Prince Arthur is married to Catherine of Aragon.
1502	Prince Arthur dies.
1503	James IV of Scotland and Henry VII's daughter, Margaret, are married. Construction begins on Henry VII's chapel at Westminster Abbey.
1504	Henry VII places an embargo on Anglo-Flemish trade. Henry VII holds his seventh parliament. Guilds and trade companies are placed under supervision of the crown.
1505	Christ's College, Cambridge, is founded.
1509	Henry VII dies.

Overview

John and Sebastian Cabot (1425–1500, 1474–1557) Born in Genoa, John Cabot settled in Bristol in the 1480s. In 1496 Henry VII issued letters patent to Cabot and other Bristol merchants authorising them to discover new lands and to monopolise any trade that might ensue, with a third of the profits being awarded to the crown. In 1497 Cabot and his son, Sebastian, reached Newfoundland, but Cabot failed to return from a second voyage a year later. Sebastian Cabot explored the east coast of America in 1499 and continued to lay the foundations for the exploitation of Newfoundland's vast resource of cod. Henry VII's patronage of men like the Cabots is indicative of an imaginative approach to government and interest in the development of English commerce.

The length of Henry VII's reign (24 years) and the fact that the dynasty he founded would occupy the throne for the whole of the sixteenth century are testimony to his adept handling of the day-to-day business of government. John Guy has described him as the most able businessman ever to wear England's crown. Like a good businessman, he knew how to deal with people, how to raise capital, how to save and how to spend wisely. He was very wary of imposing additional or increased taxes on his subjects, however, and preferred to resort to the Yorkist device of benevolences where possible. His interest in the crown's financial affairs is shown by his signature which appears on a daily basis in the royal accounts. He probably did not leave a great hoard of treasure to his heir but he did stay solvent and, despite a reputation for avarice, maintained one of the most conspicuously wealthy courts in Europe. Between December 1491 and his death in April 1509, he spent over £128,000 on jewels, and foreign dignitaries visiting Windsor Castle slept under throws of woven cloth of gold.

Henry VII sought to make his kingdom richer, too, by promoting trade abroad, although his hands often were tied by more pressing political considerations. To this end, he supported the voyages of **John and Sebastian Cabot**. He made a number of trade treaties with various countries, including the *Magnus Intercursus* (Great Commercial Exchange) with Maximilian I, the Holy Roman Emperor, in 1496. This confirmed favourable trade arrangements with Holland and, perhaps more importantly for Henry, secured the Emperor's promise to stop aiding Yorkist rivals. His support of merchants through the Navigation Acts of 1485 and 1489, which were designed to prevent the carriage of certain goods in non-English vessels, also had a political as well as economic objective. He could rely on the support of merchants when he wished to hire their ships in order to form a fleet for defensive or offensive purposes.

Henry Tudor surrounded himself with a number of able councillors, around 70 at any one time. While he promoted those who had supported him during the period of his exile abroad, he also forgave and then promoted former enemies. Thomas Howard, son of the duke of Norfolk, fought against him at Bosworth in 1485, where his father was killed. By 1501, however, he had been made lord treasurer.

In many ways Henry VII's was a traditional, even medieval, approach to kingship and government. Although he took initiatives, notably in the setting up of two new, although fairly short-lived, tribunals in Star Chamber for handling particular types of legal cases, he was more concerned with making an old system work effectively than replacing it with a new.

How well did Henry VII manage his financial affairs?

The conventional view of Henry's skill in government was that he was very competent but miserly. He certainly was accomplished in the art of government but he was no miser, as he kept a magnificent and lavish court. His miserly reputation is founded on the fact that, despite his spending, he managed his financial affairs well, he was unerringly efficient in claiming his dues, and he died leaving a full treasury. The contemporary historian, Polydore Vergil, declared in his *Anglica historia* (1537) that avarice was his only failing, and one to which he only succumbed in the latter part of his reign as he tried to safeguard his son's inheritance:

> This avarice is surely a bad enough vice in a private individual, whom it forever torments; in a monarch indeed it may be considered the worst vice, since it is harmful to everyone, and distorts those qualities of trustfulness, justice and integrity by which the state must be governed.

Henry followed in the footsteps of Edward IV in trying to extend his personal control over financial matters. His closest servants, members of the Privy Chamber, took on important treasury roles as the royal household was transformed into a government department. The highest office, treasurer of the chamber, was filled by two men during the reign, Sir Thomas Lovell (1485–92) and Sir John Heron (1492–1521). The king also relied heavily on the advice of Sir Reginald Bray, chancellor of the duchy of Lancaster, who was instrumental in increasing the revenue raised on royal estates, and who assisted Heron in the chamber.

Ordinary revenue

The king's ordinary revenue was largely earned by the land owned by the crown. The king's estates were vast, much having been gained through the extinction of family titles on the battlefields of the recent wars, or confiscation following Acts of Attainder. He inherited all the Yorkist and Lancastrian lands on becoming king and, unlike Edward IV, he proved reluctant to give them to his supporters. He had comparatively few family obligations in this respect, having no brothers and a single son after the death of Prince Arthur in 1502. He outlived both his mother and his wife and their lands too became his when they died.

Under the guidance of Bray his estates were managed more profitably from the early 1490s, and the annual income from crown land increased from £29,000 in 1485 to £42,000 in 1509.

The tenants-in-chief, those who had received land from the crown, were expected to fulfil certain feudal obligations. If an estate was inherited by a minor it was placed under the control of the king in his capacity as guardian, until his ward was old enough to take full possession. The ending of this wardship would be marked by another feudal obligation called 'livery', in which a payment had to be made before the lands were returned. A kind of death duty known as 'relief' had to be paid as lands were passed on, and the crown could even profit from the marriage of heiresses by selling suitors the right to marry them or, if an heiress wished to be free to choose, selling her the right instead.

The care Henry took over the collection of feudal dues is revealed in his establishment of special commissions to identify ways of increasing such revenues. New positions, surveyor of the king's wards (1503) and surveyor of the king's prerogative (1508), were created for the same purpose.

Initially the revenue collected from customs duties was even greater than that gathered from the crown lands. Like Edward IV before him, Henry took measures to identify ways in which such revenue could be increased, such as introducing the book of rates, which clarified valuations of particular goods and rates to be paid, and placing a greater emphasis on the need for documentary evidence recording transactions between merchants. Corrupt officials and smugglers were dragged before the courts in large numbers where they could expect to receive severe fines. The amount of income from this source was of course mainly reliant upon the health of the economy and the scale of its import and export trade. In this Henry was fortunate in that his reign coincided with a trade boom based upon greatly increased cloth exports. As S. J. Gunn has pointed out in *Early Tudor government* (1995), 'Henry was not merely lucky, he had in part made his own luck' by adopting a foreign policy which, whenever possible, encouraged trade.

A significant part of Henry's revenue was made up of fines paid by those found guilty in the law courts. For many offences, fining became the norm, even for quite serious crimes that might, technically, have warranted lengthy prison terms or execution. In addition, enormous fines were imposed upon those who fell out of favour and became attainted.

How did Henry VII try to increase his income from ordinary revenue?

Extraordinary revenue

An important function of parliament was to grant the king extraordinary means of raising money. In times of national crisis, Henry turned to parliament for financial assistance, as in 1496 in the face of threats from Perkin Warbeck and Scotland. The emergency taxes levied in these situations sometimes proved deeply unpopular. This was especially true when the projected wars for which the taxes were raised were never fought. Resentment over parliamentary taxation was a key element in the risings of 1489 and 1492 in Yorkshire and 1497 in Cornwall. For this reason, and because of the opportunity it gave parliament to make demands of the king in return, Henry was reluctant to rely on such sources and tried instead to 'live of his own'.

A less dangerous extraordinary means of raising cash was by asking the wealthiest families for loans. These were both granted and paid back because of the king's and his subjects' mutual interests: to refuse the request would imply an absence of loyalty and this might well result in the imposition of **bonds and recognisances**. The crown's failure to repay the loan might justify a noble's support for some pretender or other challenger to the throne.

bonds and recognisances These were payments in return for privileges, or fines imposed upon those whose loyalty was doubtful.

Forced loans or gifts, known as benevolences, were less welcome. These were introduced by Edward IV to finance an invasion of France in 1475. It was assumed that this obligatory 'loan', paid by the rich and for which there was no recompense, was made willingly as a token of loyalty to, and affection for, the king. No wonder then that Polydore Vergil, when he came to write about the subject, suggested a payment of this kind might more appropriately be called a 'malevolence' than a 'benevolence'.

It was customary for monarchs in the period to squeeze money out of the church, too, and Henry was no exception. Like parliament, the church was also expected to raise revenue by taxation in times of crisis. The sale of clerical offices (simony), by which the crown profited, was normal practice. Bishoprics might be left vacant for up to 12 months, while the crown received the revenue from the see before a new appointment was made. The vacancies might arise through the death of an incumbent or because bishops were moved from see to see by royal instruction. Inevitably, appointment to a new bishopric would be accompanied by a 'fine', payable to the crown.

Henry's income was further supplemented by the 'pension' paid by the king of France. This had been negotiated by Edward IV in 1475 and was renewed by Henry in 1492. In return for the pension (around £5,000 per annum) Henry agreed to remove his troops from France and not interfere with French dynastic interests.

Estimates of Henry VII's annual revenue from the main sources		
Crown lands	£40,000	(average 1502–5)
Customs	£37,000	(average 1485–1509)
Parliamentary taxation	£12,000	(average 1485–1509)
Wards and liveries	£9,400	(average 1504–6)
Total revenue	£104,800	(average 1502–5)

What was Henry VII's relationship with the English nobility?

Henry would have known, when he seized the crown from Richard III at Bosworth, that his own survival as king depended upon his dealings with the other great noble families. His success in containing noble aspirations caused early commentators to identify Henry with an 'anti-noble' policy but this is now considered inaccurate. Henry certainly did restrict the extension of aristocratic influence in a number of cases and, as the history of opposition to his reign reveals, a number of the more rebellious lords were destroyed by Acts of Attainder, imprisonment or execution. However, he also promoted the interests of loyal men, noble and non-noble alike, as demonstrated by his generosity in the weeks and months following Bosworth.

There are a number of reasons for supposing, at first sight, that Henry was anti-aristocratic.

- He was a great deal more reluctant to create new peers than other monarchs such as Edward IV and Henry VIII, and during his reign the nobility diminished in size whereas under Edward it had expanded (see tables below).

The creation of new earls and new barons		
	New earls	**New barons**
In the reign of Edward IV	9	13
In the reign of Henry VII	1	5

The total number of nobles in the reigns of Edward IV and Henry VII			
1461 (Accession of Edward IV)	42	1483 (Death of Edward IV)	46
1485 (Accession of Henry VII)	50	1509 (Death of Henry VII)	35

- He promoted the interests of commoners, sometimes over and above those of peers. He relied heavily on two lawyers of non-noble birth, Edmund Dudley and Richard Empson, who did much of the work of collecting noble debts in the form of bonds and recognisances. Dudley and Empson were impeached and executed, accused of challenging Henry VIII's accession, in 1510.
- He curbed the might of the nobility by passing, in 1485, 1487 and 1504, laws restricting the keeping of retainers, potential armies of servants and supporters identified by the wearing of their lord's livery.
- Over half of the peerage in Henry's reign was obliged to give recognisances to the crown, many nobles giving more than one. In most cases these recognisances were not collected in, but peers lived under the threat of having to make possibly crippling payments should they offend the king. This carefully organised use of recognisances in order to guarantee good behaviour was very different to the haphazard approach of Henry's predecessors.

As his leniency towards many of those who opposed him demonstrates, Henry could, however, be generous in his dealings with the nobility.

- Although new peerages were limited, this was compensated to an extent by his bestowing the order of the garter on 37 loyal subjects. This was a cheaper alternative for the crown since, unlike the creation of a new peer, it was not traditionally accompanied by a gift of land. Thus, much of the land received by the crown through the extinction of noble families was retained.
- Henry's ability to forgive and then reward is most strikingly demonstrated by the career of Thomas Howard, the earl of Surrey. Despite fighting on the other side at Bosworth, being attainted (hence having all his estates confiscated) and ending up in the Tower, his good behaviour resulted in a gradual restoration. His loyal service to the crown, particularly in containing threats from the north and Scotland, enabled him to regain the greater part of his inheritance and to secure the office of lord chancellor.
- Henry was not the first monarch to attempt limiting the military capacity of the nobility. His Acts against retaining reinforced, and made more effective, Edward IV's of 1468. Retaining was not totally prohibited and the private armies of loyal families were employed in royal campaigns.

The nobility remained important and powerful in the reign of Henry VII. However, circumstances and royal policy enabled the king to keep noble aspirations in check more effectively than had been the case in previous reigns.

What possible explanations are there for the contraction in the size of the nobility during the reign of Henry VII?

Acts of Attainder, bonds and recognisances

Henry VII's dealings with the nobility remain a controversial subject. Although the 'anti-aristocratic' tradition is inaccurate, a case can be made for claiming that Henry's treatment of noble families was more rigorous and interventionist than that of his Yorkist predecessors. His dealings with the nobility continue to be seen by some historians as part of a general revolution in government, initiated by Henry VII and completed in the reign of his son, Henry VIII.

The following sources have been selected to draw attention to important elements in this debate. Read each one carefully and try to answer the questions that follow.

1 Attainders

An Act of parliament was passed to stage an execution without trial. The title and possessions of the attainted passed to the crown. This was the method favoured by the Tudors for ridding themselves of opponents.

Source: Rosemary O'Day, *The Tudor age*, Harlow, 1995, p. 252

2 Attainders under Edward IV, Richard III and Henry VII

Number of attainders passed in Edward IV's reign	140
Number of attainders reversed	42
Number of attainders passed in Richard III's reign	100
Number of attainders reversed	1
Number of attainders reversed by Henry VII directly after Bosworth	99
Number of attainders passed in Henry VII's reign	138
Number of attainders reversed	46

Source: John Guy, *Tudor England*, Oxford, 1988, p. 8

3 The reversal of attainders

It used to be argued that Edward IV and Henry VII launched calculated attacks on the power of the nobility after 1461, but this view is refuted by the fact that 84 per cent of noble attainders were reversed.

Source: John Guy, *Tudor England*, Oxford, 1988, pp. 7–8

4 An Act of Attainder, 1491

Forasmuch as Sir Robert Chamberleyn . . . knight, and Richard White . . . gentleman . . . traitorously imagined and compassed the death and destruction of our said sovereign lord, and also the subversion of all this realm, then and there traitorously levied war against our said sovereign lord and adhered them traitorously to Charles the French king, ancient enemy to our said sovereign lord and this realm, against their duty and liegance; Be it therefore ordained and enacted by authority of this present parliament that the said Robert and Richard stand and be attainted of high treason, and forfeit all manors, lands, tenements, rents, reversions and all other hereditaments . . .

Source: *The statutes of the realm*, 1817

5 Recognizances

In their most basic form, bonds are simply written obligations to pay some kind of penalty if certain conditions are not met. Recognizances were a form of bond, which referred to some previous action or misconduct and would impose penalties if good behaviour were not maintained in the future. It was a system not dissimilar to the modern procedure of being bound over to keep the peace.

Source: David Grossel, 'The reign of Henry VII', in John Lotherington (ed.), *The Tudor years*, London, 1994, p. 48

6 Bonds

Number of peers placed under bond in the reign of Edward IV	7
Number of peerage families placed under bond in the reign of Henry VII (out of total 62)	36

Source: John Guy, *Tudor England*, Oxford, 1988, p. 8

7 Bond and recognisance, 24 December 1507

Indenture between the king and the same George, Lord Burgavenny: whereas George is indebted to the king in £100,000 [equivalent to between £20 and £30 million today] or thereabouts for unlawful receivers done, retained and made by him in Kent contrary to certain laws and statutes, as was found by inquisitions certified into the King's Bench and adjudged after free confession by him in the said court in Michaelmas term last; and whereas for execution and levy of this debt, being clearly due both in law and conscience, the king may attach his body and keep him in prison and take all the issues of his lands till the whole sum be paid; the king is graciously contented, at his suit for avoiding the extremity of the law, to accept as parcel of the debt the sum of £5,000 payable over ten years at Candlemas and the Purification; for which payments, as well as the residue of the debt, George binds himself and his heirs.

Source: *Calendar of the close rolls*, vol. 2, no. 825

It is . . . certain that the policy of imposing heavy fines was, in part at least, political in intent and designed to weaken potential opponents: it was part of Henry VII's attack on over-mighty subjects. Not uncommonly fines were remitted, wholly or in part, which shows that they were often intended to be deterrent rather than punitive. This fact makes it difficult to know what profit the king derived from them. They were not usually collected in cash: the victim gave a bond for his debt which he might take years to pay off. The policy was much resented, but it is by no means clear that it was unjust or even unduly harsh.

Source: G. R. Elton, *England under the Tudors*, 2nd edn, London, Routledge, 1974, p. 51

Historical-source questions

1 According to your own knowledge, did Acts of Attainder always result in execution?

2 What percentage of the total number of Acts of Attainder were reversed in the reign of a) Edward IV and b) Henry VII?

3 According to the information in Sources 2 and 3, were attainders more likely to be reversed in aristocratic or non-aristocratic cases?

4 What factors need to be taken into consideration before attempting to use the statistics in Source 2 to find out the relative severity of different reigns with regard to imposing attainders?

5 Why was Lord Burgavenny (Source 7) fined £100,000 in 1507?

6 How far does the evidence of Source 7 agree with the claims of Source 8?

7 Examine Henry VII's relations with the English nobility during his reign. To what extent did the nobility threaten the king, or the king the nobility?

king's council Five or six ineffective great councils met in Henry VII's reign – large assemblies of peers together with the king and the king's councillors. By the beginning of the sixteenth century the great council's role was becoming duplicated, ultimately to be replaced, by the upper house (the 'House of Lords' as it came to be called in the reign of Henry VIII).

How was England governed during the reign of Henry VII?

The king's council

Fifteenth-century government was centred upon the king and his immediate circle of advisers: members of the **king's council**. Henry's council, it has been suggested, differed from those of his predecessors in that councillors were selected according to merit and, once chosen, were expected to provide real service. Many of Henry's leading councillors had participated in previous governments. No doubt their experience helped shape the new king's policies as he tried to avoid the mistakes of previous monarchs. It is clear, however, that Henry himself was very much in control of his council and the other institutions through which he governed the realm.

THE COUNCIL IN STAR CHAMBER

Between 4 and 40 councillors met in the STAR CHAMBER in Westminster Palace, so called because of its decorated ceiling. Concerns included internal security, defence of the realm, foreign affairs. (Financial policy was dealt with elsewhere by a select group of councillors that originally included chancellor, Archbishop Morton, and secretary, Bishop Fox.) The council, dominated by clerics, was managed by the **lord chancellor** (John Morton, archbishop of Canterbury, 1487–1500, William Warham, archbishop of Canterbury, 1504–15), supported by the king's **secretary of state**, the **keeper of the privy seal** and the **treasurer**. The work of the council was dealt with by various, often overlapping, courts and committees.

TRIBUNAL FOR LAW ENFORCEMENT

Established by the Star Chamber Act of 1487, this tribunal was once, mistakenly, identified as the original Court of Star Chamber. Mainly concerned with internal security, it dealt with such matters as maintenance and livery, and riots.

COURT OF GENERAL SURVEYORS

This court was concerned with auditing revenue from crown lands.

COUNCIL LEARNED IN THE LAW

This council was established by 1495, concerned at first with feudal dues and the enforcement of bonds and recognisances, and eventually all aspects of financial policy-making. As a debt-collecting agency it was deeply unpopular. It was presided over by Sir Reginald Bray until 1503 and then by Sir Richard Empson in association with fellow lawyer, Sir Edmund Dudley, until 1509. Resentment resulted in their impeachment and execution (1510).

THE KING'S COUNCIL

CENTRAL COMMON LAW COURTS

These courts were located at Westminster, each headed by a **chief justice** or equivalent. They comprised:
KING'S BENCH,
COURT OF COMMON PLEAS,
EXCHEQUER.

CHANCERY

The **chancellor's** court of equity, for issuing writs and dealing with cases unresolved, or not satisfactorily resolved, in the common law courts.

COURT OF REQUESTS

This court heard poor men's requests regarding trade and landholding.

THE PROVINCIAL COUNCILS

THE COUNCIL OF WALES AND THE MARCHES

Established in 1471, this council was effectively restored after its termination in 1483 when Prince Arthur Tudor was made earl of March. The council was based at Ludlow, Shropshire.

THE COUNCIL OF THE NORTH

This council, serving similar functions to the council at Westminster, with a particular interest in maintaining law and order and preventing foreign invasion, met intermittently during the reign. Initially Henry VII pursued a policy of placing it in the hands of the Marcher lords, heads of powerful local families such as the Percys and Dacres. Following the murder of royal tax collector, the earl of Northumberland, in 1489, Henry modified this policy by dividing responsibility for the council between Lord Dacre and a southern aristocrat, Thomas Howard, the earl of Surrey.

THE COUNCIL IN THE MARCHES

This was an unofficial council in the Midlands established in 1499 and presided over by the queen mother, Margaret Beaufort, from her seat near Stamford, Lincolnshire.

A Lancastrian red rose drawn on the roll of the King's Bench in 1500. The red rose became the most popular emblem of sixteenth-century England.

The composition of the king's council helped create the traditional image of Henry as the monarch who distrusted, and undermined, the nobility. In fact, nobles continued to fill important posts on the council – the earl of Oxford, for example, was appointed lord great chamberlain and his former opponent at Bosworth, the earl of Surrey, later became lord treasurer. Of Henry's councillors, 30 had also served in the councils of Edward IV and/or Richard III. In addition to these, however, a number of non-noble men (though several had aristocratic connections), such as Edmund Dudley and Thomas Lovell, received high office on the basis of their ability, not birth. The experience of estate management offered by those born into gentry families was invaluable to a king anxious to extract the greatest profits from crown lands, and so too was the legal training of some of his councillors.

The council was both an advisory and administrative body. Of the total 227 councillors recorded for Henry's reign, no more than 40 at any one time were likely to be sitting in council and most of its work was done by rather smaller groups numbering seven or eight. In this inner circle of regular councils, more councillors than previously were trained lawyers. The most prominent of these, until his death in 1500, was Cardinal Morton who attended nearly all recorded meetings of the council. However, more than 40 of Henry's councillors never attended a single meeting.

Different types of business, issues related to maintenance and livery for example, were handled by sub-councils and committees, some of which emerged under Henry. The most important of these, and the most unpopular, was the Council Learned in the Law (established in 1495), which was principally concerned with the extraction of feudal dues and collection of bonds and recognisances.

In addition to the central council at Westminster, there were two provincial councils serving a similar function, the Council of the North and the Council of Wales. Henry increased the extent to which the activities of these councils were overseen from the centre and they were placed in the hands of his most trusted servants, such as Jasper Tudor for Wales. In appointing the earl of Surrey to the north, he broke with tradition in giving authority to a noble without particular personal interests in the region in terms of lands or family.

In what ways did the character of government change under Henry VII?

Parliament

> Since Henry VII governed England as his private estate through his council and household, parliament played no role at all in policy-making but acted as a working instrument of government underpinned by feudal notions ...
>
> John Guy, *Tudor England*, Oxford, 1988, p. 58

Parliament met seven times under Henry VII: in 1485, 1487, 1489, 1491, 1495, 1497 and 1504. Its sessions totalled a mere 21 months in a reign of over 23 years. The two parliaments after 1495 sat for just 120 days. During this time it was mostly concerned with financial matters and issues concerning law and order. Acts were passed, for example, to protect the English cloth industry, to clarify the responsibilities of justices of the peace, to regulate wages, and to prevent the keeping of retainers. Every part of every Act was signed by the king; Henry kept the same tight control over parliamentary affairs as he did with the council. The franchise was restricted to the elite among burgesses in borough elections and those who held freehold land worth at least 40 shillings per annum in county elections. Prospective MPs had to be knights or men of similar standing.

Henry did not launch major campaigns abroad and he, like Edward IV, was granted the customs on wool and woollen cloth exports by his first parliament. This freed him from some of the financial constraints that necessitated the summoning of parliaments in order to impose extraordinary taxes.

Parliament in Henry VII's reign, to paraphrase Roger Lockyer, was not yet a regular or integral part of the machinery of government.

Although its 'revolution', in terms of an extended role in government, did not come until after 1529, parliament had an undeniably important role in early Tudor government:

- It brought together peers, prelates, gentry and urban dignitaries and in so doing provided a sounding board for how proposed royal initiatives might be received. Its backing, while technically not essential, was of great value as the institution which most realistically could claim to represent national public opinion.
- Although Henry could, and often did, rule by proclamation, statute law made by parliament was the highest law in the land and even kings were subject to the common law. Parliament, therefore, was a crucial means of extending royal authority. Attainders were imposed by Act of parliament and more were passed by his last parliament of 1504 than any before. Parliament's recognition of Henry's right to rule and its legalising of his methods for dealing with troublesome members of the nobility and gentry were highly important to a king trying to establish the credibility and strength of a new dynasty.

What place did the church have in the government of the realm?

> The overall picture of the *Ecclesia Anglicana* [the English church] in Henry VII's reign is that of an institution which, despite its obvious flaws, commanded the voluntary allegiance of the great majority of the English people, from the king downwards.
>
> Roger Lockyer, *Henry VII*, 2nd edn, Harlow, 1983, p. 57

With a council dominated by clerics, the influence of the church in secular affairs was considerable. Clerical skill in legal matters (15 of the 33 bishops appointed by Henry had degrees in law – see table below) was as influential in shaping careers as spirituality or theological knowledge. The appointment of such men to ecclesiastical sees enhanced the management of the church, although the demands of council affairs restricted the time that men such as **Archbishop Morton** could spend on church matters and amplified the old problem of **non-residence**. The other 'flaws' mentioned above included **pluralism**, the widening gulf between the highly paid clerical elite and lesser clergy, and a general decline in monastic standards.

Archbishop Cardinal Morton (*c.* 1420–1500) After the death of Edward IV, Morton became an early supporter of Henry Tudor's cause. He was rewarded for his support in 1486, when Henry made him chancellor, and he received the archbishopric of Canterbury in 1493. Morton was a doctor of civil law and his appointment as master of rolls in 1472, in the reign of Edward IV, was highly significant; from this point on it was filled with graduates in civil law who brought a new professionalism to the institution.

non-residence The term 'non-residence' describes the absence of holders of multiple church appointments from their sees or monasteries.

pluralism Pluralism means the common practice of holding more than one church office at any one time.

The expertise of bishops appointed in the reigns of Edward IV and Henry VII		
	Edward IV	**Henry VII**
Bishops trained in the law	50%	57%
Bishops trained in theology	38%	21%
Other appointments were made mostly in reward for administrative services		

Through Archbishop Morton, Henry secured good relations between the state and the church and he was also careful to retain the pope's support. This he did by maintaining an entirely orthodox approach to ecclesiastical affairs. He tried to gain the pope's ear by appointing a cardinal protector – a cardinal who agreed to pay particular attention to all papal business that affected England. In line with the general concern for improving the quality of English law, an Act concerning church law was passed in 1489. This addressed the loopholes in the current system whereby the accused might evade common law justice by exercising the privileges of those in holy orders. To demonstrate basic literacy by reading a verse of scipture might be enough, even for a layman, to gain access to the more lenient ecclesiastical courts rather than the ordinary courts under **benefit of clergy**. Moreover, the taking of refuge (sanctuary) in a religious building could save even those accused of treason from arrest. Sanctuary was now restricted, a papal bull having been secured to make an exemption for traitors, and an Act in 1489 limited the benefit of clergy. Those seeking the privilege a second time had to prove they were in holy orders.

John Colet was prominent in the movement to reform the most glaring abuses of the church. He was much admired by the great humanist, Erasmus, when Erasmus first came to England in 1499. Despite the fact that comparatively little was done to improve matters in the reign of Henry VII, Colet and his circle, which included Thomas More, were supported by the establishment. He found supporters in such influential clerics as John Fisher and **Richard Fox**, and the king was sufficiently impressed to make him dean of St Paul's in 1504.

While willing to take on board the new humanism, Henry did not tolerate heresy and, during his reign, 73 suspected heretics were brought to trial, of whom 11 were burned.

Henry VII, in his religious devotions, was inspired by both political and pious intentions. The sense of divinity in late medieval/early modern kingship prompted kings to assert their role as defenders of the faith, particularly if the nature of their accession was of dubious legitimacy. Henry VII founded new Franciscan houses and ordered prayers to be said throughout the country in

benefit of clergy This phrase describes the privilege granted to those in holy orders which exempted them from punishment by the ordinary secular courts for certain offences. The test for this privilege was the ability to read a verse of scripture. It was abolished in 1706.

Richard Fox (c. 1447–1528) Fox had accompanied Henry VII on his invasion of England in 1485. After the Battle of Bosworth, he was made secretary of state, keeper of the privy seal and bishop of Exeter. In 1491 he became the bishop of Bath and Wells, bishop of Durham in 1494 and bishop of Winchester in 1501. Though a committed humanist, he was more a statesman than a churchman and he left his episcopal duties in the hands of a suffragan (assistant bishop) until his retirement from his other public duties in 1516.

support of the king of Spain's crusade against the Moors. His instruction for the completion of Henry IV's chapel at King's College, Cambridge, and Edward IV's chapel at Windsor strengthened his claim to be the one who had managed to reconcile the houses of York and Lancaster.

Historical interpretation: Was Henry a 'modern' or 'medieval' ruler?

Historians sometimes try to order the past. They organise history into manageable chunks which they label with terms like 'era', 'age', 'epoch', 'period'. In order to determine where one ends and the next starts they look for differences in human behaviour and social organisation. They can, however, run the risk of overstressing the changes and underestimating things that remain the same across time. For some time now, the sixteenth and seventeenth centuries in England have been termed the 'early modern' period. 1485 has been described as a 'watershed' year, after which things were very different. The Tudors, therefore, Henry VII included, have been regarded as monarchs with a 'modern' approach to government. Recent work in this area, however, questions the extent to which the transition from the medieval to the modern can be clearly seen and pinned down to any particular events or period in the past.

Arguments can be made which support both the 'medievalist' and 'modernist' interpretations of Henry's rule. For example, one might stress his interest in regal mythology: how he, or at least his propagandists, traced his dynasty back beyond 'history' to supposed reigns of such enigmatic figures as King Arthur as described in the influential work of Geoffrey of Monmouth in the early twelfth century, the *History of the kings of Britain*. On the other hand, Henry commissioned an Italian, Polydore Vergil, to write a new, more trustworthy, history of the English monarchy.

Medieval monarchs ruled by 'divine right' – a powerful myth that a monarch would not give up lightly. Henry was careful to endorse the myth, to express the institution's divinity through lavish and awe-inspiring display. J. D. Mackie, in *The earlier Tudors* (1952), wrote of his sense of the 'sacrosanctity' and 'superstition' surrounding the concept of kingship, and commented on the spectacular funerary arrangements he devised for himself in his declining years:

> For some years foreign observers had noted his failing health, and on 21 April he died at the age of 52 in his Palace of Richmond. A few days later, after magnificent obsequies, his body was buried in the great chapel which he had begun to build in 1503 and for which he had designed the tomb which to this day attests his good taste and

the skill of Torrigiano ... Chapel [and] tomb ... are eloquent of Henry's mind. It was essentially a medieval mind.

In terms of ostentation, G. R. Elton, in *England under the Tudors* (1974), maintained that Henry was even more of a 'medieval' monarch than those who came before him:

> The most obvious way in which Henry's kingship differed from that of his predecessors was in the greater stress he laid upon it. Even this far from impressive-looking man fostered the visible dignity of the office and took good care that the greatest of his subjects should appear small by his side. The Tudor court, with its red-coated guard and its vast expenditure on silks, satins, and velvets was always a gorgeous affair, and ceremonial was one thing on which Henry invariably spent in a prodigal manner. The feasts and joustings and displays which attended the visits of foreign potentates, the coronations and weddings of the reign, were things to marvel at, impressive even to the cynical eyes of Venetian and Milanese ambassadors ... Henry VII built up the formal and ceremonial element in medieval kingship to new heights, even as in other ways he greatly developed its practical attributes.

The real debate, however, revolves not around the trappings of kingship but the nature of its administration. A 'modern' approach would imply centralised control and a professional and efficient bureaucracy. Compared to his namesake, Henry VI, Henry was very much more in control of his people. The handing over of power into the hands of over-mighty magnates was very much less evident. However, recent commentators like J. A. F. Thomson in *The transformation of medieval England, 1320–1529* (1983) have seen Henry VI's reign and the chaotic, anarchic era of the Wars of the Roses as an unusual rather than a typical profile of medieval styles of kingship:

> It is fair to say that Henry VII's approach to government was strongly traditional, and that parallels to it, notably in his reliance on professional administrators, can be traced in the fourteenth century. It was the reign of Henry VI, when magnate influence was excessive, which in fact deviated from customary practice. The search of historians for a 'new monarchy' or a 'more modern' form of kingship, whether of the Yorkists or the Tudors, is in that sense the pursuit of a myth. In political terms, however, there is some justification in regarding Henry VII's accession as the start of a new

According to Thompson, what factors determined the level of royal authority?

epoch, because the dynastic change brought with it in the long run a more securely based royal authority than had previously existed.

This argument is shared by another 'post-revisionist' historian, Alexander Grant, who in *Henry VII* (1985) has endeavoured to prove that 'the contrasts between Henry VII's reign and Edward IV's are more important than the continuities':

> ... the level and extent of Henry's personal control was much greater than his predecessors ... Moreover, Henry VII's personal government ... was very different from that of his predecessors ... The most important revolution in government of the [early Tudor] period was surely the restoration of a high degree of peace and stability throughout most of the country, and its architect was Henry VII. For this reason, his victory over Richard III in August 1485 deserves to be re-established as a major turning point in English history.

Circumstances more than any conscious plan enabled Henry and his Tudor successors to develop aspects of their government. Factors such as the destruction of actual and potential opposition, and the general weariness of war in the noble families blighted by decades of conflict, provided the dynasty with the right conditions in which to extend its authority and might. In this sense, Henry did pave the way for a 'new', more confident monarchy, and the staggering achievements of his illustrious son – the supreme autocrat, King Henry VIII.

The history of Richard III's reign was originally written almost exclusively by his critics. Henry's early chroniclers were his supporters. Often, they unashamedly, in the case of Edward Hall, for example, produced gushing Tudor propaganda to enhance the reputation of the living monarchs they served and thus promote their own interests. Although Henry VII comes across as a less colourful and attractive character than, say, Edward IV, it remains hard to deny the conclusions of his first biographers. In Hall's view, he was a peculiarly shrewd and consistent monarch, and one hard to fault in either personality or policy:

> And so the king, living all his time in the favour of fortune, in high honour, riches and glory, and, for his noble acts and prudent policies, worthy to be registered in the book of fame, gave up his spirit at the last, which is undoubtedly ascended into the celestial mansion where he has the sure fruition of the godhead, and the joy that is prepared for such as shall sit on the right hand of our saviour, for ever world without end.

Henry VII

1 Portrait of Henry VII by an unknown artist, painted from a sitting in 1505

2 Polydore Vergil on Henry's appearance

His body was slender but well built and strong; his height above the average. His appearance was remarkably attractive and his face was cheerful, especially when speaking; his eyes were small and blue, his teeth few, poor and blackish; his hair was thin and white; his complexion sallow.

Source: Polydore Vergil, *Anglica historia 1485–1537*, D. Hay (ed. and trans.), Camden Series, 1950

3 Mortuary bust of Henry VII by Pietro Torrigiano, c. 1508–9

Historical-source questions

1 Which one of these three sources do you consider the most reliable as a record of Henry's appearance?

2 How do you account for the discrepancies between Sources 1 and 2?

3 Henry died in April 1509. Sources 2 and 3 were produced posthumously. How might this fact affect their reliability?

Summary questions

1 How far do you agree that the way in which Henry VII financed his government contributed to the stability of his rule?

2 Assess the importance of three institutions through which England was governed in the reign of Henry VII.

3 Identify and explain any two reasons why Henry VII has been associated with the concept of 'new monarchy'.

4 Explain how Henry VII controlled England's nobility.

6 Social and economic change in the late fifteenth and early sixteenth centuries

Focus questions

◆ What changes affected the nobility?

◆ What were the most important changes for other social groups?

◆ How did the English economy develop?

◆ What was the condition of religion?

◆ What were the main cultural developments?

Significant dates

1450	Normandy is lost to the French.
1455	The Wars of the Roses begin.
1456	Mobs attack foreigners in London.
1457	Further riots against foreigners break out in London. Bishop Pecock is condemned for heresy.
1461	The first reign of Edward IV begins.
1463	A Sumptuary Law is passed.
1468	A naval war breaks out with the Hanseatic League.
1469	Thomas Malory completes *Le morte d'Arthur*.
1470	The readeption of Henry VI occurs.
1471	The second reign of Edward IV begins.
1474	The Treaty of Utrecht is signed.
1476	William Caxton sets up England's first printing press.
1483	Richard III's reign begins.
1484	A papal bull condemns witchcraft.
1485	Henry VII's reign begins.
1496	Henry VII commissions John Cabot to find a new trade route to Asia.
1499	John Colet meets Erasmus at Oxford.
1503	Henry VII begins to build his chapel in Westminster Abbey.
1505	Christ's College, Cambridge, is founded.
1509	Henry VII dies.

Overview

> England hath long been mad, and scarred herself;
> The brother blindly shed the brother's blood,
> The father rashly slaughtered his own son,
> The son, compelled, been butc er to the sire:
> All this divided York and Lancaster.
>
> William Shakespeare, *Richard III* Act V Scene v

The second half of the fifteenth century was an era of civil war but not a time of cultural or economic stagnation. It was an epoch of change.

In all spheres developments can be identified. The social order, with the decline of medieval feudalism and an expansion of the 'middle classes', was acquiring a 'modern' hue; the growth of education and greater levels of literacy among the laity provided new opportunities; in religion, even before the **Reformation**, the pope was becoming a more remote figure; in warfare the cannon had begun to have a role; finished cloth began to dominate the export trade in place of the traditional raw wool; explorers were starting to reshape the world-picture; professional bureaucrats, appointed on merit not birth, were beginning to take the helm of an ever more sophisticated ship of state.

Much of the old survived too. The legacy of the Black Death of the mid-fourteenth century was still felt. Bubonic plague remained one of many fearsome diseases that could decimate populations and bring a sudden and unforewarned death. The medieval vision of the hereafter, of Paradise and Hell, was as real and terrifying in the later-fifteenth century as it had ever been. The illiterate masses, propertyless and having no political power, struggled to survive on the land. They led short, harsh lives that were only a little better than those of their fourteenth-century predecessors.

'The choice of the year 1485 as marking the division between medieval and modern England is nowhere more patently absurd than in the matter of religion.' So wrote A. R. Myers in *England in the late Middle Ages* (1978). The church in the reign of Henry VII continued to provide men for some of the highest secular posts in the land, it retained its internationalism as a part of the pope's spiritual kingdom, 'Christendom'. Although monasticism, perhaps, was in decline, the church continued to attract the unquestioning loyalty of the masses. It also attracted the money of those who were able to buy silver and gold plate and build chantries where prayers were offered for the dead. If anything, the church, which owned at least a fifth of all the land in England, was getting richer. Although people might criticise the church as an institution – its wealth and worldliness, for example – the teachings of the greatest English heretic of the fourteenth century, Wycliffe, were the interest of a tiny minority. Ecclesiastical buildings were still the focal point of every

Reformation The movement for religious renewal and reform of clerical practices which, from the early sixteenth century, led to the fragmentation of the medieval church and the emergence of the Protestant and Anglican churches.

Peasants ploughing, harrowing and sowing seed. In fifteenth-century England most of the population worked on the land.

community, the church dominated education, and religious observances were part and parcel of secular, economic and domestic activity.

What changes affected the nobility?

> The nobility, who are endowed with great honours, possessions and riches, can be compared to the firm ground while the lower people, who lack such endowments, can be likened to the unstable, running water . . . the reason why the nobles need to agree and listen to each other is that the well-ordered government of every region depends on the nobility . . .
>
> John Russell, bishop of Lincoln and chancellor of England, 1484

In 1436 the nobility were required to pay an income tax. The surviving record of how much they were worth in terms of the amount of land they held provides the historian with a useful profile of the peerage in the middle of the fifteenth century, before the upheaval of the Wars of the Roses. Of the fifty or so lords, three, the earls of Warwick and Buckingham, and the duke of York, were much larger landowners than the rest. Even before the Wars of the Roses, England's nobility was divided by the struggle for royal patronage and arguments over the ownership of land. Old rivalries between the great families helped make possible civil wars fought, by and large, by noblemen's retainers.

Fifteenth-century kings were challenged by the threat of 'overmighty nobles'. On the one hand, they relied on the might of the nobility to protect their interests, and fight with and for them if necessary, on the other, they felt the need to curb the power of those that could find reason to oppose them. In an era of civil war, the allegiance of the great magnates was of supreme importance. Edward IV was remarkably lenient and forgiving in his dealings with former enemies. During, his reign a clique of nobles acquired enormous power and virtual independence in the areas they administered – his brother, Richard, duke of Gloucester, for example, in the north, the Stanleys in Cheshire and Lancashire, the Woodvilles in Wales. The accumulation of power in the hands of a favoured few instilled resentment in families less fortunate. When one of the lucky families happened to be one which previously was ignoble, as in the case of the Woodvilles, resentment turned to anger.

The Wars of the Roses did not diminish the nobility at large but they did help undermine the phenomenon of the 'super-noble'. The deaths of heads of houses leaving estates in the hands of minors and royal wards, the acquisition by the crown of attainted nobles' territory, and shrewd marital arrangements for members of the king's family, all reduced the potential for successful rebellion in the reign of Henry VII. Henry was far less willing than his immediate predecessors (although similar to Henry V and the earlier Lancastrian kings) to court popularity by awarding titles. The growth of the nobility, seen in the years of Yorkist rule, slowed down. He further controlled the nobility by imposing 'recognisances' on many aristocrats, by which agreed fines would be payable in the event of their failing to fulfil their obligations to the king, such as the collecting of taxes.

The ownership of land and titles changed dramatically during the civil-war years. Lands forfeited through defeat in Edward IV's reign provided the means for the creation of a new Yorkist nobility. The leading beneficiaries were the king's brothers, the duke of Clarence and Richard, duke of Gloucester (later Richard III). Edward, however, created far fewer peerages in his second reign than his first, a principle to which Henry VII also adhered. The reign of Edward IV witnessed the meteoric rise of certain gentry families, most notably that of his wife, the Woodvilles, and also the Herberts from Wales. His growing reliance on these 'new' nobles proved disastrous in 1469 when Warwick rebelled. Their rise eclipsed Warwick and the previously dominant Neville clan. The final straw was the marriage of William Herbert's heir to the queen's sister, Mary Woodville. Such an alliance was intolerable to Warwick. The success of his rebellion, making the king his effective prisoner and being able to purge the court of the Woodville clique, was testimony to the unpopularity of the new nobility, and it demonstrated the danger of a reliance on magnates who lacked well-established gentry loyalties.

The Yorkist kings failed to maintain a dynasty, in part because they invested too much power in too few hands. Richard III died defeated on Bosworth Field because he lacked the grassroots loyalty of his subjects. Although Henry VII did not create many new peers he was skilful in the handling of patronage. While he was careful to contain the custom of retaining among his wealthier subjects, he established his own vast retinue, awarding countless, sometimes redundant, offices, each of which brought with it a fee and certain privileges. With the duchies of both Lancaster and York in his possession, Henry VII had the means, as well as the wisdom, to build dependency upon, and hence support for, his house.

Of all sections of society, the nobility had been the one that was most affected by years of dynastic struggle. Fortunes had been won and lost, new noble families had emerged and some older ones had disappeared. Numerically little had changed and the peerage at the turn of the century numbered just 55. The era of the 'super-noble' had, perhaps, passed, and government was more assured and centralised. The nobility, nevertheless, remained enormously important in local politics and constitutional affairs. The landowning elite would continue for a further couple of centuries to wield pretty much the whole of the political, economic and social power. By the end of Henry VII's reign, the divisions between the great families, to a degree, had been removed and the conditions for civil war eradicated.

How did the position of the nobility change in the second half of the fifteenth century?

What were the most important changes for other social groups?

The gentry

The **Sumptuary Law** of 1463 sought to clarify distinctions within an increasingly complex order of social classes. The gentry by this time included classifications, in descending order of rank, of knights, esquires and gentlemen. By the end of the century, there were 500 knights, 800 esquires and 5,000 gentlemen. The fifteenth century largely predated the era of the 'pseudo-gentry' whose status would rely on wealth. The gentry almost certainly still had status by virtue of their ownership of land. With the aristocracy still secure, the church unreformed (and its monasteries undissolved), and a 'pre-industrial' economy, the greatest age of expansion of the gentry class was yet to occur.

If the ownership of land distinguished the nobility and gentry from other 'classes', their political status separated them. Peers were called to parliament on the personal invitation of the king and this privilege was inherited, along

Sumptuary Law, 1463
The Sumptuary Laws restricted luxury clothes (and weapons) according to wealth and status. This Act restricted velvet, satin or counterfeit silk to men above the rank of knight and their wives. The 1463 Act was the first of many.

primogeniture
Inheritance by the first-born. In most cases, for example, title and estates, this would be the first-born son.

with their estate, by their first-born sons according to the principle of **primogeniture**. Like enoblement, knighthoods were awarded as a royal prerogative. Although traditionally these were earned through military service, wealth in land (income worth £100 a year or more) had become a benchmark for the distribution of knighthoods in the emerging post-feudal, capitalist society.

The gentry relied heavily on the patronage of the nobility. Lords could provide opportunities of advancement for knights and essquires and their sons. Nobles still needed retainers and, in an era of 'bastard feudalism', when the old feudal system was breaking down, the bond between lord and retainer was frequently a cash arrangement. The retainer, in return for services and the wearing of the lord's livery, would receive a cash fee.

Although it would be wrong to detect any intent to drive a wedge between the gentry and the old noble elite, Henry VII's inclination for rewarding merit, together with an increasing bureaucratisation of government, helped raise members of the gentry to posts of considerable political importance. The elevation of whole gentry families into the peerage, however, remained extremely unusual. The spectacular rise of the Woodvilles and, indeed, a marriage between peer and gentlewoman (Edward IV and Elizabeth Woodville) were not typical of the age.

It was difficult, too, for those who had made money through trade and commerce in the towns to buy into the landed rural gentry elite. The fifteenth- and early-sixteenth-century gentry jealously held on to their land. Moreover, before the Reformation, as the population began to recover after the ravages of the Black Death, land was in short supply and rarely for sale. There was no significant shift in the size and structure of the landowning gentry until the middle years of the sixteenth century.

The peasantry

The great mass of the people owned no land and can be described in a single broad term as 'peasants'. During the fourteenth and fifteenth centuries the character of the English peasantry underwent huge changes. The principal reason for this was the dramatic reduction in the size of the population in the aftermath of the Black Death, which arrived in England, on the back of plague-infested, flea-bearing rats, in 1348. Geoffrey le Baker, a contemporary Oxfordshire cleric and chronicler, wrote:

> And at first it carried off almost all the inhabitants of the seaports in
> Dorset, and then those living inland and from there it raged so
> dreadfully through Devon and Somerset as far as Bristol and then men
> of Gloucester refused those of Bristol entrance to their country,
> everyone thinking that the breath of those who lived amongst people

who died of plague was infectious. But at last it attacked Gloucester, yea and Oxford and London, and finally the whole country of England so violently that scarcely one in ten of either sex was left alive. As the graveyards did not suffice, fields were chosen for the burial of the dead . . . A countless number of common people and a host of monks and nuns and clerics as well, known to God alone, passed away. It was the young and strong that the plague chiefly attacked . . . This great pestilence . . . raged for a whole year in England so terribly that it cleared many country villages entirely of every human being.

By the time of its passing, England's population was reduced by at least a third, perhaps even a half. Further major outbreaks followed in 1360, 1369 and 1375 – on average every four years until 1480. By the middle of the fifteenth century, the population, already in decline before the arrival of the Black Death, had fallen from around 5 or 6 million in 1300 to 2.5 million or less.

The frequent recurrence of the plague and other epidemics, such as the **sweating sickness**, a virulent influenza, was a main factor in the general 'malaise' that has been identified as a fundamental characteristic of the period. From such afflictions none was immune. In the *Registrum annalium Collegii Mertonensis* for 1485 it is noted that:

> In the same year, about the end of August and the beginning of September, a marvellous and unprecedented sickness broke out in the University which beginning suddenly with an unexpected sweat, deprived many of their lives. By the end of September this mortality was spread abroad almost without warning through the whole country. In the city of London three mayors died within ten days; and so borne on the breeze from east to west it struck down with extraordinary slaughter almost all the nobility, except however the lords spiritual and temporal. All either died or escaped within the 24 hours: but so great and cruel a massacre of wise and prudent men has not been heard of in our history for many centuries. This mortality did not last for more than a month or six weeks, at any rate with the exception of a few cases.

The condition of the English economy in a labour-intensive, agrarian age was largely shaped by factors to do with population. The Black Death had ravaged Europe and economic recovery was chiefly reliant on the recovery of population. The population of England continued to decline for a century after the Black Death, falling to barely 2 million by the middle of the fifteenth century. Recovery did not begin until the 1480s. Even by the end of the sixteenth century, the population of England was only around 4.1 million.

sweating sickness This new disease, the 'English sweat', like others, was considered by many a natural punishment for sin, confirming the inherent corruptness and degradation of human society. Dr Perne, vice-chancellor of Cambridge University, wrote in 1574:

> Although we must confess that our sins are the principal cause of this and all other plagues sent by almighty God, the secondary cause . . . so far as I understand, is not the corruption of the air as the Physicians presently claim, but partly by the apparel of one that came from London to the Midsummer fair and died of the plague in Barnwell, where the plague has been and is now most vehement.

The 'miasma' theory, of airborne disease, however, prevailed until the nineteenth century. In any case, there could be little hope in relying upon natural contrivances to cure plagues of supernatural origin.

Many of the hundreds of deserted medieval villages which archaeologists have identified in England were the direct result of the ravages of the Black Death.

For those who survived, epidemics could bring economic advantages. With a population of maybe as much as 6 million in 1300 England faced a crisis in which the total demand for food began to outstrip the supply, and people starved. Malnutrition was rife and the people prone to fall victim to plague and famine. By the end of the century, however, land and employment in many areas were in abundant supply. Rents were reduced, or even abandoned entirely, ancient feudal labour duties were commuted into services for cash payments (a process that in some areas predated 1348), wages went up while food prices came down. The era of the Lancastrian kings was one of economic prosperity for the peasantry at large and of depression for the great landlords. Although the Ordinance and Statute of Labourers in 1349 and 1351 was designed to fix maximum wage rates, many employers from the start were inclined to pay more than regulations allowed. In some places peasants, for the first time in their history, were sufficiently well off to start building their own stone houses. Old **feudal structures** began to break down as the peasantry prospered and began to acquire greater economic independence. The buying and selling of land between peasants, or for that matter the changing of the old feudal dues to cash payments, was not unheard of before the Black Death, but the rate of change in the structure of rural society became much

feudal structures In return for their small-holdings serfs (peasants without 'freeman' status) owed certain services to the lord of the manor. These included work on the lord's land, typically three days in each week. They were not allowed to leave the manor or get married without the lord's permission. By the end of the fifteenth century, this arrangement was rare.

more rapid in the later fourteenth and fifteenth centuries. By 1500 differences in wealth among the peasantry were more marked than ever before: some had become prosperous independent farmers, while others remained landless peasants. Many left the land completely, attracted by the high wages offered to craftsmen and labourers in England's 700 or so towns. Marxist historians, interested in the emergence of the modern industrial working class, consider this a major development in the creation of the capitalist economy. The growth of the cash economy stimulated a growing number of bakers, tailors, shoemakers, carpenters, smiths, butchers and other artisans. Many of these divided their labour between their specialised craft and land husbandry, investing the cash gains of the one in the expansion of the other. Landowners, of course, were less likely to benefit. Low prices for their wheat and wool, coupled with their labourers' demands for higher wages, resulted in severely reduced profits.

In addition to a high mortality rate, the birth rate for the fifteenth century was significantly lower than it had been in the fourteenth. Women in the late fourteenth century tended to marry in their mid or late teens. During the fifteenth century, couples typically married in their mid twenties and a much higher proportion did not marry at all. According to the evidence of wills for the period 1430–80, 24.2 per cent of males died unmarried.

> What effect did the decline in population have on the fifteenth-century economy?

How did the English economy develop?

England's main industries in the fifteenth century were the same as those of the early Middle Ages. These were cloth, mining, salt production, fishing at sea, metal-working, and building. Although **fulling mills** were now used in the process in preparing wool for weaving, few technological advances had been made. Compared to the highly capitalised Flemish cloth industry, the industry in England was unsophisticated. Traditionally, most wool was exported in a raw state to be worked by the weavers of Antwerp and the Low Countries. Wool was so central to medieval England's prosperity, that the chancellor in parliament sat on a symbolic woolsack. During the closing decades of the century significant changes occurred, with a 60 per cent increase in the export of cloth and a 30 per cent decrease in the export of wool. During Henry VII's reign, there was a corresponding increase in total imports of around 50 per cent.

Increased trade promoted an expansion of the merchant class. Business was conducted through the various trade companies, each specialising in a particular commodity. The Mercers were associated with silk, the Grocers with spices, the Merchant Adventurers with woollen cloth, and the Merchant Staplers with raw wool. The merchants' status was asserted through the

> **fulling mills** In the medieval cloth industry, fulling was the only part of the process of production to be carried out mechanically. Woven cloth and fuller's earth were pounded together with wooden hammers, water powered at a fulling mill. The fuller's earth scoured and cleaned the material.

building of magnificent town houses and the wearing of fine clothes. The most successful traders invested in land and joined the ranks of the gentry, distinguished from others by the wearing of a sword and the bearing of a coat of arms.

A great deal of England's trade was conducted through the Hanseatic League, an organisation of German merchants which had secured special trading privileges in Germany, Scandinavia and Russia and monopolies in the purchase and carriage of certain goods. The merchants brought fish, furs, softwoods and other commodities to England in return for English wool and cloth, coal, tin and other valuable raw materials. In England they too had a privileged position: they were exempt from customs duties, much to the chagrin of English merchants. They operated all along England's east coast with a main base in London – an autonomous community on the Thames called the Steelyard. Venetian merchants had a similar control over trade between England and the eastern Mediterranean.

Fifteenth-century English kings, particularly Edward IV and Henry VII, tried to secure equivalent privileges for English merchants abroad and to undermine the activities of monopolists like the Hanse merchants. In 1485 and 1489, for example, Navigation Acts were passed in order to try to prevent the carriage of certain imported goods in foreign ships.

The 1450s marked the lowpoint in fifteenth-century English trade, culminating in civil war from 1459 to 1461. Henry VI's struggles with Charles VII of France brought the prosperous trade with Gascony to a virtual halt, worsening the effect of the loss of Henry V's French kingdom. Piracy at the time was rife in the waters around Europe and English **privateers**, sanctioned by the government, had seized goods belonging to the Hanseatic League from a great merchant fleet of Flemish and Dutch ships in 1449. In retaliation the Hanse merchants took English possessions abroad and, worse still, forbade the passage of English cloth to the east. Riots against foreigners in London in 1456 and 1457, which undermined the activities of foreign merchants in the capital, further damaged international relations, particularly since the English government proved incapable of quelling the disturbances. English merchants, in turn, were further alienated from their government when, by way of compensation, Italian merchants were issued with letters of pardon for past trading offences. Such misfortunes and malpractice led A. R. Myers in *England in the late Middle Ages* (10th edn, 1978) to the following conclusion:

> At the crisis of its fate the Lancastrian regime had therefore not only lost the support of the English merchants but had alienated every commercial power in Europe. No wonder English merchants looked for better things from Yorkist rule.

privateers Privateers engaged in their own private wars at sea but they did so with the permission of the government. In return for attacking the shipping of a rival state the privateer was entitled to keep any booty seized. Pirates acted independently and without any licence from the government.

Relations with Burgundy improved after 1467 and the new French king, Louis XI, did not share his father's opinion that political hostilities should necessarily impact upon trade. This led to the beginnings of a recovery in the 1460s. The old squabble with the Hanseatic League, however, continued and, by the end of the decade, English and Hanse merchants were engaged in open warfare at sea. The cutting-short of Edward IV's first reign in 1470 brought the quarrel to an end, to the advantage of the Hanseatics. In 1471 Edward returned to England in a flotilla which included 14 Hanseatic ships and, in return, by the Treaty of Utrecht of 1474, their privileges, which hindered England's direct trade to the east, were fully restored. The new relationship with the League reopened markets abroad and was an important factor in the comparative commercial prosperity of the second half of the fifteenth century.

The kingdom's 3,000 market places, all authorised by royal charter, fell to just about a thousand as the population declined in the wake of the Black Death. The greatest commercial centres were all ports and included Bristol, Hull, Plymouth, Southampton and, of course, London. Here the streets were said to be paved with gold and people flocked to the city, expanding its population from around 50,000 at the start of Henry VII's reign (1485) to an estimated 120,000 by the end of Henry VIII's (1547).

The growth of the cloth industry and international trade during the second half of the fifteenth century might seem surprising considering the fact that for 32 years (1455–87) Englishmen, Yorkists and Lancastrians were at war with one another. The number of woollen cloths exported trebled between 1470 and 1500: a crucial development for the crown since customs duties were its greatest source of revenue. In the same period, the value of land increased, largely because of the cloth trade and also because the population began to grow. Great landowners, notably the king himself, could therefore charge higher rents. The industry also stimulated the growth of an entrepreneurial class of capitalist clothiers, who organised the work of spinners, fullers, weavers and dyers, keeping the ownership of the raw materials in their own hands throughout. They took the lion's share of the profit when the finished product finally arrived at the market place. Eventually the activities of the clothiers became so large-scale and widespread, that historians enquiring into the eighteenth-century 'industrial revolution' have coined a phrase, 'proto-industry', to acknowledge the sophistication of the industry in its pre-factory age.

Why did the woollen cloth industry prosper and expand, despite the civil war, during the second half of the fifteenth century?

Agriculture was still the main economic activity. Different environments resulted in different types of land exploitation. In the mid-nineteenth century an agricultural enthusiast, James Caird, divided the country into two 'zones' – the 'highland' and 'lowland'. The moorland and mountainous regions of the highland zone encouraged a pastoral economy, while the lowland zone was better suited to arable farming. The lowland zone continued to be more densely populated and richer. Its great open fields, farmed in strips, supported numerous small, concentrated, 'nuclear' villages. In the highland zone the settlements were more dispersed and farms frequently isolated. In both zones the vast majority of the population was settled in the countryside and worked on the land. Incomes were supplemented by a huge variety of other jobs, such as spinning and weaving. Spinning was such an integral part of a female's working life that unmarried women came to be known as spinsters. Increasingly, cloth manufacture was located in the countryside. This was partly because the restrictive practice of **craft guilds** that had taken root in the towns kept new entrants out of the industry, but mainly because of the growing need for water power to turn the fulling mills. These began to increase in numbers after the twelfth century.

Population pressure in the thirteenth century had stimulated more intensive use of the land and more sophisticated farming techniques. In some areas, particularly on the big monastic estates, specialisation was developing. The Cistercian monks at Rievaulx and Fountains Abbeys, for example, raised vast flocks of sheep for the wool trade. The scarcity of labour led to a decline in arable farming, as more lords turned their land over to cattle- and sheep-rearing, which was less labour intensive. Although self-sufficiency was still the order of the day for some isolated hamlets, particularly in the highland zone, most villages produced a surplus for sale at nearby or even distant markets. This, of course, stimulated the growth of towns during the period, towns which, in turn, represented the principal market places in any locality.

The dramatic decline in population during the fourteenth century resulted, in part, in the decline of the feudal system for the reasons outlined above. The old arrangement whereby work was an obligation to one's overlord and benefactor was fast disappearing in the fifteenth century, as services were commuted to money payments. As early as the late 1200s, kings were relying on paid soldiers, in addition to their feudal **vassals**, to fight their campaigns.

Despite bouts of civil war, the late-fifteenth-century economy was relatively stable. Agricultural wages in southern England for routine work stood at around four pence a day until the 1540s, and wheat prices, despite considerable fluctuations from year to year, on average rose scarcely at all until the reign of Henry VIII. Overall, the unskilled agricultural labourer of the late fifteenth century was likely to be considerably better off than his late-sixteenth-century counterpart, with a wage that could well command at least twice as much purchasing power.

London in the fifteenth century

The most prosperous of English towns was London, which thrived on the wool and cloth trades with the Netherlands. Unlike other eastern ports such as

craft guilds Craft organisations or guilds originated in English towns in the twelfth century for the mutual benefit of their members by providing charitable help for those in need. They developed into protective organisations designed to restrict entry into a particular trade by establishing strict rules of apprenticeship. Sometimes they endeavoured to monitor and control the quality of the goods produced and services provided. The greatest guilds established guildhalls which, as in the case of that built by York's Merchant Adventurers in the mid-fourteenth century, might contain meeting rooms, a chapel and a hospital.

vassals A term that describes those who receive land and protection from their lord in return for the payment of feudal dues.

Newcastle which specialised in coal, London had a diverse trade which made her less susceptible to economic fluctuations. London's merchants lent money to the government which, usually, sat in their town. Great merchant families, such as the Boleyns, joined the gentry as they acquired the status of country seats and official titles. In 1334, just 2 per cent of England's taxable lay wealth was located in London, by 1515 it was 9 per cent. The most powerful merchants formed the Merchant Adventurers Company, which dominated all trade, except that in wool, with the Low Countries. Resentment, particularly among traders based outside London, of the Adventurers' virtual monopoly prompted Henry VII, in 1505, to lower the cost of entry into the company. Very rapidly, as evidenced by Anne Boleyn's marriage to Henry VIII in 1533, the families of London merchants were learning to aspire to the highest places in English society.

Why was London so prosperous in the fifteenth century?

What was the condition of religion?

The condition of the church in the decades before its reformation under Henry VIII in the 1530s is a controversial subject. In the 1960s A. G. Dickens identified a church in trouble. Clerics were criticised for abusing their positions, their secular and ecclesiastical authority was in decline, and the church, it was widely believed, was in need of reformation.

According to Dickens, the power and influence of the church in England was more apparent than real. The church no longer inspired, and lacked the unity and intellectual supremacy it needed to be the truly 'supranational' body it once represented.

More recently, historians have painted a very different picture of the pre-Reformation church. J. J. Scarisbrick, for example, studied about 2,500 wills dating from the first half of the sixteenth century and covering most parts of England. He found that the majority left bequests to the church, an indication, he presumed, of its continuing popularity. Most experts in the field would now agree with Christopher Haigh, who has claimed that Catholic Christianity was flourishing and that the Reformations of the 1500s in themselves do not prove otherwise.

The wealth of the church

The scores of beautiful **Perpendicular** churches built in the fifteenth century, particularly in areas associated with the wool and cloth trades, give some indication of the wealth of the church and its benefactors during the last century of Roman Catholic England.

Church income was derived from a variety of sources. Bequests to the parish church might take the form of property that could be rented out.

Perpendicular
Perpendicular architecture is a style of English architecture developed in the fourteenth and fifteenth centuries. Buildings in the Perpendicular style have slender verticals, large expanses of windows, panel tracery and fan vaulting. The chapel of King's College, Cambridge, sponsored by Henry VI, is usually cited as one of the finest examples of a building in the Perpendicular style in Britain.

Church land (the glebe) was farmed for profit, flocks of sheep being the mainstay for many of the greatest monasteries and the humblest parishes. Of great importance, too, was the tithe, the obligatory payment of a tenth of each man's income collected in cash or kind. Traditionally, in agrarian communities, this would be a portion of the harvest, stored by the church in a great barn known as the 'tithe barn'. These can still be seen in many parts of England, particularly in the south and west. Although people sometimes resented having to pay the tithe, just as people in more recent times might resent paying income tax, the comparative rarity of tithe suits brought to court during the period suggests that, in principle, the payment of tithes was generally accepted. Although there were prolonged and bitter disputes, sometimes involving large numbers of parishioners arrayed against their priest, as at Barfreston in Kent in 1511, it has been the mistake of some historians to see these really exceptional cases as evidence of general hostility.

Complaints against tithe payments were frequently concerned with the 'mortuary', theoretically the exaction of tithes unpaid during the lifetime of the recently deceased, in practice a death duty. Again, the principle seems to have been accepted and disputes were most likely to arise when a cleric was seen to break with tradition concerning such payments. This was the complaint of the bailiffs of Kingston-upon-Thames in 1509 who accused their vicar of 'taking mortuaries otherwise than hath been taken and used since time out of mind'.

Other traditional payments were voluntary, collections for the Paschal candle at Easter, for example, and money raised at the 'gatherings' of men on Hock Monday and women on Hock Tuesday. Such revenue might buy the church's sacramental silver plate, a new bell, candles or new vestments for the priest. Further petty cash was raised from the sale of church ale, special brews sold to parishioners in association with the various church holidays. For major projects such as the building of a steeple, the church wardens might impose an obligatory rate known as a 'cess' but most parishes appear to have managed without resorting to additional and unpopular impositions.

The greatest patron of the church was the crown. In this era of usurpers and pretenders, the king had every reason to secure the ecclesiastical, and better still, papal blessing. Henry VI and Henry VII were renowned for their great piety. Henry VI wrought a triumph of architecture in the Perpendicular style when he commissioned the building of King's College Chapel in Cambridge, and Henry VII constructed the wonderful chapel in Westminster Abbey, originally intended as a shrine for Henry VI, but which became his own mausoleum.

Why did Henry VII show such public reverence for the body and memory of Henry VI?

Popular religion

For the illiterate masses of the fifteenth century, the church was a focus for a deep-seated belief in the supernatural, pagan as well as Christian. Superstition and myth were a part of daily life. Fairies and pixies were real phenomena, spells and charms were thought to have magical effect. Many pre-Christian festivals and rituals associated with pagan sites, such as holy wells and standing stones, had survived a thousand years or more of institutionalised Christianity. The Devil, too, was a very real entity, although, as the ultimate shape-changer, he might appear in many guises. The witches with whom he communed were acquiring a higher profile in western Europe in anticipation of the witchcraft mania of the sixteenth and seventeenth centuries. A papal bull of 1484, quoted in Vivian Green's *A new history of Christianity* (1996), provided official condemnation of witchcraft, confirmed its existence, described its practices, and ordered its suppression:

> . . . many persons of both sexes unmindful of their own salvation . . .
> have abandoned themselves to devils . . . and by their incantations,
> spells, cojurations, and other accursed charms . . . have slain infants
> yet in the mother's womb, as also the offspring of cattle, have blasted
> the produce of the earth, the grapes of the vine, the fruit of the trees
> . . . The witches, furthermore, afflict and torment men and women . . .
> they blasphemously renounce the faith which is theirs by the
> Sacrament of Baptism, and at the instigation of the enemy of
> mankind they also shrink not from committing and perpetrating the
> foulest abominations and the filthiest excesses to the deadly peril of
> their own souls.

Why did people in the fifteenth century believe in witches and witchcraft?

The medieval Christian church created an imaginary landscape which could be as terrifying as that of any pagan culture. Damnation, which awaited every unrepenting and unforgiven sinner, was a truly terrible prospect. According to one early-fifteenth-century preacher, Richard Alkerton, the wicked would be 'boiled in fire and brimstone without end. Venomous worms . . . shall gnaw all their members unceasingly, and the worm of conscience shall gnaw the soul . . . This fire that tormenteth you shall never be quenched, and they that tormenteth you shall never be weary neither die.' And he was not speaking metaphorically.

Various devices existed for reducing the chances of this dread fate. Pilgrimage to the shrines of saints for example might be a requirement of penitents, as well as those who sought the miraculous healing properties of the array of sacred relics that awaited them at their journey's end. Even after death the rich could speed their passage through **purgatory** to salvation by leaving money to chantry priests to say masses on their behalf.

purgatory The church taught that only those without sin could enter Heaven, and since most people were sinners to a greater or lesser degree the concept of Purgatory had developed. This stated that the soul, after death, would be purged of all sin in Purgatory before entering Heaven. By the early sixteenth century it was common practice to purchase 'indulgences'. These were written statements, authorised by the church, which would shorten the time in Purgatory in return for good deeds or the payment of a sum of money.

English humanism

> . . . rites and ceremonies neither purify the spirit nor justify the man.
>
> John Colet, 1466–1509, dean of St Paul's

Criticism of the church from within came from the humanists, inspired particularly by the ideas of the great Dutch humanist, Desiderius Erasmus. Humanism challenged the orthodox theology that man was born sinful and only through divine intervention was he capable of virtue. The humanists placed destiny in human hands with their belief that each individual has the potential to choose a virtuous path through life. Erasmus, encouraged by the example of the English theologian, John Colet, whom he met at Oxford in 1499, adopted a scientific approach to the study of sacred texts. In place of a theology based upon traditional interpretations of ecclesiastical texts, humanists studied the scriptures in their earliest existing form. To this end, Erasmus studied Greek and produced his much celebrated Greek New Testament. The historical approach to the Bible, as adopted by scholars such as Colet, revealed to humanists the disparity between religious traditions and the original sources, as well as the potential for interpreting a single text in radically different ways. At their most optimistic, humanists believed their methods could help resolve religious differences by revealing the common inspiration for different beliefs. While advocating tolerance for different traditions and interpretations, humanism also promoted a simpler, less ritualistic approach to religion. The humanists have been seen as a crucial link in the transition from English Catholicism to Protestantism. As well as challenging certain deeply held theological beliefs, such as transubstantiation, they highlighted clerical abuses. Colet, for example, was critical of excessive tithes, 'money extorted by bitter exactions under the name of tithes and obligations'. In a sermon delivered in 1510, he found the clergy guilty of 'lust of the flesh', 'covetousness', 'pride of life', and 'worldly occupation'. He went on to call for a 'reformation of ecclesiastical affairs'.

transubstantiation
Transubstantiation is the belief that, when consecrated by the priest, the communion bread and wine becomes Christ's body and blood.

What did early sixteenth-century humanists consider to be faults in contemporary religious practice?

Historical sources

English humanism – a 'half-way house' towards Protestantism?

The sources which follow have been selected to help you appreciate the nature of humanism in the late fifteenth and early sixteenth centuries. Read each one carefully and then try to answer the questions which follow.

1 The position of Colet

Nevertheless, Colet's exposition of Romans [St Paul's epistle] cannot be regarded as more than a half-way house toward that of Luther . . . He apparently believed in transubstantiation, held the mass to be a propitiatory sacrifice [an act designed to win God's forgiveness], accepted all seven sacraments and accompanied his denunciation of papal scandals by an acknowledgment of the papal supremacy. Nevertheless, one cannot be surprised that he was admired by the Lollards and accused of heresy by Bishop Fitzjames. He is a Catholic with a special place in the history of Protestantism. The latter was above all a biblical religion, and Colet's chief distinction lies in the fact that he stressed, well before Luther and Tyndale, the extreme relevance to contemporary religious problems of the Scriptures, historically, humanly and literally considered. He stands both among the causes and the symptoms of that climatic change which swept across English intellectual life during the early decades of the century.

Source: A. G. Dickens, *The English Reformation*, London, 1964

2 Another view of Colet

Colet's cry for reform was not provoked by a decline in the morals or commitment of priests; rather it stood in a long tradition of Christian protest against the contamination of God's priests by man's ambition. Before Colet there had been Gascoigne in the fifteenth century, Langland in the fourteenth, Grosseteste in the thirteenth, and Bernard of Clairvaux in the twelfth; all critics of clergy who followed the ways of Mammon rather than the path of Christ. The cry for moral reform is a constant theme in Christian history, not the precursor of crisis, and it is unwise to read realities from the claims of crusaders. Colet was not a proto-Protestant, disgusted with the ecclesiastical structure and the sacramental system; he was a high clericalist, anxious to maintain the privileges of priests by raising their prestige.

Source: Christopher Haigh, *English Reformations*, Oxford, 1993

3 Colet's own words

. . . the diseases which are now in the church were the same in former ages . . . The need, therefore, is not for the enactment of new laws and constitutions, but the observance of those already enacted.

Source: Bishop Colet, message to the Canterbury Convocation, 1510

4 A sermon against greed for money

We must avoid and keep far from ourselves that grasping, deadly plague of avarice for which practically every priest is accused and held in disrepute before the people, when it is said that we are greedy for rich promotions, or harsh and grasping in retaining or amassing money, and spend but little or nothing on works of piety. For shame! How notorious are we for cunning in making contracts! How absorbed we are in careful purchases or profitable sales! These men take up the fields, the richest pastures, so that their herds of cattle and flocks of sheep may enjoy the finest grazing, but they take neither thought nor care for the tending of their own souls. Because of such people is the honour of the holy priesthood profaned and defiled.

Source: William Melton, chancellor of York Minster and friend of Bishop Colet, in a sermon to the ordinands in the diocese of York, c. 1510

Historical-source questions

1. What do you understand by the term 'transubstantiation' and the phrase 'a biblical religion'?
2. On what points in their discussion of Bishop Colet do Dickens and Haigh agree, and in what ways do they differ?
3. Do Colet's own words in Source 3 substantiate the position taken by Dickens or that of Haigh? Explain your answer.
4. How might Source 4 be used to support both sides in the debate?
5. What considerations should be made before accepting as fact the claims of Source 4?
6. To what extent do you consider humanism both a cause and a symptom of change in English religious practice in the first half of the sixteenth century?

Lollards

Lollards were the followers of the remarkably outspoken Yorkshireman, John Wycliffe, an Oxford don who was condemning clerical abuses in the early 1380s. He denied certain fundamental sacramental beliefs, including that of transubstantiation; those in holy orders he likened to 'ravening wolves' and 'fat cows'; his description of the pope as 'a limb of Lucifer' made him a marked man, saved from papal arrest only through the intervention of his powerful patron, John of Gaunt, son of Edward III. He utterly rejected the notion that clerics, by definition, were virtuous, and considered that priests devoid of 'grace' were worthless. Most importantly he stressed the authority of the Bible and, with his Oxford disciples, produced the first English translation since the Norman Conquest. This challenged the privilege of clerics by enabling men other than Latin scholars to read and interpret the scriptures independently.

By the early years of the fifteenth century, the Lollard movement was losing momentum and was widely viewed as heretical. Known Lollards were obliged to wear on their clothing a badge showing a faggot, a symbol of the bundles of sticks used to burn condemned heretics. The movement was driven underground, its followers meeting secretly and the token of their belief, the English Bible, being carefully hidden from the prying eyes of servants and visitors. Over 70 people were put on trial for heresy in Henry VII's reign, of which three were probably burned. By the early sixteenth century Lollards were to be found only in a number of enclaves scattered around southern England, particularly in small towns and villages.

The Lollard movement spawned the most important theological works written in England and, uniquely since Anglo-Saxon times, in English in the late Middle Ages. Bishop Reginald Pecock, convinced Lollardy was on the increase, produced many books designed to convert Lollards. His was an intellectual approach to the heresy, which supported the notion that discussion and education were more effective forms of combat than the threat of burning. By doing so, he offended both religious reactionaries and reformers alike. On the one hand, he appealed to reason and arbitration to resolve the dispute with Lollards, in treatises that extended participation in theological discussion beyond the reach of only those who could read Latin, while, on the other hand, he defended the church and certain of its 'abuses' including the non-residence of bishops who had other duties to attend to. He ended up being condemned for heresy himself in 1457, his critics having taken his words out of context and contrived to misinterpret them. His cause was championed by Pope Calixtus III, but Rome abandoned him when Pius II became pope in 1458. He spent the rest of his life, in some comfort, imprisoned by the church authorities. This stifling of intellectual and philosophical enquiry into religion, which combined reason and faith, would make the church all the less attractive to educated men of the sixteenth century as the European Renaissance unfolded and took root in England.

What were the main cultural developments?

Education, literacy and printing

The Lollards championed learning. Back in 1384 a group of them even petitioned parliament for the disendowment of the church with a view to using its wealth in the founding of new universities. Lollardy had its origins in the learned discussions of Oxford academics before gaining popularity among poorly educated artisans. They recognised that a growth of education, together with making the scriptures more accessible by having them

An early-sixteenth-century woodcut of a lesson in morals. Education advanced and literacy levels rose during the fifteenth and sixteenth centuries.

translated into the vernacular, would have a profound effect upon religious practices and popular beliefs.

No new universities were established in England in the fifteenth century, although three were founded in parts of France still under English rule in the 1430s and 1440s (Poitiers, Caen and Bordeaux). New colleges were founded at Oxford (Lincoln in 1429, All Souls in 1438 and Magdalen in 1448) and Cambridge (King's in 1441 and Queens' in 1448). Many new grammar schools were also established during the period. In 1441 Henry VI founded Eton College. Richly endowed by the royal purse, Eton and King's, Cambridge, each soon housing 70 scholars, became two of the greatest centres of learning in pre-Reformation England. While Cambridge University grew in size and reputation, Oxford was in decline and had no more than 600 students by the mid-fifteenth century. Parents began to choose Cambridge over Oxford because of the latter's association with John Wycliffe and the disgraced Bishop Pecock.

Why did an association with Wycliffe and Pecock dissuade parents from sending their sons to Oxford?

It is not possible to measure accurately the level of literacy in late-medieval Britain. Detailed statistical data from the period does not exist and what constitutes 'literacy', in any case, is open to question. A measure of literacy for more recent times is the frequency with which marriages are confirmed in parish registers with signatures as opposed to crosses. This, of course, helps identify levels of absolute illiteracy but is unhelpful as a device for measuring the *extent* of any individual's literacy.

The historian of the fifteenth century must use a wide variety of sources in order to estimate literacy levels. Customs accounts reveal the numbers of books imported, while private papers and business records reveal the relative importance of documentation. The records of ecclesiastical courts can be used in much the same way as later parish registers, and wills sometimes contained specific reference to valuable manuscripts and devotional books. The careful analysis of such evidence reveals certain facts:

- Literacy was increasing.
- Literacy was no longer restricted and largely confined to the clergy.
- Reading and writing skills extended beyond the nobility and clergy to merchants and skilled artisans. Terms of apprenticeship for some craft guilds required minimum levels of literacy.
- More commercial, legal and government business was conducted through the written word than before.
- English, as opposed to French or Latin, was becoming more common as the language in which even officialdom communicated.
- Literary interests (establishing personal libraries, reading and writing verse, going to plays) became increasingly popular leisure pursuits.

All of these developments would be greatly enhanced by the arrival of the **printing press**, first introduced to England by William Caxton in 1476. Caxton printed over 18,000 pages on a hand press which was essentially a modified wine press. This technology was invented by his fellow printers in the Rhine Valley in the 1440s. His enterprise made nearly a hundred affordable books available between 1476 and 1491, covering a wide range of topics. The print-runs were small, numbering tens or, at best, hundreds, but, like modern periodicals, their circulation among the purchaser's acquaintances was usually wide. Caxton was typical of the new 'literate class'; not a cleric but a rich, educated wool merchant. Besides the clergy, he catered for the tastes of kings, aristocrats, and middle-class landowners and businessmen. The diversity of his output is revealed in the titles of his first publications: *The recuyell of the historyes of Troye* (1475), *The game and playe of the chesse* (1476) and *Dictes and sayenges of the phylosophers* (1477). He printed most existing English literature, including Sir Thomas Malory's *Le morte d'Arthur* and Geoffrey Chaucer's *Canterbury tales*.

Such volumes were instrumental in helping to forge a common English language. England at this time abounded in dialects. In some extreme cases, like that of Northumbrian and Cornish, for example, dialects were virtually different languages. Without a dictionary to guide him, in an age that had no rules regarding accurate spelling and grammatical structure, the printer faced a dilemma. As William Caxton put it in his *Preface* to Virgil's *Aeneid*:

printing press The printing press would provide a vehicle for the religious propaganda of the early sixteenth century which helped prepare the ground for the reform of the church under Henry VIII and his successors.

Certayn marchauntes were in a shippe in Tamyse and for lacke of wynde thei taryed atte Forlond and wente to lande for to refreshe them; And one of theym . . . cam in-to an hows and axed for mete; and specyally he axyed after eggys; and the goode wyf answerde that she coude speke no Frenshe . . . And theene at laste another sayd that he wolde haue 'eyren' then the goode wyf sayd that she vnderstod hym wel. Loo, what sholde a man in thyse dates now wryte, 'egges' or 'eyren'?

That we say these days 'eggs' is in part due to Caxton's books. The language Caxton selected was that in common use in London among the well-to-do circles in which he moved. This language in turn was derived largely from the dialects of the Midlands, reflecting a migration of many Midlanders to the capital during the fourteenth and fifteenth centuries. Thus the English language came to be standardised in Caxton's work according to his own principle of writing 'English not over rude, nor curious, but in such terms as shall be understood by God's grace.'

Architecture and building

Perhaps the greatest architectural statement of the age was King's College Chapel, Cambridge. Henry VI laid its foundation stone in 1446 and proceeded to fund the finest piece of fifteenth-century building in the Perpendicular Gothic style. It was unfinished and had already cost £16,000 when Henry was deposed in 1461. Work on it was not resumed until 1480, not to be finished until after the reign of Henry VII. Edward IV spent over £1,000 each year between 1477 and 1483 developing St George's Chapel, also in the Perpendicular style, for the glorification of his dynasty. Similar work was continued during the period at Gloucester Abbey, completed around the time of the accession of Henry VII.

Why did the rich put so much money into ecclesiastical building during the fifteenth century?

Building on such a grand scale during this period, however, was rare. Other examples include the nave of Winchester Cathedral and the west front of Beverley Minster. Many less grandiose parish churches were built during these turbulent years. This shows, in part, that the 'middle classes', engaged in the wool and cloth trades, continued to prosper while the fortunes of the aristocracy fluctuated. Many were adorned with spectacular woodwork, shaping their roofs, rood screens and misericord seats. Many churches were sumptuously decorated, too, with wall paintings created by local firms of commercial artists. Typically they might reflect society's preoccupation with mortality by depicting the Last Judgement or a picture of St Christopher: a talisman against death, for he who gazed on his image would be spared for the rest of that day.

The Last Judgement. Belief in life after death and particularly in the Last Judgement could have a profound effect upon the way people lived their lives.

The arts

The era of the Wars of the Roses was not a great period in terms of the written and visual arts. In previous and at contemporary courts in more settled parts of Europe the arts were stimulated by royal and noble patronage. While little formal courtly poetry of particular merit was produced, this was an age in which less elitist verse flourished in the form of carols, religious songs and narrative ballads. It is likely, for example, that it was during the fifteenth century that many of those particularly English tales of the struggle for justice in unruly and dangerous times – the adventures of Robin Hood and his merry men – were first composed in ballad form.

Portraiture in the fifteenth century was developing a more realistic style and, by the end of the century, portraits of kings and their courtiers were pictures of actual people rather than mere generalisations. The tradition of profile portraiture had also given way to the more informative 'three-quarter face' portrait with the sitter's face painted at an angle, revealing aspects of both the right and left.

The early part of the century, encouraged particularly by the patronage of Henry IV, had been a rich one for courtly and devotional music. During Henry V's reign, English music was a powerful influence on the development of music elsewhere in Europe, as English musicians and composers mingled with their continental counterparts in Henry's French provinces. The civil wars, however, stifled this art like others during the 1450s and 1460s, when music continued to flourish only in its popular forms.

Civil war, culture and creativity

One of the most interesting questions about the period concerns the extent to which the Wars of the Roses impaired the development of English society and culture. The conclusion most historians draw is that the general impact of civil war has, in the past, been exaggerated, and important positive developments in political, economic and religious spheres can be identified for the period 1450 to 1509, some, perhaps, even accelerated by war. Even in the short term, the immediate effects of war were mild when compared to those of the Hundred Years' War fought across the scorched earth of mainland western Europe in preceding decades.

The wars did impinge upon civilian life, with ordinary men pressed into service and with the land in the path of the armies exploited for provisions. War, however, was not continuous nor was it large scale. Some battles were over in a few hours or less, leaving just a few hundred dead on the battlefield. Any damage sustained by English merchants and other tradesmen in the period was far more likely to be the result of international diplomacy than the immediate consequences of dynastic war fought on English soil. In fact, while the fortunes of the great magnates were both won and lost, the gentry and merchant classes continued to prosper. Royal investment in magnificent ecclesiastical buildings at times languished, but many parishes continued to raise the capital necessary to create the beautiful churches for which the age is renowned.

Historical interpretation: the social and economic impact of the Wars of the Roses

Nineteenth-century historians assumed the civil wars were catastrophic in every respect; a period of virtual anarchy, dislocation, social and economic collapse. Modern historians are less convinced, like John Warren, in *The Wars of the Roses and the Yorkist kings* (1995):

> ... to argue that the Wars came close to destroying the economic life
> of the country, or left devastated villages in their wake, or
> irreparably damaged the relationship between noble and monarch,
> is simply inaccurate.

Such opinions seem confirmed by the accounts of the wars' contemporaries. Philippe de Commynes, Louis XI's councillor, commented:

> England enjoyed this peculiar mercy above all other kingdoms, that
> neither the country nor the people, nor the houses were wasted,
> destroyed or demolished; but the calamities and misfortunes of the
> war fell only upon the soldiers, and especially on the nobility.

Compared to the savagery of the French wars of the fifteenth century the civil wars in England must have seemed tame to a French observer. To those on the receiving end, however, if we accept this account of the prior of Crowland writing about the aftermath of the Battle of Wakefield (1460), the violence off the battlefield was real enough:

> ... fancying that every thing tended to insure them freedom from
> molestation, paupers and beggars flocked forth from those quarters
> in infinite numbers, just like so many mice rushing forth from their
> holes, and universally devoted themselves to spoil and rapine,
> without regard of place or person ... [they] rushed, in their
> unbridled and frantic rage, into churches and other sanctuaries of
> God, and most nefariously plundered them of their chalices, books,
> and vestments ... When the priests and the other faithful of Christ
> in any way offered to make resistance, like so many abandoned
> wretches as they were, they cruelly slaughtered them in the very
> churches or churchyards. Thus did they proceed with impunity,
> spreading in vast multitudes over a space of thirty miles [50 kilo-
> metres] in breadth and, covering the whole surface of the earth just
> like so many locusts, made their way almost to the very walls
> of London ...

Although the security of London, as on this occasion, was threatened during the wars, towns and cities were remarkably unscathed by, and uninvolved in, the fighting. Few towns, and certainly no major towns, were sacked, and their trading activities, by and large, remained intact. Townspeople, following the lead of their city fathers, endeavoured to maintain a neutral, non-participatory role; the Wars of the Roses were fought, in the main, by countrymen. According to David Cook, in *Lancastrians and Yorkists: the Wars of the Roses* (1994), the conduct of

Why is it difficult for historians to draw firm conclusions regarding the impact of the Wars of the Roses?

Le morte d'Arthur
Thomas Malory probably completed this masterpiece in 1470, shortly before he died (although his exact identity, like Shakespeare's, is open to question). There were several mid-fifteenth-century Thomas Malorys, but the most likely candidate for the authorship of *Le morte d'Arthur* was a knight from Newbold Revel in Warwickshire who spent several years in prison for theft and rape: a surprising history for the writer of the most celebrated account of chivalry and courtly love. *Le morte d'Arthur* revived the old stories and reverence for the hero-king. The association of King Arthur with the Romano-Celts defending Britain against the invading Germanic tribes meant that legend gave him a base somewhere in the west of England. Henry Tudor, with his Welsh ancestry, eagerly exploited tradition by stressing his own dynastic link with Arthur and naming his first-born son and heir after him.

Margaret of Anjou's army after Wakefield was the exception and not the rule – she and the other figureheads had no desire to turn public opinion against the cause, and the logic of civil war dictated the desirability of preserving the prosperity of the territory across which the battles were fought. J. R. Lander's conclusion in *The Wars of the Roses* (1965), that the wars 'had little or no effect upon agrarian and commercial life' is, in the broadest terms, true, although quite serious localised disruption at different stages must also have occurred.

A period of 30 years of sporadic campaigning amounted to just a few months of actual 'warfare'. J. R. Lander, writing in 1965, estimated that the campaigns lasted as little as 13 weeks while A. J. Pollard, writing in 1983, estimated that they lasted almost two years. Many parts of the country were untouched. While kings struggled to raise the capital to complete grand-scale architectural projects, lesser lords, bishops and wealthy merchants continued to build great new homes with comfort and aesthetics, and not war, in mind. Beautifully proportioned Perpendicular ecclesiastical buildings, utterly lacking in the defensive measures associated with contemporary European architecture, mushroomed in town and country alike. Conversely, the number of grants for improving town defences were little higher in the era of the wars than in preceding decades. This implies that there was little heightened sense of insecurity for those who might reasonably have considered themselves a likely target of the belligerents (as they certainly were during the Civil War of the 1640s). The slump in high-status building activity during the 1450s and 1460s can be explained by a general economic malaise rather than any sudden outburst of violence.

This was, by modern standards, a violent and, at times, a lawless age. Chaos afflicted war zones during the crises of 1459–1461 and 1469–1471 but there was no general breakdown of law and order. Before and between the civil wars men in high places, and elsewhere, literally got away with murder. Charles Ross, in *The Wars of the Roses* (1976), related the remarkable, but unexceptional, case of Sir Thomas Malory, author of the greatest Arthurian romance, **Le morte d'Arthur**:

> Although he sat in parliament on no less than three occasions, Malory was also a flagrant law-breaker. In late 1449 or early 1450, with a gang of 26 men, he tried to ambush and murder the duke of Buckingham; in May 1450 he committed rape and extortion, and again in August. The next year he stole several hundred head of livestock, terrorised the monks of Monks Kirby, stole deer from the duke of Buckingham's park at Caludon, broke into Combe Abbey to

steal money and ornaments, and came back the next day with a hundred men to insult the monks and steal more money.

His further offences included two successful gaolbreaks. The example amplifies Ross's point that 'The high level of violence which characterised late-medieval society, and the difficulties of obtaining justice, were . . . not products of the civil war.' Indeed the soldiery at large appears to have been remarkably well-behaved according to J. R. Lander, in *The Wars of the Roses* (1965), 'Looting was not unknown' but 'complaints of it were singularly rare.' Where, in a continental campaign, 'scorched earth' and requisitioning policies might have been the order of the day, pillaging in the Wars of the Roses was likely to carry the death penalty.

Tradition once had it that the wars all but destroyed the political power and autonomy of the old feudal lords. Certainly many peers died on the battlefield or in the subsequent bouts of retribution. Even so, this rarely extinguished noble families; the failure to produce male heirs was far more likely to cause extinction. Henry VI and Edward IV each more than compensated for the loss in the nobility's numbers by their inclination to create new peers. The new nobility, however, did not entirely take the place of the old. In any case, the male line in such families typically died out every three or four generations; the creation of new nobility was no novelty and the 'old' nobility was not necessarily very old. Kings continued to rely on the nobility and governed trusting to the loyalty of a handful of mighty magnates. If any significant change in the period occurred at all in the political involvement of the English nobility, it lay in the beginnings of a new reluctance among the great families to participate in the deadly conflicts of kings and kingmakers.

law and order On gaining the throne, Edward's priority was the establishment of law and order. To this effect 'livery and maintenance', the practice of paying men to join the private armies of magnates, was banned. Courts throughout the land were unusually busy in the early 1460s bringing murderers and other criminals to justice and Acts of Attainder were brought against prominent Lancastrians, including Henry VI himself and his queen. A great deal of property was confiscated and redistributed to loyal supporters of the new king. The retribution for some, like the earl of Oxford, who suffered at the hands of John Tiptoft, was truly dreadful.

Summary questions

1 Identify and explain any two reasons for economic developments in England between 1450 and 1509.

2 Assess the causes of change in English society in the late fifteenth and early sixteenth century.

3 How was the nobility affected by civil war in the second half of the fifteenth century?

4 Compare the importance of at least three social and economic developments in England between 1450 and 1509.

The Wars of the Roses, 1450–85

Significant dates

1450	Normandy is lost to the French.
	Suffolk is murdered.
	Cade's rebellion takes place.
1451	Thomas Yonge petitions that the duke of York be named heir to the throne.
1454	York is appointed as protector during Henry VI's insanity.
1455	The First Battle of St Albans takes place. Somerset dies.
1459	The Battle of Blore Heath takes place.
1460	The Battle of Northampton is fought.
	Richard of York is killed at the Battle of Wakefield.
1461	The Battle of Mortimer's Cross, the Second Battle of St Albans and the Battle of Towton are fought.
	Edward IV's reign begins.
1464	Edward IV marries Elizabeth Woodville.
1465	Henry VI is captured.
1469	Robin of Redesdale's rebellion breaks out.
	George, duke of Clarence, marries Warwick's daughter, Isabel Neville.
	Edward IV is captured by Warwick at Edgecote.
1470	The Battle of Empingham takes place.
	Clarence and Warwick flee to France.
	Warwick invades and Edward IV flees to the Low Countries.
	Henry VI regains the throne.
1471	Edward IV returns to England and is restored as king.
	Battles are fought at Barnet and Tewkesbury.
	Warwick, Henry VI and Prince Edward all die.

1475	Edward IV invades France and makes the Treaty of Picquigny with the French.
1478	Clarence is put to death for treason.
1483	Edward IV dies.
1483	*April* Edward V is proclaimed king. *June* Lord Hastings is executed. The princes in the Tower are supposedly murdered. The duke of Gloucester is proclaimed King Richard III. *October* Buckingham's rebellion takes place.
1484	Richard III's son and heir, Edward, dies.
1485	Richard III's wife dies. Henry Tudor invades England. Richard III is killed at the Battle of Bosworth.

Overview

The study of history is founded on the analysis of primary sources. These include the visible evidence of portraits, the physical evidence of buildings and, above all, the written evidence of documents. Modern academic history tries to provide a plausible account of the causes and effects of historical events which is based upon a balanced interpretation of all this available evidence. The evidence, inevitably, is fragmentary, often misleading and frequently contradictory. Even the most eloquent writer who has to handle a mass of material, and take other experts' interpretations into consideration, is likely to produce a history which, to the lay reader, can seem overwhelmingly complex. For this reason it is sensible to approach any research by first reading a simple account of events before moving on to more sophisticated works.

The fifteenth century served modern historians well by leaving a rich legacy of chronicles, all of which tell a story in a direct and readable way. The chronicler rarely shared the modern historian's desire to be objective and would readily reject evidence which might challenge his own beliefs. All studies into the dynastic history of this century sooner or later lead to a consideration of one or more of the chronicles and, to a very considerable degree, we still rely on them for our knowledge and understanding of the time of the Wars of the Roses. Only when other contemporary sources, such as letters and official papers, refer to the same issues can we hope to check on their accuracy. Consequently, much of the debate surrounding themes like the supposed murder of the princes in the Tower revolves around the reliability of the chroniclers themselves.

This chapter focuses on such sources and it is designed to stimulate an appreciation of the very real importance of the source material while cautioning against taking it at face value. Some of the documents were written at the same time as the events described, some were written a while afterwards. Many are eye-witness accounts, others are hearsay. Sometimes they are the work of Englishmen, sometimes of foreign observers. Some writers are guided by religious convictions, others have more secular concerns. All the sources, however, provide an insight into a distant age with a clarity and freshness that modern commentators can scarcely hope to better.

Document study: Why did civil strife break out in England in 1455?

Government and opposition

1 Taxation

The closing lines of Adam of Usk's Chronicle

. . . our lord the king . . . designs to return again to France in full strength. But, woe is me! mighty men and treasure of the realm will be most miserably fordone about this business. And in truth the grievous taxation of the people to this end being unbearable, accompanied with murmurs and with smothered curses among them from hatred of the burden, I pray that my liege lord become not in the end a partaker . . . of the sword of wrath of the Lord!

Source: Adam of Usk, *Chronicle*, 1421, ed. and tr. by E. Maunde Thompson, quoted in J. R. Lander, *The Wars of the Roses*, Stroud, 1965

2 Complaints against bad government

The views of another chronicler

In this same time, the realm of England was out of all good governance, as it had been many days before, for the king was simple and led by a covetous counsel, and owed more than he was worth. His debts increased daily, but payment was there none; all the possessions and lordships that pertained to the crown the king had given away, some to lords and some to other lesser persons, so that he had almost nothing left to own. And such impositions as were put to the people, as taxes and tallages [taxes like tolls or customs duties], all that came from them was spent in vain, for he held no household nor maintained any wars . . . The queen with such as were of her affinity ruled the realm as she liked, gathering innumerable riches . . . The queen was defamed and slandered, that he that was called prince, was not her son, but a bastard gotten in adultery; wherefore she, dreading that he should not succeed his father as king of England, allied unto her all the knights and squires of Cheshire . . .

Source: J. S. Davies (ed.), *An English chronicle of the reigns of Richard II, Henry IV, Henry V and Henry VI*, c.1465, Camden Society, 1856

3 Opposition to the king's advisers

The view of Jack Cade

The king should take about his noble person men of true blood from his royal realm, that is to say, the high and mighty prince, the duke of York, exiled from our sovereign lord's person by the suggestions of those false traitors the duke of Suffolk and his affinity.

Source: Jack Cade's Manifesto, quoted in Sarah Newman, *Yorkists and Tudors, 1450–1603*, Oxford, 1989, p. 42

4 Opposition in parliament

The words of a chronicler concerning Thomas Yonge's plea in parliament

In the same parliament Thomas Yonge of Bristol, apprentice in law, moved that because the king had no offspring, it would be for the security of the kingdom that it should be openly known who should be heir apparent. And he named the duke of York. For which cause the same Thomas was afterwards committed to the Tower of London.

Source: *Annales rerum anglicarum*, May 1451, in J. Stephenson (ed.), *Letters and papers illustrative of the wars of the English in France during the reign of Henry VI*, 2 vols., Rolls Series, 1861–64

Document-study questions

1 Study Document 1. How useful is this document, written in the reign of Henry V, for explaining the crises in the reign of Henry VI?
2 Study Document 2. From this document and your own knowledge explain what was meant by 'owed more than he was worth'.
3 Study Documents 2 and 4. How far does 2 confirm the implication of 4 that 'the security of the kingdom' depended on recognition of an 'heir apparent'?
4 Use all the documents and your own knowledge to explain how far you agree with the view that Henry VI was the author of his own downfall.

The madness of King Henry

5 The king fails to recognise his son

A contemporary letter describing the king's madness

. . . at the prince's coming to Windsor, the duke of Buckingham took him in his arms and presented him to the king in goodly wise, beseeching the king to bless him; and the king gave no answer . . . the queen came in, and took the prince in her arms and presented him in like form as the duke had done, desiring that he should bless it; but all their labour was in vain, for they departed thence without any answer or countenance saving only once that he looked on the prince and cast down his eyes again . . .

Source: James Gardner (ed.), *The Paston letters, 1422–1509*, 6 vols., 1904

6 A warrant from the king's council, 1454. It is signed in the middle by Richard of York in his capacity as protector for the duration of the Henry VI's illness.

This warrant was signed during the period of the duke of York's protectorate in 1454. Beneath York's signature in the middle of the document are those of Salisbury and Warwick (R Warrewyk).

7 The recovery of Henry VI

Edmund Clere to John Paston, 9 January 1455

And on that Monday afternoon the queen came to him, and brought my lord prince with her. And then he asked what the prince's name was, and the queen told him Edward; and then he held up his hands and thanked God thereof. And he said he never knew till that time, nor wist not what was said to him, nor wist not where he had been whilst he hath been sick till now.

Source: James Gardner (ed.), *The Paston letters, 1422–1509*, 6 vols., 1904

8 Somerset is reinstated

A contemporary account of Somerset's release from the Tower

On 6 February, the duke of Somerset was released from the Tower of London on bail. Very shortly afterwards the duke of York resigned his office to the king at Greenwich, after he had governed England most excellently for a whole year, miraculously calming rebels and villains, according to the laws and without unnecessary violence; and he reigned his office much honoured and much loved.

Then the king, in response to the intercession of the Archbishop of Canterbury and the duke of Buckingham, pardoned all those who had entered into recognisances for the duke of Somerset. Once more, the duke of

Somerset became head of the government under the king, although in the past he had almost ruined the whole of England with his misrule.

Source: John Benet, *Chronicle*, G. L. Harriss and M. A. Harriss (eds.), Camden Miscellany, XXIV, Camden 4th Series vol. 9, Royal Historical Society, 1973

Document-study questions

1 Study Document 8. From this document and your own knowledge explain what was meant by 'recognisances'.
2 Study Document 6. How useful is this document as evidence for the protectorship of Richard of York?
3 Study Documents 5 and 8. To what extent does Document 8 confirm the evidence of Document 5 that the king was completely incapacitated during his mental illness?
4 Use all these documents and your own knowledge to explain how far you agree with the view that 'it was not Henry's madness but the recovery of his sanity which made the Wars of the Roses inevitable'.

The duke of Somerset and Queen Margaret

9 Henry VI's behaviour towards his wife

From the writings of a Carthusian monk who was one of Henry VI's chaplains

. . . King Henry was chaste and pure from the beginning of his days. He eschewed all licentiousness in deed or word while he was young; until he was of marriageable age, when he espoused the most noble lady, Lady Margaret, daughter of the king of Sicily, by whom he begat one only son, the most noble and virtuous Prince Edward; and with her and toward her he kept his marriage vow wholly and sincerely, even in the absences of the lady, which were sometimes very long: never dealing unchastely with any other woman. Neither when they lived together did he use his wife unseemly, but with all honesty and gravity.

Source: J.R. Lander, *The Wars of the Roses*, Stroud, 1965, pp. 26–27

10 The loss of Maine

Henry VI to Charles VII of France, 22 December 1445

To the most high and powerful prince, our very dear uncle of France [Charles VII] . . .

Most high and powerful prince, our very dear uncle, knowing that you would be very glad that we should make deliverance of the city, town and castle of Le Mans, and all that we have and hold within the comté of Maine, to . . . the king of Sicily and Charles of Anjou, his brother . . . who have most affectionately upon your part required us so to do, and moreover informed us that it appeared to you that this was one of the best and aptest means to arrive at the blessing of a peace between us and you . . . favouring also our most dear and well-beloved companion the queen, who has requested us to do this many times . . .

Source: *Annales rerum anglicarum*, May 1451, in J. Stephenson (ed.), *Letters and papers illustrative of the wars of the English in France during the reign of Henry VI*, 2 vols., Rolls Series, 1861–64

11 Differences of opinion about foreign policy

A chronicler, Jean de Waurin, explains the situation in 1449

At the time we are talking about, there were, in the kingdom of England, two parties contending for the government and administration of the king and his people. In one of these parties there was Humphrey, duke of Gloucester, King Henry's uncle, Richard, duke of York, and several other princes and notable barons; the other was an alliance between the dukes of Somerset and Suffolk, Lord Say, the Bishop of Salisbury and several others not named here . . .

William, duke of Suffolk . . . was the principal advisor to the king, and also well loved by the queen. It was through her and Edmund, duke of Somerset, and other men of his party that they managed to talk to the king in private, and point out to him that Normandy was costing him a lot to maintain, in wages to the soldiers he was keeping there under the duke of York and in other sundry daily expenses. So they recommended to him that the country of Normandy should be handed back to the French . . .

Source: Jean de Waurin, *Chroniques*, H. T. Riley and E. Hardy (eds.), Rolls Series, London, 1884

12 Trouble between Somerset and York

An account of the chronicler, Jean de Waurin

. . . the duke of Somerset, who despised the duke of York . . . found a way to harm him. He was well liked by the queen of England, Margaret of Anjou, daughter of René, duke of Anjou, and the king of France's niece. She worked on King Henry, her husband, on the advice and support of the duke of Somerset and other lords and barons of his following, such that the duke of York was recalled from France to England. There he was totally stripped of his authority to govern Normandy, which he had done well and for some time, and despite his having acted commendably throughout the whole English conquest of France. In York's place, the duke of Somerset was appointed due to the solicitation and exhortation of the said queen and of some barons who, at that time, were in positions of power in the kingdom.

Source: Jean de Waurin, *Chroniques*, H. T. Riley and E. Hardy (eds.), Rolls Series, London, 1884

1   Study Document 10. How reliable is this document as evidence about the character of Henry VI?
2   Study Document 11. From this document and your own knowledge explain what was meant at the time by the phrase 'the kingdom of England'.
3   Study Documents 11 and 12. How far does Document 11 confirm the view in Document 12 that the duke of Somerset initiated the changes in Henry VI's policy regarding the administration and fate of Normandy?
4   Use all these documents and your own knowledge to explain how far you agree with the view that foreign affairs were a principal cause of civil war in England in the reign of Henry VI.

Richard, duke of York

13 The duke of York's rebellion

A London chronicler describes the confrontation between York and the king in 1452
The king heard that the duke of York, the earl of Devonshire and Lord Cobham were marching towards London, with twenty thousand men, so he rode to Northampton and sent the Bishop of Winchester, the count of Eu and Lord Stourton to the duke of York, to tell him not to rise up in arms.

The duke replied, commending himself to the king's good grace and saying that he had never rebelled against the king and would obey him always. He asserted that his uprising had been directed against those who betrayed the king and the kingdom of England and that he was not against the king and desired nothing but the good of England. He wished to tell the king of those who were encompassing the destruction of his two kingdoms, that is to say, of England and France. And these men were Edmund, duke of Somerset, who had been responsible for the shameful loss of all Normandy, and John Kemp, the Archbishop of York, who was a cardinal and the Chancellor of England.

Source: *Annales rerum anglicarum*, May 1451, in J. Stephenson (ed.), *Letters and papers illustrative of the wars of the English in France during the reign of Henry VI*, 2 vols., Rolls Series, 1861–64

14 Enmity between York, Somerset and Buckingham

The anonymous London chronicle for the year 1455
Soon after Easter [1455], another dispute arose between the noble duke of York, on the one hand, and the evil duke of Somerset and the duke of Buckingham, on the other. For Somerset was plotting the destruction of the noble duke of York. He offered advice to the king, saying that the duke of York wished to depose the king and rule England himself – which was manifestly false.

Because of this, around the middle of May, the duke of York and with him the earls of Shrewsbury and Warwick, approached London, with seven thousand armed men. When the duke of Somerset heard this news, he suggested to the king that York had come to usurp the throne. For this reason, the king sided with the duke of Somerset.

Source: John Benet, *Chronicle*, G. L. Harriss and M. A. Harriss (eds.), Camden Miscellany, XXIV, Camden 4th Series vol. 9, Royal Historical Society, 1973

15 The First Battle of St Albans

An account, written within five days of the events described, probably by a foreigner resident in England

When the duke of Somerset and those who were of his party then being in the City of London, heard that the duke of York and many other lords in his company were advancing against them with a force of five thousand men and when he considered what he had done against the said duke of York and that he was also in very bad odour with the people of London, he came to the conclusion that he should not remain in the City of London for fear that the people would fall upon him the moment he [the duke of York] arrived. For which cause he persuaded the king to sally forth against the said duke of York . . .

. . . the king sent a herald to the duke of York to know the cause for which he had come there with so many men and that it seemed to the king something quite new that he, the duke, should be rising against him, the king. The reply made was that he was not coming against him thus, [he] was always ready to do him obedience but he well intended in one way or another to have the traitors who were about him so that they should be punished, and that in case he could not have them with good will and fair consent, he intended in any case to have them by force. The reply that was made from the king's side to the said duke of York was that he [the king] was unaware that there were any traitors about him were it not for the duke of York himself who had risen against his crown. And even before this reply came to the duke of York there begun the skirmish before the village by one side and the other. And thus when the duke of York had the aforesaid reply the battle became more violent and both sides with banners displayed began to fight.

Source: Quoted by C. A. J. Armstrong in 'Politics of the Battle of St Albans, 1455', in *Bulletin of the Institute of Historical Research*, XXXIII, 1960

Document-study questions

1   Study Document 14. How reliable is this document as evidence for the duke of York's motives in early 1455?
2   Study Documents 13 and 15. How far do these documents reveal a consistency in the duke of York's thoughts and actions between 1452 and 1455?

3   Use all these documents and your own knowledge to explain how far you agree with the view that the duke of Somerset was most to blame for the start of civil war in England in 1455.

Document study: How effective a king was Edward IV?

Edward IV, Elizabeth Woodville and the earl of Warwick

1 The marriage between Edward IV and Elizabeth Woodville

John Warkworth describes the circumstances in which the marriage took place

In that year, the earl of Warwick was sent into France to look for a wife for the king. The fair lady in question was the niece of the king of France, and the earl of Warwick managed to arrange this wedding. However, while the earl of Warwick was away in France, the king was married to Elizabeth Woodville, a widow, whose husband Sir John Grey had been slain in battle on King Henry's side, and whose father was Lord Rivers. The wedding took place in great secrecy, on the first day of May 1464.

Source: John Warkworth, *A chronicle of the first thirteen years of the reign of King Edward the Fourth*, J. O. Halliwell (ed.), Camden Society, 1839

2 The view of the nobility

The Italian chronicler, Dominic Mancini, writing in December 1483

Edward IV, though he was then king of England, allowed himself to be ruled by his appetites in all things. In his choice of his wife too he was governed by lust. For he married a woman of low stock, called Elizabeth, against the wishes of the magnates. They would not stoop to show regal honour in accordance with her exalted rank to a woman of such humble origins, who was, moreover, a widow with two sons.

. . . The marriage caused the nobles to turn against Edward – later, indeed, he was even obliged to make war on them – while the members of Edward's own house were bitterly offended. His mother was furious and offered to submit to a public enquiry, asserting that Edward was not the child of her husband, the duke of York, but was conceived in adultery. For this reason, she claimed, he had no right to be king.

Source: Dominic Mancini, *The usurpation of Richard III*, 2nd edn, C. A. J. Armstrong (ed.), Oxford, 1969

The account of a contemporary chronicler for 1486

At this marriage [that of Margaret of York, Edward IV's sister, and the duke of Burgundy], Richard Neville, earl of Warwick, who had for some years appeared to favour the party of the French against the Burgundians, conceived great indignation. For he would greatly have preferred to have sought an alliance for the said Lady Margaret in the kingdom of France, by means of which a favourable understanding might have arisen between the monarchs of those two kingdoms; it being much against his wish, that the views of Charles, now duke of Burgundy, should be in anyway promoted by means of an alliance with England. The fact is, that he pursued that man with a most deadly hatred.

This, in my opinion, was really the cause of the dissensions between the king and the earl, and not the one which has previously been mentioned – the marriage of the king with Queen Elizabeth.

Source: N. Pronay and J. Cox (eds.), *The Crowland chronicle continuations 1459–86*, London, 1986

4 The Woodville family tree

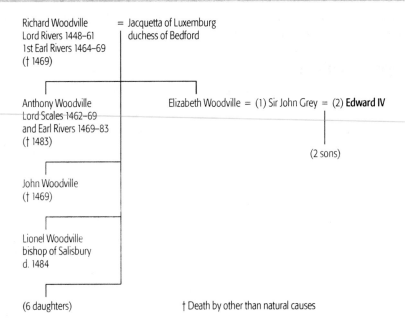

Richard Woodville
Lord Rivers 1448–61
1st Earl Rivers 1464–69
(† 1469)

= Jacquetta of Luxemburg
duchess of Bedford

Anthony Woodville
Lord Scales 1462–69
and Earl Rivers 1469–83
(† 1483)

Elizabeth Woodville = (1) Sir John Grey = (2) **Edward IV**

(2 sons)

John Woodville
(† 1469)

Lionel Woodville
bishop of Salisbury
d. 1484

(6 daughters)   † Death by other than natural causes

Document-study questions

1 Study Document 2. From this document and your own knowledge explain what was meant by 'against the wishes of the magnates'.
2 Study Document 2. How reliable is this document as evidence for the Woodville marriage crisis?

3 Study Documents 2 and 3. How far does Document 3 challenge the view in Document 2 that the Woodville marriage was the main cause of strife between the king and the nobility?

4 Use these documents and your own knowledge to explain how far you agree with the view that Edward IV's marriage to Elizabeth Woodville was disastrous.

Edward IV and his brothers

5 Edward IV's brothers' view of his marriage

The Italian chronicler, Dominic Mancini, writing about 20 years after the events described

Edward had two brothers then living and they, for their part, were sorely displeased at Edward's marriage. The duke of Clarence, who was closest in age to Edward, showed his anger more openly. He criticised Elizabeth's humble origins bitterly and in public and asserted that the king ought to marry a virgin, not a widow, which was contrary to established custom.

The other brother, however, Richard, duke of Gloucester, was better able to dissemble his thoughts and was in any case, because of his youth, less influential. He said and did nothing that might have been used against him.

Source: Dominic Mancini, *The usurpation of Richard III*, 2nd edn, C. A. J. Armstrong (ed.), Oxford, 1969

6 Henry is restored with the assent of Edward's brothers

From John Warkworth's chronicle

. . . in the beginning of the month of October . . . 1470, the Bishop of Winchester, by the assent of the duke of Clarence and the earl of Warwick, went to the Tower of London where King Henry was in prison . . . and brought him to the Palace of Westminster, and so he was restored to the crown again . . .

Source: John Warkworth, *A chronicle of the first thirteen years of the reign of King Edward the Fourth*, J. O. Halliwell (ed.), Camden Society, 1839

7 Edward's brothers quarrel

***From the* Crowland chronicle**

It is my intention here to insert an account of the dissensions which arose . . . between the two brothers of the king . . . After the son of King Henry, to whom the Lady Anne, the youngest daughter of the earl of Warwick, had been married, was slain at the Battle of Tewkesbury, Richard, duke of Gloucester, sought the said Anne in marriage. This proposal, however, did not suit the views of his brother, the duke of Clarence, who had previously married the eldest daughter of the same earl . . . as he was afraid of a division of the earl's property, which he wished to come to himself alone in right of his wife, and not be obliged to share it with any other person . . . In consequence of this, such violent dissensions arose between the brothers, and so many arguments were, with the greatest acuteness, put forward on either side, in the king's presence, who sat in judgement in the council chamber, that all present, and the lawyers even, were quite surprised that these princes should find arguments in such abundance by means of which to support their respective causes. In fact, these three brothers, the king and the two dukes, were possessed of such surpassing talents, that, if they had been able to live without dissensions, such a threefold cord could never have been broken without the utmost difficulty . . .

Source: N. Pronay and J. Cox (eds.), *The Crowland chronicle continuations 1459–86*, London, 1986

8 The queen plots against Clarence

The Italian chronicler, Dominic Mancini, writing in 1483

The queen remembered the insults to her family and the calumnies with which she was reproached, namely that according to established usage she was not the legitimate wife of the king. Thus she concluded that her offspring by the king would never come to the throne, unless the duke of Clarence were removed; and of this she easily persuaded the king. The queen's alarm was intensified by the comeliness of the duke of Clarence, which would make him appear worthy of the crown: besides he possessed such mastery of popular eloquence that nothing upon which he set his heart seemed difficult for him to achieve. Accordingly whether the charge was fabricated, or a real plot revealed, the duke of Clarence was accused of conspiring the king's death by means of spells and magicians. When the charge had been considered before a court, he was condemned and put to death. The mode of execution preferred in this case was, that he should die by being plunged into a jar of sweet wine.

Source: Dominic Mancini, *The usurpation of Richard III*, 2nd edn, C. A. J. Armstrong (ed.), Oxford, 1969

Document-study questions

1   Study Document 5. From this document and your own knowledge explain what was meant by 'Elizabeth's humble origins'.
2   Study Document 8. How reliable is this document as evidence for the fate of the duke of Clarence?
3   Study Documents 7 and 8. How far does Document 8 confirm the impression of the duke of Clarence in Document 7?
4   Study all these documents. Use these documents and your own knowledge to explain how far you agree with the view that Clarence's execution in 1478 was necessary for the security of the realm.

The appearance and personality of Edward IV

9 The beauty of Edward's children and his Catholic faith

The view of the Crowland chronicler

In those days you would have seen a royal court worthy of a leading king-dom, full of riches and men from almost every nation, and above all with fine looking and most delightful children, the offspring of his marriage to Elizabeth Woodville. They had ten children, of whom three had died and seven were living at the time [1482]. Of these latter, the two boys, Edward, Prince of Wales, and Richard, duke of York and Norfolk, had not yet reached manhood. There were five beautiful girls . . . Although in earlier years solemn embassies and pledges of faith in the words of princes had been despatched, with letters of agreement drawn up in due form, concerning the marriage of each of the daughters, it was not now thought that any one of the marriages would materialise, for everything was susceptible to change given the unstable relations between England and France, Scotland, Burgundy and Spain.

 . . . This prince, although at the time [1483] it was thought that he indulged his desires and passions to excess, was a Catholic of the truest faith and a most stern enemy of heretics, a most benevolent patron of learned men, scholars and clerics, a most devoted observer of the sacraments of the church and most penitent of sinners.

Source: N. Pronay and J. Cox (eds.), *The Crowland chronicle continuations 1459–86*, London, 1986

10 Edward's character

The Italian chronicler, Dominic Mancini, writing in 1483

Edward was of a gentle nature and cheerful aspect: nevertheless should he assume an angry countenance he could appear very terrible to beholders. He was easy of access to his friends and to others, even the least notable . . . he seized any opportunity that the occasion offered of revealing his fine stature more protractedly and more evidently to on-lookers. He was so genial in his greeting, that if he saw a newcomer bewildered at his appearance and royal magnificence, he would give him courage to speak by laying a kindly hand upon his shoulder . . . He was more favourable than other princes to foreign-ers, who visited his realm for trade or any other reason. He very seldom showed munificence, and then only in moderation, still he was very grateful to those from whom he had received a favour. Though not rapacious of other men's goods, he was yet so eager for money, that in pursuing it he acquired a reputation for avarice.

Source: Dominic Mancini, *The usurpation of Richard III*, 2nd edn, C. A. J. Armstrong (ed.), Oxford, 1969

11 A portrait of Edward IV, based on an engraving dated before 1472 and painted around 1534 to 1540

12 Edward at the Battle of Barnet, April 1471

The official Yorkist account

. . . the king, trusting verily in God's help, our blessed Lady's and St George . . . with the faithful, well-beloved and mighty assistance of his fellowship that in great number dissevered not from his person, and were as well assured unto him as to them was possible . . . he manly, vigorously and valiantly assailed them in the midst of the strongest of their battle, where he, with great violence, beat and bore down before him all that stood in his way, and then turned to the range, first on that one hand, and then on that other hand, so beat and bear them down that nothing might stand in the sight of him and that well-assured fellowship that attended truly upon him.

Source: J. Bruce (ed.), *Historie of the arrivall of King Edward in England*, Camden Society, 1839

Document-study questions

1 Study Document 9. From this document and your own knowledge explain what was meant by 'a leading kingdom'.

2 Study Document 11. How reliable is this document as evidence for the appearance of Edward IV?

3 Study Documents 10 and 11. How far does Document 11 confirm the impression of the man described in Document 10?

4　Use all these documents and your own knowledge to explain how far you agree with the view that Edward IV was a 'model' fifteenth-century king.

Government, law and order in the reign of Edward IV

13　Civil disorder

The views of some of his subjects

. . . in divers parts of this realm great abominable murders, robberies, extortions, oppression and other manifold maintainences, forcible entries . . . affrays, assaults be committed and done by such persons as either be of great might, or else favoured under persons of great power . . . yet remain unpunished . . . a number of people have been slain, some in Southwark . . . and some here at Westminster Gate, regardless of your presence here at your Palace of Westminster, or that your high court of Parliament is in session . . . [showing] contempt of your highness . . . to the great emboldening of all rioters and misgoverned persons.

Source: Sarah Newman, *Yorkists and Tudors 1450–1603*, Oxford, 1989, p. 67

14　Debasement of the coinage

The Italian chronicler, Dominic Mancini, writing in 1483

[In the year] 1464, Edward IV changed the coinage of England, which proved most profitable to him. He made an old noble a royal, the value of which was declared to be ten shillings; but the new coins contained some alloy, which reduced their value and made them weigh more; and he changed the design. He also made a groat worth threepence and an Angle noble worth six shillings and eightpence, and with all these changes caused great harm to the common people.

Source: Dominic Mancini, *The usurpation of Richard III*, 2nd edn, C. A. J. Armstrong (ed.), Oxford, 1969

15　Edward exhorts a benevolence from his subjects

Robert Fabyan, a London draper, writes about events in Edward's reign in 1473

This year this king, intending to make a voyage over sea to France, called before him his lords . . . to know their good minds, what of their free wills they would aid and depart with him toward the said voyage. And after he had known their good disposition towards him, he sent for the Mayor of London and his brethren, the aldermen, assessed each one and exhorted [them] to aid and assist him toward the great journey, of which the mayor for his part granted £30, and the aldermen some 20 marks, and the least £10. And that done, he sent for all the trusty commoners within the said city, and them exhorted in like manner, of whom most granted to him the wages of half a man for a year . . . And after that he rode about [the kingdom] . . . and raised thereby notable sums of money, the which way of the levying of this money was after named a benevolence.

Source: Robert Fabyan, *The new chronicles of England and France in two parts*, 1473, H. Ellis (ed.), London, 1811

16 The effects of the war with France

The words of a contemporary chronicler

When they [some soldiers after the French campaign of 1475] got back home they gave themselves up to theft and pillage to the extent that no road in all England was safe for merchants or pilgrims.

The king was thus compelled to travel through his own kingdom with his justices, sparing no one, not even from his own household, from being hanged if they were arrested for theft or murder. Wherever it was enforced, this severe justice eliminated highway robbery for a long time to come . . . [The king] was aware that he had reached a position where he no longer dared demand subsidies from the English people . . . Accordingly he devoted all his attention to how he might in future gather funds commensurate with his position as king from his own resources and by his own endeavour.

When parliament had been summoned, he took back almost all the royal patrimony from all those, whoever they were, on whom it had been conferred and devoted it entirely to bearing the crown's costs. He appointed as overseers of tolls at every port of the kingdom hand-picked men who were reputedly excessively hard on the merchants.

The king himself fitted out cargo ships and loaded them with fine wool, cloth, tin and other commodities of the kingdom and, like any other merchant, he traded for goods . . . He studied the Chancery registers and rolls and from those persons discovered to have trespassed on inheritances without observing due legal procedure he demanded heavy fines . . . the income from these and similar snares – more than could be devised by someone inexperienced – made the king very rich over the next few years. Indeed, in the collecting of gold and silver vessels, tapestries, valuable ornaments, both regal and religious, in the building of castles, colleges and other important places, in the acquisition of lands and estates, none of his predecessors could equal his outstanding achievements.

Source: N. Pronay and J. Cox (eds.), *The Crowland chronicle continuations 1459–86*, London, 1986

Document-study questions

1 Study Document 15. From this document and your own knowledge explain what was meant by a 'benevolence'.

2 Study Document 13. How useful is this document as evidence for the state of law and order during the reign(s) of Edward IV?

3   Study Documents 13 and 16. How far does the evidence of Document 16 corroborate that of Document 13?

4   Study all the documents. Use these documents and your own knowledge to explain how far you agree with the view that England was efficiently and effectively governed in the reign of Edward IV.

Document study: Why did the Yorkist dynasty fail to maintain its hold on the crown?

Usurpation and murder

1 The murder of Hastings, the king's chamberlain

The Italian chronicler, Dominic Mancini, writing in 1483

Having got into his power all the royal blood in the land, yet he [Richard, duke of Gloucester] considered that his prospects were not sufficiently secure, without the removal or imprisonment of those who had been the closest friends of his brother, and were expected to be loyal to his brother's offspring. In this class he thought to include Hastings, the king's chamberlain; Thomas Rotherham, whom shortly before had been relieved of his office; and the bishop of Ely . . . Therefore the protector [Richard] rushed headlong into crime . . . One day these three and several others came to the Tower about ten o'clock to salute the protector, as was their custom. When they had been admitted to the innermost quarters, the protector, as pre-arranged, cried out that an ambush had been prepared for him . . . Thereupon the soldiers, who had been stationed there by their lord, rushed in with the duke of Buckingham, and cut down Hastings on the false pretext of treason; they arrested the others, whose life, it was presumed, was spared out of respect for religion and holy orders.

Source: Dominic Mancini, *The usurpation of Richard III*, 2nd edn, C. A. J. Armstrong (ed.), Oxford, 1969

2 The death of Edward, prince of Wales, and Richard, duke of York

From a contemporary source, 1483

Item: this year King Edward V, late called prince of Wales, and Richard, duke of York, his brother, King Edward IV's sons, were put to death in the Tower of London on the instruction of the duke of Buckingham.

Source: R. F. Green (ed.), 'Historical notes of a London citizen', 1483–88, in *English Historical Review*, vol. 96, 1981

3 The murder of the two princes

From a history written by Sir Thomas More in the second decade of the sixteenth century

I shall rehearse you the dolorous end of those babes [Edward and Richard: 'the princes in the Tower'], not after every way I have heard, but after that way that I have so heard by such men and such means me thinketh it were hard but it should be true . . .

King Richard, after his coronation, taking his way to Gloucester . . . devised as he rode to fulfil that thing which he before had intended. And for as much as his mind gave him that, his nephews living, men would not reckon that he could have right to the realm, he thought therefore without delay to rid them, as though the killing of his kinsmen could amend his cause and make him a kindly king.

. . . Sir James Tyrell devised that they should be murdered in their beds. To the execution whereof, he appointed Miles Forest, one of the four that kept them, a fellow fleshed in murder before-time. To him he joined one John Dighton, his own horse-keeper, a big broad, square, strong knave. Then, all the others being removed from them, this Miles Forest and John Dighton, about midnight (the silly [ie innocent] children lying in their beds) came into the chamber and suddenly lapped them up among the clothes, so bewrapped them and entangled them, keeping down by force the feather bed and pillows hard unto their mouths, that within a while, smothered and stifled, their breath failing, they gave up to God their innocent souls into the joys of heaven, leaving to the tormentors their bodies dead in bed. Which after that the wretches perceived, first by the struggling with the pains of death, and after long lying still, to be thoroughly dead: they laid their bodies naked out upon the bed, and fetched Sir James to see them. Which, upon the sight of them, caused those murderers to bury them at the stair foot, meetly deep in the ground, under a great heap of stones.

Source: Sir Thomas More, *The history of King Richard III*, R. S. Sylvester (ed.), New York, 1963

4 The removal of the princes to the Tower

The Italian chronicler, Dominic Mancini, writing in 1483

Richard's actions up until now had given reason to think he was aiming for the crown. Yet some hope remained that this might not be his intention, for he had not yet gone so far as to lay claim to the throne itself. Indeed, he declared that he acted as he did only so that treason might be avenged and past wrongs righted. Moreover, all private deeds and official documents continued to bear the titles and name of Edward V. However, after the removal of Hastings, the attendants who had previously ministered to the young king's needs were all kept from him. He and his brother were transferred to the inner chambers of the Tower. Every day their appearances behind the windows grew less frequent and eventually they ceased to appear altogether. The doctor, Argentine, was the only one of Edward's former retinue who still attended him. He told how the young king, like a victim prepared for sacrifice, sought remission for his sins by daily confession and penance, believing that death was close at hand . . . And after he disappeared I saw many men moved to weeping and lamentation at the mention of his name. However, I have not yet been able to establish whether he was done away with and, if so, by what means.

Source: Dominic Mancini, *The usurpation of Richard III*, 2nd edn, C. A. J. Armstrong (ed.), Oxford, 1969

Document-study questions

1   Study Document 1. From this document and your own knowledge explain what was meant by 'Having got into his power all of the royal blood in the land'.
2   How reliable is Document 1 as evidence about Richard III's usurpation of power in 1483?
3   Study Documents 2 and 3. How far does Document 3 confirm the evidence of Document 2?
4   Study all the documents. Use these documents and your own knowledge to explain how far you would agree with the verdict that Richard III murdered the princes in the Tower.

Richard III and contemporary opinion

5 The death of Prince Edward

The words of a contemporary chronicler

One afternoon in February almost all the lords spiritual and temporal of the realm and the most powerful knights and esquires of the king's household foregathered, at the king's specific command, in a downstairs room off the corridor leading to the queen's quarters. Each man put his name to a new oath . . . pledging their allegiance to Edward, King Richard III's only son, as their supreme lord, if anything should happen to his father. Soon afterwards, however, it was made plain how fruitless are the plans of men when they wish to arrange their own affairs without God.

The following April, on a day close to the anniversary of King Edward IV's death, this only son on whom rested all hope of the royal succession, expressed in so many oaths, died in Middleham Castle after a brief illness. Then you would have seen both the father and the mother, when they received the news in Nottingham where they were staying, go almost out of their minds for a time with sudden grief.

Source: N. Pronay and J. Cox (eds.), *The Crowland chronicle continuations 1459–86*, London, 1986

6 The death of Queen Anne

The words of a contemporary chronicler

It was said by many that [by the beginning of 1485] the king was concentrating all his attention on contracting marriage with Elizabeth [of York, daughter of Edward IV], either after the death of the queen – for which he was waiting – or through a divorce for which he considered he had sufficient grounds. He could see no other way of confirming his position as king nor of depriving his rival of hope. A few days later, the queen fell seriously ill and died and her weakness was considered to have worsened because the king entirely forsook his consort's bed . . . Towards the middle of March 1485, on a day when a major eclipse of the sun took place, Queen Anne died . . .

The king's intention and plan to marry his niece, Elizabeth of York, was finally reported to certain people who did not favour it and, after he had summoned the council, the king was compelled to make a lengthy denial to the effect that this idea had never entered his head. There were those in the council who were quite aware that this was not true. Those who objected most strongly to this marriage, and whose opinion the king himself rarely dared oppose, were Sir Richard Ratcliffe and William Catesby, a member of the royal bodyguard. They told the king to his face that if he did not repudiate this plan . . . the northerners, on whom he principally relied, would rise up against him, accusing him of the death of the queen, the daughter and one of the heirs of the earl of Warwick, through whom he had obtained his first honour, in order to satisfy his incestuous desire for his close relative, in defiance of God. Furthermore they brought forward more than twelve doctors of theology to state that the pope could not grant a dispensation covering that degree of consanguinity.

Source: N. Pronay and J. Cox (eds.), *The Crowland chronicle continuations 1459–86*, London, 1986

7 Rumours of murder

A contemporary account

Slander and rumour, spread among the people by evil disposed individuals to the very great displeasure of the king, claims that the queen, by the consent and will of the king, was poisoned so that he might marry Lady Elizabeth, eldest daughter of his brother, the late king of England . . .

. . . the king sent for and had before him at St John's yesterday the mayor and aldermen . . . in the great hall there, in the presence of many of his lords and many other people, he showed his grief and displeasure and said it never came to his thought or mind to marry in such manner, nor did he wish the death of his queen but was sorry and in heart as heavy as a man might be . . .

Source: L. Lyell and F. D. Watney (eds.), *Acts of court of the Mercers' Company, 1453–1537*, 1936

8 A seditious libel

The words of a contemporary chronicler

In these days [1484] the king's chief advisers were Lord Lovell, and two gentlemen named Mr Ratcliffe and Mr Catesby of the whom a seditious rhyme was made and fastened upon the Cross in Cheap and other places of the city which went as follows: 'The cat, the rat, and Lovell our dog, rule all England under a hog.' This was to mean that these three ruled England under the king who had a white boar as his symbol. A great search was made for the devisers of this rhyme and finally two gentlemen named Turberville and Collingbourne were charged for that and other offences, arrested and cast into prison . . . Collingbourne was convicted . . . he was drawn into Tower Hill and there full cruelly put to death, at first hanged and straight after cut down and ripped open, and his bowels cast into a fire. The punishment was so speedily carried out that when the butcher pulled out his heart he spoke and said 'JESUS JESUS'.

Source: A. H. Thomas and I. D. Thornley (eds.), *The great chronicle of London*, London, 1938

Document-study questions

1 Study Document 5. From this document and your own knowledge explain what was meant by the phrase 'the king's household'.
2 Study Document 6. How reliable is this document as evidence for Richard III's marital plans in early 1485?
3 Study Documents 6 and 7. How far does Document 7 refute or endorse the implications of Document 6 concerning allegations that Richard III intended to marry Elizabeth of York and may even have poisoned his own wife?
4 Study all the documents. Use these documents and your own knowledge to explain how far you agree with the view that misfortune more than misadventure undermined Richard III's position between 1483 and 1485.

The Battle of Bosworth, 22 August 1485

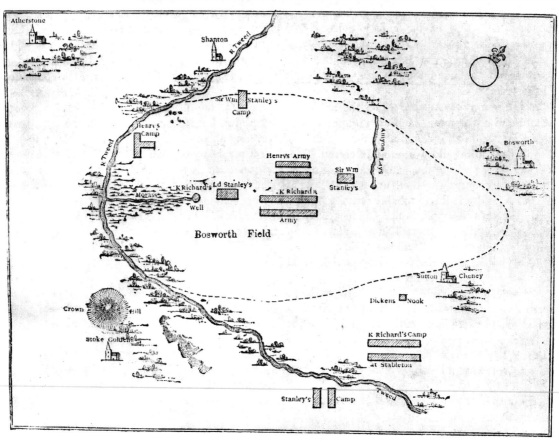

Why would the allegiances of the Stanleys be of such importance once Richard III's and Henry Tudor's armies came to blows?

10 Events leading up to the Battle of Bosworth

The words of John Rous, a contemporary chronicler

Shortly before these men landed [Henry Tudor's invasion force], Thomas Stanley, steward to the king's household, had received permission to cross into his native Lancashire to see his home and family from whom he had been absent for a long time; but he was not permitted to stay there unless he sent his eldest son, George, Lord Lestrange, to the king at Nottingham in his place. This he did.

After the landing at Milford Haven in Wales . . . the rebels advanced along difficult and out-of-the-way routes in the northern part of the province where William Stanley, brother of the steward, had sole command as chamberlain of north Wales.

The king sent word to Thomas, Lord Stanley, that he should appear before him at Nottingham without delay. The king was afraid that the mother of the earl of Richmond [Henry Tudor], who in fact was married to Thomas Stanley, would persuade her husband to support her son's faction. However, Lord Stanley was unable to come, claiming the sweating sickness from which he was suffering was his excuse.

Meanwhile his son, George, who had secretly prepared his escape from the king, was discovered and taken in an ambush. After revealing a conspiracy to support the cause of the earl of Richmond involving himself, William Stanley, his uncle, and Sir John Savage, he asked for mercy and promised that his father, Thomas, would come to the king's aid as quickly as possible with all his forces. In addition he wrote to his father informing him of the danger he was in, and of his wish that this help should be forthcoming.

Source: John Rous, *Historia regibus Angliae*, A. Hanham (trans.), in *Richard III and his early historians*, Oxford, 1975

11 The Battle of Bosworth

A record of the events of August 1485, probably based on eye-witness accounts

. . . though he [Henry Tudor] were of noble courage . . . yet he was in great fear, because he thought that he could not assure himself of Thomas Stanley, who, as I have shown, feared the danger that King Richard might do his son [effectively held hostage in the king's entourage], did incline as yet to neither party . . . Moreover he heard that King Richard, with an host innumerable, was at hand . . . After that he went privily to Atherstone, where Thomas Stanley and William lay encamped. Here Henry did meet with Thomas and William, where taking each other by the hand, and yielding mutual salutation, each man was glad for the state of the others, and all their minds were moved to great joy. After that they discussed tactics should they come to blows with King Richard, whom they heard to be not far off.

Source: Polydor Vergil, *Anglica historia*, 1485–1537, D. Hay (ed. and trans.), Camden Series, 1950

12 The behaviour of King Richard III

The words of John Rous, a contemporary chronicler and, until 1485, a Yorkist

This King Richard, who was excessively cruel in his days, reigned for three years and a little more, in the way that Antichrist is to reign. And like the Antichrist to come, he was confounded at his moment of greatest pride. For having with him the crown itself, together with great quantities of treasure, he was unexpectedly destroyed in the midst of his army by an invading army, small by comparison, but furious in impetus, like a wretched creature.

For all that, let me say the truth to his credit: that he bore himself like a soldier and despite his little body and feeble strength, honourably defended himself to his last breath, shouting again and again that he was betrayed, and crying 'Treason! Treason! Treason!'

Source: John Rous, *Historia regibus Angliae*, A. Hanham (trans.), in *Richard III and his early historians*, Oxford, 1975

Document-study questions

1 Study Document 10. From this document and your own knowledge explain what was meant by 'her son's faction'.
2 Study Document 12. How reliable do you find this document as evidence for Richard III and his defeat at Bosworth?
3 Study Documents 11 and 12. How far do each of these documents confirm the view that the allegiance of the Stanleys was critical to the outcome of the Battle of Bosworth?
4 Study all the documents. Use these documents and your own knowledge to explain how far you agree with the view that Henry Tudor's victory over Richard III in 1485 was unexpected and remains surprising.

Richard Crouchback

13 Richard III's abilities as a ruler

The view of John Rous before he turned his pen against Richard III

The most mighty Prince Richard, by the grace of God king of England and of France and lord of Ireland . . . all avarice set aside, ruled his subjects in his realm full commendably, punishing offenders of his laws, especially extortioners and oppressors of his Commons, and cherishing those that were virtuous, by the which discreet guiding he got the great thanks of God and the love of all his subjects rich and poor and the great praise of the people of all other lands about him.

Source: John Rous, *The Rous roll*, Stroud, 1980

14 Richard III's appearance and character

The view of the historian, Polydore Vergil

He reigned two years and so many months, and one day over. He was little of stature, deformed of body, the one shoulder being higher than the other, a short and sour countenance, which seemed to savour of mischief, and utter evidently craft and deceit. The while he was thinking of any matter, he did continually bite his nether lip, as though the cruel nature of his did rage against itself in that little carcase . . . his courage . . . failed him not in the very death, which, when his men forsook him, he rather yielded to take with the sword, than by foul flight to prolong his life . . .

Source: Polydor Vergil, *Anglica historia, 1485–1537*, D. Hay (ed. and trans.), Camden Series, 1950

15 Shakespeare's portrait of Richard III

From the play written around 1592

But I, that am not shap'd for sportive tricks,
Nor made to court an amorous looking-glass,
I, that am rudely stamp'd, and want love's majesty
To strut before a wanton ambling nymph;
I, that am curtail'd of this fair proportion,
Cheated of feature by dissembling nature,
Deform'd, unfinish'd, sent before my time
Into this breathing world scarce half made up,
And that so lamely and unfashionable,
That dogs bark at me as I halt by them;
Why, I, in this weak piping time of peace,
have no delight to pass away the time,
Unless to spy my shadow in the sun,
And descant on mine own deformity:
And therefore, since I cannot prove a lover,
To entertain these fair well-spoken days,
I am determined to prove a villain . . .

Source: William Shakespeare, *Richard III*, Act I, Scene ii

16 A reaction to the death of Richard by Yorkist sympathisers in the north

Minutes of a meeting of York city council on receiving the news of Richard's death

King Richard, late mercifully reigning upon us, . . . with many other lords and nobility of these northern parts, was piteously slain and murdered, to the great heaviness of this city.

Source: R. Davies (ed.), *York records: extracts from the municipal records of the City of York*, 1843, p. 218

Document-study questions

1 Study Document 13. Explain what was meant by the phrase 'king of England and of France and lord of Ireland'.
2 Study Document 15. How useful is this document as evidence about the character and personality of Richard III?
3 Study Documents 14 and 15. How far does Shakespeare appear to replicate Polydore Vergil in his description of Richard III?
4 Study all the documents. Use these documents and your own knowledge to explain how far you agree with the view that Richard III was a 'villain'?

Further reading

Chapter 1

A helpful introduction to late medieval kingship can be found in the opening chapter of John McGurk, *The Tudor monarchies*, Cambridge, 1999. Two useful biographies for the further study of the reigns of Henry VI and Edward IV are B. P. Wolffe, *Henry VI*, London, 1981; and C. D. Ross, *Edward VI*, London, 1984. The same authors have also written shorter accounts of the two kings which are available in an excellent collection of essays on the period: B. P. Wolffe, 'The personal rule of Henry VI', in S. B. Chrimes, C. D. Ross and R. A. Griffiths, *Fifteenth-century England 1399–1509*, Stroud, 1972; and C. D. Ross, 'The personal rule of Edward VI', in S. B. Chrimes, C. D. Ross and R. A. Griffiths, *Fifteenth-century England 1399–1509*, Stroud, 1972.

Chapter 2

The conflicts of the 1450s and 1460s are superbly documented in Alison Weir, *Lancaster and York: the Wars of the Roses*, Pimilico, 1995. Shorter accounts, catering specifically for the student market, are John Warren, *The Wars of the Roses and the Yorkist kings*, London, 1995; and D. R. Cook, *Lancastrians and Yorkists: the Wars of the Roses*, Harlow, 1994.

Chapter 3

The historiography and iconography of Richard III's reign is explored in the interesting and lavishly illustrated A. J. Pollard, *Richard III and the princes in the Tower*, Stroud, 1991. A thorough and critical account of the reign is Desmond Seward, *Richard III: England's black legend*, Harmondsworth, 1982. Another biography worth consulting for a fair verdict on Richard III is C. D. Ross, *Richard III*, London, 1991. The story of Richard III's reign has been told by Keith Dockray in a fascinating tapestry of contemporary and near-contemporary sources in Keith Dockray, *Richard III: a reader in history*, Stroud, 1988.

Chapter 4

A long-established A level text concerning the reign of Henry VII is John Lockyer, *Henry VII*, Harlow, 1968. A more recent monograph of similar length and equally well suited to A level study is Caroline Rogers, *Henry VII*, London, 1991. Henry VII is discussed in some detail in the early part of John Guy's magnificent account of Tudor monarchs, *Tudor England*, Oxford, 1988. For a comprehensive, highly crafted and impeccably researched biography read S. B. Chrimes, *Henry VII*, London, 1972.

Chapter 5

For an interesting contribution to the 'new monarchy' debate consult Alexander Grant, *Henry VII*, London, 1985. A useful account of the nature of Henry VII's government is S. B. Chrimes, 'The Reign of Henry VII', in S. B. Chrimes, C. D. Ross and R. A. Griffiths, *Fifteenth-century England 1399–1509*, Stroud, 1972. Another useful source is S. J. Gunn, *Early Tudor government 1485–1588*, London, 1985. Henry VII's foreign policy is covered efficiently in Susan Doran, *England and Europe 1485–1603*, Harlow, 1986.

Chapter 6

An excellent introduction to the social and economic history of the fifteenth and sixteenth centuries is Nigel Heard, *Tudor economy and society*, London, 1992. An older, but still useful, account is A. L. Myers, *England in the late Middle Ages*, Harmondsworth, 1952.

Document study

Useful collections of primary-source material concerned with the Wars of the Roses can be found in J. R. Lander, *The Wars of the Roses*, Stroud, 1965; and David R. Cook, *Lancastrians and Yorkists: The Wars of the Roses*, Harlow, 1984. A richly illustrated account of the era, with the story told through modern translations of contemporary chronicles, is Elizabeth Hallam (ed.), *The chronicles of the Wars of the Roses*, Godalming, 1988. The most extensive collection of primary sources is the massive compendium, A. L. Myers (ed.), *English historical documents*, vol. 4, *1327–1485*, Cambridge, 1969.

Index

CPSIA information can be obtained at www.ICGtesting.com
Printed in the USA
LVOW13s1104090714

393568LV00005B/28/P